Edition

KEEPING TIME

The History and Theory of Preservation in America

WILLIAM J. MURTAGH

Keeping Time

Keeping Time

The History and Theory of Preservation in America

Third Edition

William J. Murtagh

WILEY

John Wiley & Sons, Inc.

Published by John Wiley & Sons, Inc., Hoboken, New Jersey
Published simultaneously in Canada

For general information about our other products and services, please contact our Customer Care Department within the United States at (800) 762-2974, outside the United States at (317) 572-3993 or fax (317) 572-4002.

Wiley also publishes its books in a variety of electronic formats. Some content that appears in print may not be available in electronic books. For more information about Wiley products, visit our Web site at www.wiley.com.

Library of Congress Cataloging-in-Publication Data:

Murtagh, William J.
  Keeping time : the history and theory of preservation in America / William J. Murtagh—3rd ed.
     p. cm.
  Includes bibliographical references and index.
  ISBN-10: 0-471-47377-4 (pbk)
  ISBN-13: 978-0-471-47377-0
  1. Historic preservation—United States. 2. Historic buildings—Conservation and restoration—United States. 3. Architecture—Conservation and restoration—United States. 4. Historic preservation—United States—History. 5. Historic buildings—Conservation and restoration—United States—History. 6. Architecture—Conservation and restoration—United States—History. I. Title.

  E159.M875 2005
  363.6'9'90973—dc22

                                                                                    2004061237

Printed in the United States of America

10 9 8 7 6 5 4 3 2 1

FRONTISPIECE: Galena, Illinois, is representative of the rich variety of built resources which succeeding generations of Americans have produced. Its buildings, once considered expendable under the philosophy "new is better," have been preserved and recycled through adaptive use because of a series of legal developments spurred by preservationists who recognize the collective economic worth of such material culture and the important role of such vernacular buildings to American communities.

To the members of the National Conference of State
Historic Preservation Officers, whose collective efforts
have been pivotal to the success of the National Historic
Preservation Act of 1966.

Contents

Preface

I t has been approximately seventeen years since the first edition of this book saw print and about eight years since the last soft cover edition. These years have been singularly unnotable in preservation, with none of the legislative activity that distinguished the 1960s and little of the educational and economic developments of the 1970s or the seminal technical amendments of the 1980s that ushered in new parameters: thinking about land, minorities, and the concerns of Native Americans in relation to their traditional culture. The 1970s saw the establishment of many preservation training programs in universities as well as changes in our tax structure that made historic structures financially recyclable for the commercial real estate development world. With increasing restrictions on these tax credits and the consequent reduction in economic attractiveness, their use all but disappeared in the late 1980s—but not before having energized massive rehabilitation projects across the country. These projects worked hand in glove with the then new attention to the Main Street program of the National Trust for Historic Preservation, focused on the commercial hearts of towns and cities alike.

Since 1998, the National Park Service reports what appears to be a stable use of the tax credit system at 1,000 to 1,200 projects per annum, representing investments in restoration and rehabilitation of approximately $2 billion per year. This would indicate that big developers are syndicating large projects using the tax credit system in such examples as Rockefeller Center and Radio City Music Hall in New York; the Ferry Building and the Embarcadero in San Francisco; and the Atlantic City Convention Hall in New Jersey.

University degree programs, combined with the entrepreneurism that the tax credit system injected into the field, have collectively led to the emergence of a managerial cum business-oriented preservation practitioner heretofore unknown in American mainstream preservation. Add to this development the preservation planning concept introduced with the establishment of the first historic district in Charleston, South Carolina, as early as 1931. The more recent recognition (and flourishing) of cultural heritage corridors, areas consisting of massive land areas to which conservation-oriented environmental concerns are applied, adds yet another dimension. The result is a broad, multifaceted preservation involvement, touching a greater base of American society than ever before.

In the downsizing economic era we are now experiencing, with the attendant withdrawal of public monies to which the preservation field has become accustomed, younger preservationists may feel threatened by a potential loss of job/professional opportunities in the field. Such need not be the case, although, admittedly, the spots of opportunity may change. Preservationists who worked in the field prior to 1966 know that the private sector historically fueled the mainstream of preservation in our country long before government saw fit to join the dance. Yet even if preservation activities were to return once more to a primary reliance on the private sector for financial support, the preservation picture would still not be as it was before 1966, for two reasons. The first is the check-and-balance system formed by Section 106 of the National Historic Preservation Act, which created and requires the Advisory Council on Historic Preservation to consider federally funded or licensed threats to cultural property on the National Register of Historic Places. The second is the National Conference of State Historic Preservation Officers, the group of governor-appointed preservation representatives and their staffs in each state and territory of the United States. Irrespective of whether they are locally perceived to function satisfactorily or not, they exist, and the preservation of our national heritage is the better for it. What is more important, however, is that the preservation ethic appears to have become internalized in a broader base of American society than ever before, tied as it is in most minds to a search for cleaner and better-looking environments in which to work and live.

One final observation on the impact of the National Historic Preservation Act of 1966 is in order now that forty years have passed since its passage by the Congress of the United States. Prior to 1966, the private sector was the primary engine which drove the preservation movement while government's vision focused on conservation of open land and the development of the world-class national parks system we enjoy today. Not only did the private sector exercise leadership through money, interest, and energy, but it provided the nascent preservation movement with a personality base upon which it operated, whether through philanthropy or through the rare opportunities for employment in what was then, in most respects, a national volunteer effort. Ann Pamela Cunningham, the savior of Mount Vernon; John D. Rockefeller, Jr., and Williamsburg, Susan Pringle Frost, initiator of Charleston, South Carolina's historic district; and Emily Edwards, founder of the San Antonio Conservation Society in Texas, all come to mind. Even at the national level, early in the development of the National Trust, this private sector personality leadership would have named Helen Bullock, paid historian of the Trust due to her constant travel, speaking engagements, and representation of the organization at meetings and conferences. All of this essentially changed with the passage of the National Historic Preservation Act in 1966, after which a system of law and regulations replaced private individual personality recognition in the identification of what preservation is and how it functions. The Keeper of the National Register of Historic Places, the Director of the Advisory Council on Historic Preservation, the Director of the National Conference of State Historic Preservation, Officers, and the network of State Historic Preservation Officers, for example, are now components of an established system more important for name recognition than the incumbents who head up the individual parts of the system. This is not to say that the traditional generosity of the private donor to preservation, so unique to this country, has ceased and disappeared. Such is not the case. They and their support are more important than ever. However, the 1966 legislation made the conservation-conscious public sector more strongly concerned for the preservation of the man-made environment, setting the stage for the cementing of the public and private sectors in this interest to a degree heretofore not observable since the founding of the National Park Service. That was in 1916 when the first director, drawn from private industry to head up the then new Interior bureau, personally and financially underwrote the costs of things he felt important to achieve in order to get the new program off the ground.

In addition to those mentioned in the Preface of the previous edition, there have been a number of individuals who have been generous with information and time in regards to this newest edition.

I am very much indebted to Gustavo Araoz, Executive Director of the United States Committee of the International Council on Monuments and Sites (USICOMOS) for reading and commentary on the new chapter on International Preservation, as well as Russell Keune FAIA, Resident Fellow, International Relations, American Institute of Architects, for further valuable contributions.

Within our National Park Service, Carol Shull, Keeper of the National Register of Historic Places, has been of great assistance, as has Brenda Barrett, National Coordinator for Heritage Areas, and her assistant Suzanne Copping, Charles Bernbaum, Office of Historic Landscape Initiative, Barbara Baxter in the office of the Chief of Communications and Public Affairs, Martin Perschler with the Historic American Buildings Survey (HABS), and Historic American Engineering Record (HAER), Sharon C. Park, FAIA, Chief of Technical Preservation Services, and Ann Grimmer, Architectural Historian.

At the National Trust for Historic Preservation, Peter Brink, Senior Vice President, Programs and Greg Coble, Vice President, Business and Finance were both very helpful, as was Joan Maynard, Trustee Emeritus.

Nancy Schamu, Executive Director of the National Conference of State Historic Preservation Officers, and John Fowler, Director of the Advisory Council on Historic Preservation, were likewise of great assistance.

At the state level, Rodney Little, State Historic Preservation Officer and Director of the Division of Historical and Cultural Programs, and his staff in the Maryland Department of Housing and Community Development served me especially well in updating preservation program developments and statistics within their state. I am indebted to them for their generous cooperation.

Interaction with Mark Baumler, State Historic Preservation Officer for Montana, and his staff, as well as Marcella Sherfy, Executive Director of the Montana Heritage Society Project in Helena, Montana, were both informative concerning oral-based Native American culture—locally and at large.

In the field of architectural preservation technology, Amy Cole Ives, historic preservationist on the staff of the Maine Preservation Commission in Augusta, directed by the State Historic Preservation Officer Earl Shettleworth, has always been helpful when called upon. So too has Hugh Miller, FAIA, Director of Theses in the preservation program at Goucher in Baltimore, Maryland.

I would be remiss on the subject of architectural preservation technology if I didn't mention Diane S. Waite, President of the Mount Ida Press; John G. Waite, Principal, John G. Waite Associates, Architects; and Professor David G. Woodcock of Texas A.&M. University who discussed and developed a plausible definition of preservation technology.

Further, mention must be made of Nathan Napoka, Branch Chief, Culture and History in the Hawaii State Historic Preservation Office, Emily Pagliaro of Kamuela, Hawaii, and Puanani Maunu of Juneau, Alaska for their interest in reading and commenting on my remarks about oral-culture-based peoples and preservation. I am much indebted to them for their assistance and input.

I am indebted to photographer Walter Smalling, Jr., who devoted considerable time to produce the cover photograph.

Sharing the labors in the preparation of much of the material for this updated edition of *Keeping Time* prior to sending it to press has been Kristen Youcis of Orland, Maine, and Charlottesville, Virginia. Hers has been a dedicated involvement and is much appreciated.

Finally, my editor Paul Drougas and his staff at Wiley have been the soul of patience during this updating process and always a pleasure to work with and I am very appreciative. Thank you.

WILLIAM J. MURTAGH
Sarasota, Florida
September 2004

Preface to the Previous Edition

THANKS, I SUSPECT, in large part to an increasing sensitivity to environmental issues in American society, preservation of the built environment seems to have enjoyed greater popular support in recent years than at any time in its history. Despite increasing positive attitudinal changes toward recycling the man-made environment, fundamental concepts of preservation can still be widely misunderstood, especially when dealing with buildings and sites of local significance in neighborhoods where the average American lives. This confusion can be readily noted when one tries to introduce and explain historic district ordinances to a town council unfamiliar with a concept such as architectural infill to a municipal board of adjustment or the limits of the National Register of Historic Places to a gathering of homeowners worried about individual property rights. Only when we understand how preservation theory has evolved from its genteel museum roots to a powerful planning tool supported by professional disciplines, including law and economics, can we make the best possible case for the broadest interpretation of preservation issues as an environmental necessity.

This book's primary purpose is to discuss the subject of historic preservation, the various forms it takes and something about its background in order to understand what it is and how it has evolved. The preservation movement today seems to be preoccupied with process and methodology, as it should be, given the many legal national, state, and local preservation building blocks that have been put in place, especially those since the passage of the National Historic Preservation Act in 1966. These progressive legal steps, however, sometimes tend to blur the vision about the subject itself. With the recent growth of new program concepts and the introduction of dedicated funds at the federal level to address the special issues of native peoples and their cultures, an understanding of what preservation is, in its broadest sense, becomes increasingly more important and timely.

In the mid-1980s, when I started this book, in the forefront of my mind were local private citizen preservation activists, caught up in local preservation controversies, in need of a quick immersion in the most basic concepts of what preservation is and what it is not. The willingness of Americans everywhere to increasingly concern themselves with their heritage and attempt to husband it for future generations has traditionally distinguished our country among the sovereign nations of the world who have tended to rely primarily on government for their leadership. Legal and programmatic developments since 1966 have tended to balance the involvement of the public sector with existing private leadership. Because the private citizen sometimes finds existing preservation laws, regulations, criteria, and standards difficult to locate, the most important of these at the federal level have been gathered in the appendices of this book for easy reference. Since preservation is essentially a humanistic opinion, exercised in the public arena of law and economics, answers to the questions are now based on whether regulations have been followed, rather than on the intrinsic value of the entity in question.

Since this book was published in 1988, I have entered the academic world and learned by personal experience how much an introductory book on this subject was needed to teach the preservation professionals of tomorrow. Testament to that observation is its reported broad use throughout academia where preservation course work and degrees are offered.

Keeping Time attempts to cover preservation in most of the forms in which it is known today, to trace the development of the preservation movement in the United States, and to outline some of the basic philosophies and actions behind that development. While it is not intended as a definitive study of the various processes and methods currently employed, such processes are treated as deemed necessary. For detailed explanations of additional facets of preservation, the reader is urged to consult the bibliography. Two growing aspects of the preservation movement that have not been addressed in this book are the work and concerns of those professionals known as scientific architectural conservators and the work and issues of native peoples. The former peer group's interests deal mostly with the illnesses of building materials in an uncontrolled environment and how to treat such problems in the restoration process. Their methodologies and solutions are scientific in nature and similar to those employed by museum personnel conserving objects in museum galleries. The difference is that the architectural conservator lacks the luxury of the gallery's controlled environment.

Native American preservation issues are distinct, necessitating evaluations and treatments worthy of and reflective of the oral cultural traditions from which they emanate. It follows that the evaluative preservation methods and systems of the predominantly written cultures of our country fall short in satisfying the preservation needs of such cultures. Only recently has the preservation movement's sensitivities begun to address these issues. Much work and progress remains to be achieved in this respect.

I am much indebted to many people who have been helpful in various ways in bringing this book to completion. I would be remiss if I did not begin the list with Robert Guter, who started this effort with me but soon discovered that the life of the freelance consultant demanded such an investment of time as to preclude his continuing with the book. I also owe a debt to Charles Hosmer, on whose well-researched volumes on the history of the preservation movement I have heavily relied. The same may be said of an equally longstanding friend and professional compatriot, Edward P. Alexander. His books on the development of the museum movement—and especially the outdoor museum—are invaluable, as is Stephen Tschudi-Madsen's book on the English attitude toward restoration for its explanation of the lineage of preservation terms.

Professor William Tischler was very helpful in dealing with the subject of landscape preservation. Samuel Stokes and Elizabeth Watson were both excellent guides on rural and small-town preservation, as was Patricia Williams on living history museums.

William Seale encouraged this project and was generous with comments and helpful criticism in general, specifically on those chapters dealing with the history of the preservation movement and the house museum.

I am especially indebted to Ann Webster Smith, Ellen Beasley, and Hugh Taylor, all of whom read and commented constructively on the entire manuscript.

The staffs of the Historic American Building Survey, the Historic American Engineering Record, the National Register of Historic Places, the Office of Graphic Research, Historic Photography Collection, and the National Historic Landmarks Program—all divisions of the National Park Service—were extremely cooperative in locating many illustrations. The staff of the National Trust was equally generous in opening its photographic archives for research, as was the Advisory Council on Historic Preservation. I am indebted to Walter Smalling, Jr., and Robert Rettig for their suggestions about the selection of illustrations. Thanks are also owed to Harold Skramstad, Jr., and to Barnes Riznik, who responded with alacrity to requests for photographs. To Barbara Kirkconnell, who assisted me in locating illustrations, much credit is due.

Permissions needed to reproduce photographs were secured by Peter Herrick. I am very grateful to him for his efficiency in handling this aspect of the work, as I am to Ernest Connally and Mark Edwards, who supplied current statistics on preservation tax credits and on Maryland's preservation activities, respectively. Diane Maddex was extremely helpful with some of the definitions which appear in the book.

Finally, I am grateful to the National Conference of State Historic Preservation Officers (to whom this book is dedicated in recognition of the officers' important role in the preservation movement), for the selfless practical assistance which they offered in preparing the manuscript. Of particular help was staff member Virginia DeMarce, who not only entered the manuscript into the NCSHPO computer, but offered helpful comments and criticism along the way. I gladly acknowledge her invaluable assistance.

WILLIAM J. MURTAGH
Honolulu, Hawaii
April 1993

Introduction

O VER THE COURSE of recent history, the initiative of American preservation has shifted from the involvement of concerned citizens—the private sector—to the achievement of an equitable balance with government—the public sector. With changes in cultural and social attitudes, dominant themes in preservation have also changed. First was the secular pietism that defined mid-nineteenth-century preservation efforts. (One reason given in 1856 for saving the Hermitage, Andrew Jackson's Tennessee home, was that "it is good policy in a republican government to inculcate sentiments of veneration for those departed heroes who have rendered services to their country in times of danger.") By the twentieth century, aesthetics (i.e., architecture) had broadened the scope of the traditional historical or associative criteria. This growth was stimulated in the new century's first decades by large-scale philanthropy and by the foundation of state and regional organizations which were to create new definitions of preservation.

Early efforts in preservation dealt with landmarks as artifacts held separate from the community for veneration, pleasure, or education. With government's increasing role in historic preservation during the 1930s, a new sensitivity to preservation issues became part of the social fabric and led to the present realization that recreation, environmental planning and conservation, housing, and economic health can all include components of preservation. Anyone who doubts that historic preservation has become a modern "growth industry" should listen to the cash registers at Boston's Quincy Market and follow the critical debates over whether preservation in the marketplace serves or defeats its own goals. The history of preservation is still being written.

In order to understand that history, a thorough understanding of its terminology is imperative. Thus, the first chapter of *Keeping Time* is devoted to the distinctions of the preservationists' language. (A glossary of terms in current usage can be found beginning on page 207.) As the next four chapters explain, the history of American preservation began to be written as early as 1812, when architect Robert Mills drew up plans—never employed and subsequently lost—for the reconstruction of the steeple of Independence Hall. The minutes of the pertinent Philadelphia City Council meetings of the late 1820s, which contain proposals by the architect William Strickland for the reconstruction of the steeple following his designs, cite the importance of rebuilding the steeple for patriotic reasons.

Patriotism fueled the energies of nineteenth-century preservationists to the exclusion of any of the other interests—education, aesthetics, the environment, or most recently, economics—which have motivated later individuals. The protection of single buildings of landmark quality and with strong historic significance was the goal of early preservationists, whose ranks were filled, for the most part, by women. As later chapters attest, such landmarks as Mount Vernon were thus secured for future generations.

The federal government's role in preservation grew out of its concern for the conservation of America's natural resources, which led in turn to the development of the great national park system that began with the acquisition of Yellowstone in 1872. Only in the early twentieth century, however, did Washington begin to take action in the direct interests of preservation, starting in 1906 with the passage of the Antiquities Act and continuing to the present with other legislative landmarks, the most pertinent of which are reproduced in Appendix A. The more recent economic incentives of the tax laws of 1976, 1981, and 1986 and the explosive changes these acts, as well as the 1966 National Historic Preservation Act, have collectively had on the preservation movement, are discussed in detail in Chapter 5.

Many of the specific forms which the preservation movement has taken during its development in the United States are outlined in the succeeding chapters. Beginning with a concentration on period rooms and single house museums, the movement has grown to encompass complexes of buildings, ranging from the outdoor museums of Colonial Williamsburg and Sturbridge Village to the historic districts of American cities and towns, in whose buildings people continue to work and live. Further, more recently, preservationists have broadened their sights to include large heritage and cultural corridors reflecting the preservationist movements increased concern for context and conservation issues. The rehabilitation of those buildings and the imaginative adaptive uses to which some of them are being put are discussed in Chapter 9. Along with a concern for the vernacular architecture of America's cities and towns has come a concern for the rural environment, which includes not only small villages, but also the farmland and wilderness areas and the landscapes that surround them. The steps being taken to preserve these landscapes and the important man-made elements of the rural American scene are outlined in Chapters 10 and 11, respectively, followed in Chapter 12 by a brief explanation of the science of archaeology, which in its many manifestations plays an important role in reconstructing and rehabilitating both the natural and the built environment.

While the primary purpose of *Keeping Time* is to explain what preservation is rather than to provide guidelines for action, the final chapter includes an example of a successful preservation state program, (Maryland), with the hope that their activities and achievements can be of utility and inspiration elsewhere.

Despite a rather long history of preservation activity in the United States, the average American's consciousness of the built environment as a conservable rather than an expendable resource is very recent. As late as 1960, no comprehensive book-length treatment on preservation had been published in the United States. The explosion of scholarly interest in the subject becomes obvious in visiting the library of the National Trust for Historic Preservation, whose multivolumes on the subject are housed at Special Collections, University of Maryland Libraries.

Opportunities for academic training in preservation are also relatively recent. In order to attract qualified young professionals to the field, the National Trust and Colonial Williamsburg launched a summer training program, the Seminar for Historical Administrators, in 1959. Yet as late as the early 1960s, volunteers far outnumbered paid personnel in the preservation-related work of historical agencies. Academe began to address the issue institutionally in the mid-1960s, when Columbia University in New York and the University of Virginia at Charlottesville launched course work which led to the establishment of degree programs in preservation. By 1973, there were about five such programs. The National Trust's *Whitehill Report,* issued in 1968, called for the establishment of an institute which would concern itself with the training of preservationists. A decade later, the Trust published the *Belmont Report,* which called for the establishment of a study group on higher education. As of 2003 the Trust's guide to undergraduate and graduate education in historic preservation listed about fifty-four institutions of higher education offering preservation programs leading to degrees and many more schools giving some course work in preservation.

It is my hope that this book will stimulate interested laymen to pursue elsewhere in greater depth those aspects of preservation that interest them, and that it will be a useful text by which academics, teaching basic preservation courses by choice or assignment, can encourage students to pursue the subject further. Finally, *Keeping Time* should provide some guidance for civic activists as they debate controversial preservation issues in their own communities, regardless of which side they choose to take in the continuing controversy.

The Language
of Preservation

THE FIRST THING anyone interested in preservation must know is how to talk about the subject. Over the years, certain terminology has been established by use and common consent, even though confusion and differences of opinion over exact meaning still tend to persist in the public mind. The distinct meanings of these terms must be grasped in order to communicate preservation concerns properly and authoritatively. We must strive for a language of preciseness, one that is universally understood and accepted.

Confusion over the definitions of terms in the preservationist's lexicon depends to a large extent on whether one comes to the subject as a museum curator or historian, or with the planner's lineage, the lawyer's interest, or the economist's concern. The purpose of this chapter is to explain the derivation of the most basic terms of preservation in common parlance today. These terms—*preservation, restoration, reconstruction*—lend themselves to the widest latitude of interpretation.

Those definitions issued in the name of the secretary of the interior's preservation programs are recommended. Not only do they have the weight of professional training and experience behind them, but they also have the authority of legal acceptance, having been developed on the basis of needs growing out of Congressional action and establishment of law. Definitions for terms not treated in this chapter are included in the glossary at the end of the book, where a full list of preservationist terms, which have grown out of the working language of preservation as new needs arose, can be found.

Today, the typical interdisciplinary team of specialists working on preservation projects and programs is composed of people united by common goals, but not necessarily by a common language. As the practice of preservation draws on expertise from an increasing number of disciplines, such specialists as the architect, historian, conservator, planner, lawyer, archaeologist, craftsman, realtor, or computer analyst may, like the builders of Babel, risk confusion and miscommunication. Such difficulties are brought on by a lack of uniformity of definition, understanding, and expression of basic terms important to preservation problems and their solutions. Lack of a precise understanding of these terms only adds controversy to what may already be a problematic situation.

The semantic legacy inherited by preservationists has been the subject of controversy for more than a hundred years. Prosper Mérimée, appointed head of the French Monument Service in 1834, distinguished restoration from reconstruction by using the words *conservation* and *re-creation*: "We understand the conservation of that which exists and the re-creation of that which definitely existed." By that statement, Mérimée was attempting to distinguish between the process of recapturing the integrity of an extant monument and the total rebuilding or reconstruction of a replica or full-scale model of a monument that no longer exists.

Somewhat later, Eugène Emmanuel Viollet-le-Duc, the influential French writer and architect and leader of the romantic rationalists of the Second Empire, defined the restoration process as the effort "to establish a completed state which may never have existed at any particular time." (See Figures 1-1 and 1-2.)

Figure 1-1
The Single Brothers' House, Salem, North Carolina, before its twentieth-century restoration under the direction of Old Salem, Inc.

This is the philosophy of what might be termed *overzealousness*: the replacement and enhancement of original fabric to produce a finished project which epitomizes the age and aesthetic of the period of its original creation. This overzealousness can easily be observed in Viollet-le-Duc's work at Carcassonne. Here the patina of time has heightened the perception of authenticity, confusing the twentieth-century observer into accepting Viollet-le-Duc's late-nineteenth-century additions as original construction of the Middle Ages.

The philosophy of nineteenth-century English architectural critic and social reformer John Ruskin was at the opposite extreme. "Restoration," he wrote, "is always alive. It means the most total destruction which a building can suffer. It's as impossible to raise the dead as to restore a building." Ruskin subscribed to what has come to be known in the twentieth century as the "let-it-alone" school of thought. To Ruskin the restoration process was nothing more or less than an intellectual process of destruction of original fabric and replacement with new materials, eradicating the patina of time in the process. Hence his attitude that restoration is "the most total destruction which a building can suffer." To Ruskin, restoration was as unacceptable as trying to make that which has died live again.

It is obvious that his fellow English architect, painter, and designer, William Morris, subscribed to Ruskin's philosophy when he wrote an anguished letter to an editor, complaining, "Sir, my eye just now caught the word restoration in the morning paper, and, on looking closer, I saw that

Figure 1-2
A postrestoration view of the same eighteenth-century building, showing the original half-timbered construction which had been hidden by the later addition of clapboard siding.

this time it is nothing less than the minster of Tewksbury that is to be destroyed by Sir George Scott." In 1879, Morris summed up his philosophy by writing that "restoration is generally speaking a modern euphemism for wholesale destruction and the worst desecration."

Morris's understanding of restoration was obviously at odds with that of Sir George Gilbert Scott, his contemporary practitioner of high-Victorian Gothic Revival design, best known for the Albert Memorial in Hyde Park, London. Such differences of opinion remain today, since the visions of amateur and even professional preservationists are inevitably colored by personal experience and unconscious bias. Clearly, as preservation grows in scope and influence, the need for commonly held definitions grows apace. Given the differences in intellectual human thought and opinion illustrated in the quotations from Morris, Ruskin, and Viollet-le-Duc, it is clear that preservation is basically a humanistic endeavor. It must be remembered, however, that today's humanistic opinions of preservation are exercised in an unhumanistic arena, increasingly oriented to the world of politics and economics.

The language of historic preservation must thus operate on at least two levels simultaneously. If its definitions help us to gain an objective understanding of the actions we take, they are also invested with inescapable subjective overtones that convey nuances of philosophy and attitude endemic to humanistic concerns.

The very word *preservation*, for example, carries a strict meaning radically different from associated terms like *restoration* and *conservation*, yet *preservation* has also acquired a generic meaning, as in "the historic preservation movement." In the second sense it is an umbrella term encompassing a host of meanings, including, but not limited to, its primary meaning: to keep from injury or destruction, to save. As the movement gained a broader foundation in architectural history and neighborhood renewal at the expense of purely associative history, shifts of emphasis were imperative. Even during the past ten years, the vocabulary of preservation has changed, altered by changing goals and the assimilation of terminology from allied fields. By today's preservation standards, some argue, the word *landmark* is misleading and the expression *historic preservation* should be shorn of the adjective *historic*. Others, feeling that the preservation movement has strayed too far from its stewardship of property and its roots in associative history, would insist that it is time we put history back into preservation.

It seems clear that the vocabulary of preservation will continue to evolve as long as the activity it describes remains a vital one. For the present, we need to pursue precision of expression not only for accurate communication but to foster high professional standards.

In 1839, A. N. Didron, a French archaeologist, originated the maxim, "it is better to preserve than to restore and better to restore than to reconstruct." This dictum, included in volume I of his *Bulletin Archéologique*, not only makes use of the three basic terms in the preservationist's lexicon, but neatly prioritizes, in order of desirability, those preservation-oriented actions one takes with entities to be saved. Out of these three basic terms—*preserve, restore, reconstruct*—an ever-enlarging glossary of terms has evolved and, indeed, continues to evolve as the concepts of preservation change and broaden. For the purposes of this discussion, only those terms considered most basic to a beginning understanding of preservation are dealt with. (See Figure 1-3.)

The following words are the most important in preservation usage and are those that have acquired specific meanings sometimes different from their connotations in common parlance. Their definitions are those of the office of the Secretary of the Interior.

> *Preservation* is defined as the act or process of applying measures to sustain the existing form, integrity, and material of a building or structure, and the existing form and vegetative cover of a site. It may include initial stabilization work, where necessary, as well as ongoing maintenance of the historic building materials.

> *Restoration* is defined as the act or process of accurately recovering the form and details of a property and its setting as it appeared at a particular period of time by means of the removal of later work or by the replacement of missing earlier work.

> *Reconstruction* is defined as the act or process of reproducing by new construction the exact form and detail of a vanished building, structure, or object, or a part thereof, as it appeared at a specific period of time.

In a broad sense, *preservation* has been defined as a concern for the rate of consumption of buildings. The implosion of an existing building to

Figure 1-3
Drayton Hall (1738–42), a National Trust property near Charleston, South Carolina, is considered one of the best examples of a preserved building in the United States. Maintained in its original condition (without electricity or plumbing), it is shown to the public without interior furnishings.

make way for new construction represents instant consumption. The original building immediately ceases to exist. The antithesis of implosion is represented by the historic house museum, where all measures possible are taken to depress the rate of wear and tear on the building. This is usually done by controlling where visitors walk and what they touch to prolong the life of the structure and its contents to the maximum extent. Between these extremes exists a gamut of ways in which a building can be used, from private residences through uses different from those for which a building was initially built (which we call *adaptive use*), all of which subject a structure to varying degrees of wear.

In an equally broad sense, one can interpret preservation as a good maintenance program. For example, the process of replacing a rotted window sill with a new sill, the profile of which follows as closely as possible that of the original, is, in the strictest sense of the word, a *restoration* procedure. The amount of replacement that must take place because of damage or inaccurate or stylistically different earlier replacements, additions, or deletions, leads one to speak of a "heavy restoration" or a "light restoration." The replacement of the accurate profile of one window sill in a building is so minuscule in proportion to the rest of the existing original fabric that it hardly merits the name *restoration*. The greater the amount of replacement necessary to accurately recover the form and detail of a property and its setting as it appeared at a particular period or periods in time, the heavier the restoration is considered. Indeed, the overzealousness of some so-called preservation practitioners to replace original materials sometimes leads to what has been called *creeping reconstruction*. This latter term has been coined to convey the idea that so much new material has been introduced into a building in the restoration process that the state of the building visually approaches the appearance of new construction. In other words, the irregularities of material surfaces that time and use have created, referred to as *patina*, have been eradicated by replacement.

No golden rule exists as a measure to be employed when restoration goes too far. The basic dictum of the professional preservationist, however, is to keep as much of the original fabric as possible. Careful adherence to this concept separates the professional preservationist from the nonprofessional. Many old buildings are destroyed in the restoration process by the very people whose aim is to do just the opposite—to preserve the building by restoring it. When in doubt, subscribe to John Ruskin's let-it-alone school of thinking. The debate over how far one takes the restoration process has indeed raged since the days of Ruskin. The question of how far to go in the replacement process is exemplified in the nineteenth-century restorations of Viollet-le-Duc, whose reputation for creating whole cloth out of fragments or imagination is well known in preservation circles.

This brings us to the question of reconstruction. One can think of a total reconstruction as a full-scale contemporary model of an earlier building that no longer exists. (See Figures 1-4 and 1-5.) How historically accurate the reconstruction turns out to be stands in direct relationship to the depth of documentation available on the nonexistent building. The

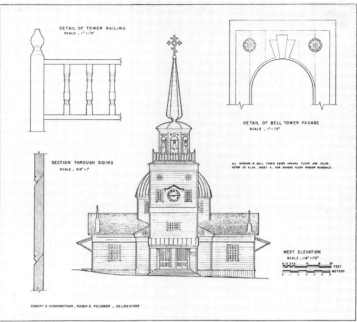

less the documentation, the less accurate the reconstruction potentially becomes. In this instance, research and documentation not only include archival research into written or sketched sources, but also archaeological research conducted by digging in the ground. The finds of the archaeologists during the excavation process often produce rich results which, when added to the historian's and archivist's work, add to or corroborate facts unearthed in both processes. The architectural historian's knowledge of style adds yet another instrument to the growing orchestra of fact. This body of documented information becomes the basis for the work of the historical architect and eventually the curator (if a museum is planned), not to mention the landscape architect.

In reconstruction, as in restoration, personal tastes must be sublimated and expressed only as reflections of the socioeconomic status of the original owner or owners and the period of the lost building with which one is dealing. If the pool of professional information is sufficient, a complete reconstruction can be chanced.

The Governor's Palace at Williamsburg is an excellent case in point. As with all reconstructed or restored buildings in this project, it was the consortium of expertise in research that produced the results one sees. If sufficient information is not available, it is better to interpret the lost building through other media, such as film, slides, dioramas, paintings, and written descriptions, than to run the risk of fabricating an expensive historical untruth. For instance, the National Park Service erected a full-scale metal outline or frame of Benjamin Franklin's house in Philadelphia (Figure 1.6) when it was concluded that insufficient information could be collected to create a creditable reconstruction of the building.

Figure 1-4 and 1-5
When St. Michael's Cathedral, Sitka, Alaska (1848–50), was destroyed by fire in 1966, a measured drawing, made by the Historic American Buildings Survey of the National Park Service prior to the conflagration, permitted a total reconstruction of the original building.

Figure 1-6
The National Park Service interpreted the site and general mass of Benjamin Franklin's eighteenth-century house as a rigid metal frame or outline to avoid the potential inaccuracy of a reconstruction. The houses in the background have been heavily restored, using documentary evidence of architectural detail common to Philadelphia residences of the eighteenth century.

The word *reconstruction* denotes new construction of once-extant buildings on their original sites. One occasionally hears two semantic refinements relating to the reconstruction process. The first, *reconstitution*, is applied when some original materials survive, although not enough to constitute what could be considered a heavy restoration *in situ*. When existing nonarchaeological fragments survive the demolition of a building, and are reassembled to approximate the lost building *in situ* or at a new location, the building can be said to have been reconstituted. A prime example of this is Boscobel in Putnam County, New York, where major fragments of architectural trim, such as fireplace mantels, doors and windows, interior stairs, and other elements have been applied to a new full-scale building which reproduces the scale and shape of the original structure on a new site.

Replication is the second variant of reconstruction. This rarely used procedure calls for duplicating an extant artifact on a site removed from the original, usually as a means of saving the original from inordinate wear by frequent use.

Since the growth of preservation as a planning process, a fourth basic term has entered the preservationists' lexicon. This is *rehabilitation*, defined by the office of the secretary of the interior as "the act or process of returning a property to a state of utility through repair or alteration which makes possible an efficient contemporary use while preserving those portions or features of the property which are significant to its historical, architectural, and cultural values."

Rehabilitation is thus the process generally applied to historic housing stock. It is usually carried out in neighborhoods designated through local zoning as historic districts, although this need not be the case. No effort to establish the rehabilitated houses as museums is implied.

In the rehabilitation process, the owner should preserve as many of the significant interior and exterior features of the property as possible to maintain its sense of historicity. Indeed, if the owner is sensitive to the building, those façades seen from the public right-of-way should be restored wherever possible, since it is the street façade or façades of the building that contribute to the sense of locality and place of the neighborhood. Rehabilitated housing stock can be seen in any of the numerous historic districts throughout the United States, such as Beacon Hill in Boston, the Battery in Charleston, the Vieux Carré in New Orleans, the Westside Neighborhood in Denver, or the Port Townsend Historic District in Washington State.

In sum, the preservation practitioner needs to be very careful about how he speaks of his activities. This is important for clarity of communication. The manner in which the professional preservationist speaks about his or her subject helps establish credibility and authority with the client and with other concerned individuals and groups.

This discussion has deliberately emphasized the four basic words of the preservationist's vocabulary, *preservation, restoration, reconstruction,* and *rehabilitation*. Without a clear understanding of the distinctions in meaning among these basic concepts, the individual is lost in a morass of misunderstanding and misconception when considering such related terms as *adaptive use* or *renovation*, as well as words relating to contemporary methodologies of preservation such as *easement, façadism,* or *townscape*.

Along with a basic understanding of what we are talking about, we also need to know *why* we are talking about it. Preservation of the built environment has a longer lineage in the United States than one might suspect. That the leadership of private citizens in this interest has been substantial considerably distinguishes our country from other parts of the world, where a primary reliance on government has been the rule. As we shall see in the following chapters, however, the responsibility of government or the public sector has increased in the twentieth century and the force of law has had an impact on the development of the preservation movement.

CHAPTER 2

The Preservation Movement and the Private Citizen Before World War II

H OW CAN a nation without a past have anything to preserve? The first generation of American writers grappled with that problem head-on. In the early nineteenth century, Washington Irving, American author and humorist, romanticized the Hudson River Valley to create a mythological recent past where cozy Dutch farmhouses and the quaint architecture of old New Amsterdam figured as prominently as headless horsemen. Somewhat later, Nathaniel Hawthorne, a contemporary of Irving's, lamented that "no author . . . can conceive of the difficulty of writing a romance about a country where there is no shadow, no antiquity, no mystery . . . ," yet his countrymen, however sporadically, had been self-consciously cultivating their own history from an early date.

As early as 1749, Peter Kalm, a Swedish botanist who traveled extensively in North America, commented in his diary on an old log cabin in the Philadelphia area. As late as the 1830s, John Fanning Watson, chronicler of early Philadelphia, made reference to some of the seventeenth-century caves of the first Old World settlers, caves which could still be seen on the banks of the Delaware. One cannot conclude anything more than a basic consciousness of the past in either of these references. By the post-Revolutionary period, however, this type of consciousness had apparently affected the painter Charles Willson Peale, who in 1786 established an art museum, including historical artifacts, in Philadelphia's Old State House (as Independence Hall was then known). Concern for the past was likewise the motivation for a group of citizens who formed the Massachusetts Historical Society in 1789. Such interests were sufficiently established by the Centennial of 1876 that approximately seventy-eight such societies were then flourishing. While the groups were principally interested in genealogy and archival materials, they were nonetheless expressive of a growing interest in who we were, where we had been, and what we had achieved as a nation and as a society.

The first known restoration activity in America did not take place until the early nineteenth century. In 1827–1828, the Newport, Rhode Island, synagogue, designed in 1765 by the local amateur architect Peter Harrison, underwent repair and restoration (Figure 2-1). The work was funded by the estate of successful shipper Abraham Touro (son of Isaac, founder of Touro Synagogue), who had died in 1822.

In 1816, Philadelphia's Old State House was rescued from demolition when it was purchased by the city from the Commonwealth of Pennsylvania. The new national Capitol was under construction in Washington, D.C., and the Old State House stood under threat of being razed, its deteriorated tower having been removed about 1790. In 1828, William Strickland, architect of the neoclassical Second Bank of the United States and the Philadelphia Merchants Exchange Building, designed the current State House tower in the Georgian style. (See Figure 2.2.) This is usually considered the first known instance in the United States of an architect sublimating the current design idiom in which he would have been expected to work in favor of what would have been an outdated style for his time. To Strickland, therefore, goes the accolade of being the first restorationist in the country.

By the middle of the nineteenth century, the importance of a national identity was focusing the attention of Americans even more strongly on past deeds and great men. When Princeton University's Nassau Hall, the site of the Continental Congress in 1783, was damaged by fire in 1855, the university trustees voted to retain as much of the historic old structure as possible and to "restore" it because of the strong associations it held for the university.

As a generator of patriotic fervor in America, no early figure could equal George Washington, and so his life became the stuff of preservation as well as hagiography. No other colonial American comes close to Washington in personifying the symbol of patriotism expressed with what approaches religious zeal. To the state legislators in New York, Washington's magnetism was sufficient to cause them to open the public treasury in his memory. In 1850, the albany lawmakers spent almost $2,000 to buy one of the many buildings used by the general as a headquarters. The Hasbrouck House in Newburgh and its surrounding

Figure 2-1
Interior of Touro
Synagogue, New-
port, Rhode Island,
considered the first
known restoration
in the United States.

acreage thus became the first publicly owned shrine to an American secular patron saint.

Many were the houses where "Washington slept," but Mt. Vernon
was indisputably the house with greatest personal association. Owned by
Washington's collateral descendants, the plantation had fallen into genteel decay by the 1850s—a condition current preservationists would recognize as "preservation by neglect." Even so, it had become a site of pilgrimage, memorialized by painters and popularized by engravers, and was
an essential stop on the itinerary of foreign as well as American travelers.

Figure 2-2   Independence Hall: its reconstructed tower, designed by William Strickland, dates from 1828.

When developers sought the house and its prime Potomac River frontage for use as a hotel, public outcry was insufficient to convince either the state of Virginia or the federal government to buy the estate. Into the vacuum left by governmental default stepped Ann Pamela Cunningham of South Carolina, a woman whose tactics and vision were to color American preservation for generations.

In 1853, realizing that the bid for government support had failed, Miss Cunningham organized a patriotic group of women who canvassed the South, and later the entire country, for contributions and support. Their gentility belied by their determination, this Mount Vernon Ladies' Association of the Union accepted no answer but "yes." In five years

Mount Vernon was theirs—and remains so today, despite subsequent offers by the government to relieve the ladies of their trust.

Ann Pamela Cunningham is described as a small spinster, frail of health, serious, and intelligent, who was reared on a plantation in up-country South Carolina (Figure 2-3). It was a letter from her mother while Miss Cunningham was in Philadelphia for medical attention which stimulated her to spearhead the creation of an organization of women to save Mount Vernon. She identified herself as "regent" and appointed vice-regents in each of the states where there appeared the hope of raising funds. Soliciting contributions was the prime responsibility of each vice-regent, assisted by a secretary. Reporting to the vice-regent were "lady managers" for each county, town, or village in the respective state. Each manager appointed assistants to help.

The seminal quality of this organizational arrangement cannot be overemphasized. It not only documents the leadership of women in preservation, but, like the efforts at Williamsburg almost three-quarters of a century later, Mount Vernon's administrative organization became an instant informational resource and blueprint for other potential preservationists to emulate. Two cases in point are the efforts of Mrs. William Holstein of Pennsylvania, who tried to save Washington's headquarters at Valley Forge and those of Colonel Andrew Jackson, adopted grandson of General and Mrs. Andrew Jackson, who was then living in the Hermitage, his grandfather's house near Nashville, after its purchase by the state of Tennessee. In both instances, efforts to create a national organization similar to that of Mount Vernon failed to live up to expectations. Although the Ladies' Hermitage Association grew out of the successful effort to save the Hermitage, it never became a motivating force as an organization of national scope.

Figure 2-3
Ann Pamela Cunningham is seated fourth from the right in this early (c. 1873) photograph surrounded by regents from nine states and the District of Columbia.

So influential was Ann Pamela Cunningham's victory at Mount Vernon that her efforts established certain presuppositions about historic preservation in America. These assumptions included the idea that private citizens, not government, were the proper advocates for preservation; that only buildings and sites associated with military and political figures were worthy of preservation; that such sites must be treated as shrines or icons; and that women would assume a dominant role in the acquisition and management of such properties. Thus was established the uniqueness of the preservation movement in America among sovereign states of the world.

Most preservation efforts throughout the end of the nineteenth century were characterized by the kind of pietism and private support typical of the Mount Vernon effort. The motives for preservation in this period were complex. Not only were we as a people using historic shrines to assert our legitimacy in an international community of venerable nations, but also, as individuals and groups, we looked to associative history for reassurance. In the face of post-Civil War affluence, established families pursued genealogy and the preservation of their ancestral homesteads as a challenge to "new money's" claims of legitimacy. Regionally, preservation was used as a defense against the cultural and political hegemony of the East. By the 1880s and '90s, Southerners showed renewed interest in the homes of their own great men, and by the beginning of the twentieth century preservation organizations could also be found in the West and Southwest.

By the turn of the century, too, another phenomenon gave fresh impetus to preservation. A new generation of immigrants, particularly eastern and southern Europeans, was seen as a threat by a middle class only recently established, a middle class which calmed its own anxieties by a veneration of the past.

From about 1850 to 1900, American preservationists held buildings to be worthy of attention for transcendent rather than intrinsic reasons. As shrines to historic personages, these structures were symbols of patriotic fervor before any consideration of their aesthetic quality. Preservationists of the time were motivated by a brand of chauvinistic fervor that sometimes strikes us as naïve today, or by social and cultural impulses of which they themselves were not always fully aware. Their accomplishments were substantial, yet part of the legacy early preservationists bequeathed to us includes a rather narrow vision of how historic buildings should be presented to the general public. The buildings and their interior furnishings were put on display in a conservative light which limited controversy and played down any unanswered questions about their authenticity. Such a subjective interpretation is inevitable as part of the evolutionary process of any movement or institution.

The relevance of historic preservation in a broader context had to wait until its artifacts were recognized not only as historic symbols but for their intrinsic aesthetic value. Not until the close of the nineteenth century did we gain the perspective for a general assessment of historic buildings as worthwhile objects in their own right. New England led the way with two early examples of architecturally motivated restoration. In

1898 the Ipswich, Massachusetts, Historical Society restored the John Whipple House. This modest seventeenth-century dwelling, representative of the region's English roots, was unremarkable from the standpoint of history. In 1905 private interests saved and restored Paul Revere's Boston house (Figure 2-4). Although associatively significant, the house attracted equal attention because it was the city's oldest surviving frame building. Restoration to what was thought to be its earliest appearance emphasized the importance of architectural merit over purely patriotic impulses.

William Sumner Appleton, New England architectural historian, preservationist, and proper Bostonian, was an active supporter of the Revere house campaign. His education and extensive travel had equipped him to thoroughly understand the lessons of that restoration. In 1910 he founded the Society for the Preservation of New England Antiquities, now known as Historic New England, introducing early in the new century a new way of thinking about preservation and history. Appleton and his colleagues were less interested in pedigrees, bloodlines, and heroes than they were in aesthetics. While they mourned the destruction of John Hancock's house, they had also witnessed the loss of houses without patriotic inferences but with much architectural meaning. Building on New England's respect for the antique, Appleton modeled public enthusiasm for historic architecture, making the SPNEA a powerful force for preservation.

Also in 1910, the Essex Institute (founded in 1848) embarked on a program to acquire, preserve, and restore the architectural treasures of Salem, Massachusetts, starting with the John Ward House, built c. 1685.

Figure 2-4 Paul Revere House, Boston, after heavy restoration. Before its restoration, the house had been heavily altered to a flat-roofed, flat-fronted clapboard building some time in the nineteenth century.

The fact that Ward had been a tradesman rather than a grandee dampened the enthusiasm of the Institute's members not a bit.

Ideas about the validity of architectural preservation did not, of course, spring full blown from the brow of William Sumner Appleton. They had been germinating in the American consciousness for more than a quarter of a century, influenced significantly by such English critics as John Ruskin and William Morris, whose ideas influenced their Yankee cousins despite the customary time lag the Atlantic Ocean then created.

The event generally credited with inaugurating a reappraisal of America's own architecture was the Centennial Exposition of 1876 which was held in Fairmount Park, Philadelphia. Some of the state exhibits, notably Connecticut's, featured colonial furniture, memorabilia, and at least a suggestion of "quaint old architecture." Even before the Centennial year, a stirring of interest in old American houses was evident. In 1874, the *New York Sketch Book* had published a photograph of the 1728 Bishop Berkeley House in Newport, and the following year there had appeared in the same paper a drawing of the Palladian doorway of Jacob Ford's pre-Revolutionary mansion in Morristown, New Jersey. Following the Centennial, more and more attention was devoted to American building types. In 1877 Charles Follen McKim, William Rutherford Mead, and Stanford White, principals in the leading beaux arts-era architectural firm of McKim, Mead and White, joined by fellow architect William Bigelow, embarked on a walking tour of selected New England towns. In what would later be known as their celebrated sketching trip, they paid serious attention to the eighteenth-century architecture of Marblehead, Salem, Newburyport, and Portsmouth. This resulted, according to Mead, in "sketches and measured drawings of many of the important colonial houses."

In a climate of enthusiasm for the antique, the newly founded *American Architect and Building News,* as well as *Century Magazine,* stimulated interest in colonial houses. In November of 1877, J. Cleveland Cady, designer of the Museum of Natural History and other important buildings, addressed the New York Society of Architects. His subject was not the European precedents for his more monumental commissions, but the modest Dutch-Colonial farmhouses of New Jersey, for which he professed admiration.

By the end of the 1880s, eighteenth-century American architecture was eliciting both popular and learned approbation. Like the English Ecclesiologists of the Oxford Movement and the Cambridge Camden Society of the first half of the nineteenth century, who associated the classical revival with secularism and equated Gothic architecture with godliness, American critics had begun to associate early American architecture with high moral purpose. John Calvin Stevens and Albert Winslow Cobb asserted in 1889 that

> wherever the democratic spirit was earliest developed and most marked, there the work done by our American Carpenter-Architects of the Colonial and early National times exhibits most of pure beauty. In and around Philadelphia and along the New England coast from

Plymouth to Portland; throughout that territory where the protest against black slavery rang out long before the protest against tyrannies of the Crown; there, especially, we find the genuine refinement and delicacy, the temperate, telling use of detail, so desirable in architectural composition.

Not only did these developments influence the emergence of a colonial revival style in architecture, but they also established architecture—i.e., aesthetics—as a criterion for preservation. True, the use of this criterion remained limited and tied to associative historical principles in many cases, but it prepared the ground for William Sumner Appleton and his successors.

The ability of Americans to look at their own architecture as part of a heritage, and not merely of time past, was hampered by a native tendency to emphasize the practical and to evaluate buildings in purely utilitarian terms. This national predilection was mitigated by a movement in English intellectual life that began to take shape in the 1840s and had powerfully influenced American thinkers by the time of the Centennial. In England, architects and designers like Augustus Welby Northmore Pugin, John Ruskin, and William Morris were busy studying and reviving past forms for a host of philosophical, social, and aesthetic reasons. Their reverence for medieval art, for example, led them to decry the industrialized degradation of their own time. Ruskin, in particular, was a polemicist of enormous impact whose books enjoyed at least as much currency in America as they did at home. His *Seven Lamps of Architecture*, which appeared in 1849, included among its principles not only Beauty and Truth but Memory, a key to the importance of the past. Ruskin's antiquarianism was humanized by his heartfelt belief in the relevance of past forms to modern life. At the age of twenty-four he journeyed to Italy, where he saw " . . . wrecks of lovely things destroyed, remains of them unrespected, *all* going to decay, nothing rising but ugliness and meanness. . . . " Two years later, he returned to find in Venice that the Grand Canal below the Rialto was adorned with " . . . *gas lamps!* . . . in grand new iron posts of the latest Birmingham fashion. The modern work has set its plague spot everywhere—the moment you begin to feel [the past], you are thrust into the nineteenth century."

Passionate utterances like these educated a generation, including Americans who took stock of what in their own brief history was worth preserving. Interest in beauty, even in the 1890s, took on environmental dimensions when the Trustees of Public Reservations incorporated in 1891 in Massachusetts to voice their concerns as private citizens for the disappearance of open space. So impressed by this concept was a group of British friends, that just a few years later, in 1894, they founded the English National Trust. Six years later C. R. Ashbee, an English preservationist, visited the United States on a fact-finding mission: the British wondered if a similar national organization could be established in America. Ashbee found that the views of local preservation groups were too disparate to allow for a unified approach at that time, and it was not until 1949, with no formal assist from the British, that the National Trust for Historic Preservation was founded.

The work of Appleton at the SPNEA and that of a growing number of local preservationists in New England created repercussions along the length of the Eastern seaboard. For one thing, the cultural establishment could no longer ignore American architecture and decorative arts. In 1925, the Metropolitan Museum of Art opened its American wing, a gift of Mr. and Mrs. Robert W. DeForest, which incorporated twenty-five rooms from colonial- and federal-era buildings. Although the rationale for the new wing was primarily an aesthetic one, regional pride and nativism had not been eclipsed totally, as the following remarks excerpted from the dedication address prove:

> American history hitherto has had no comprehensive background in our city. The gift of this building, devoted to American art, enables a realistic visualization of the past of America to every citizen of New York, a visualization hitherto only enabled by a visit to New England or other parts of the country where landmarks of our Colonial days have been preserved. Fortunately for us all, some of the old America is left.
>
> Traditions are one of the integral assets of a country. Much of America of today has lost sight of its traditions. Their stage settings have largely passed away along with the actors. Many of our people are not cognizant of our traditions and the principles for which our fathers struggled and died. The tremendous changes in the character of our nation and the influx of foreign ideas utterly at variance with those held by the men who gave us the Republic threaten, and unless checked may shake, the foundations of our Republic.

In the same decade the surviving eighteenth- and nineteenth-century houses of Fairmount Park were brought under the management of the Philadelphia Museum of Art, whose director, Fiske Kimball, had delivered a series of lectures on early American architecture at the Metropolitan Museum in 1920. (These lectures were published two years later as *Domestic Architecture of the American Colonies and of the Early Republic*.) In these developments we can see the increasing interchange between scholarly interest in American architecture and local and regional preservation efforts.

The private undertaking that was to dwarf all previous efforts of historic preservation began in 1926, when W.A.R. Goodwin, rector of Bruton Parish Church in Williamsburg, Virginia, caught the interest of John D. Rockefeller, Jr., during a Phi Beta Kappa meeting and dinner in Williamsburg, the colonial capital. Goodwin had the determination of his predecessors, Ann Pamela Cunningham and William Sumner Appleton. His vision encompassed not merely a single property of significance, nor even a string of important houses scattered throughout several states, but the restoration of an entire eighteenth-century town—houses, dependencies, public buildings, streets, and landscaping—a total environment to be resuscitated from the past. Goodwin looked upon Williamsburg as "the Cradle of the Republic" and "the birthplace of liberty." He was not only interested in rescuing the physical evidence of the past, but also in what he called "the spirit of the past." The Colonial Williamsburg Foundation's motto, "That the Future May Learn from the Past," sums up the motivating force not only of Goodwin but of Rockefeller as well. (See Figure 2-5.)

Goodwin's version appealed to Rockefeller, and, step by step, the patron's financial support fell into line with the rector's grand scheme. Such unprecedented philanthrophy made the restoration of Colonial Williamsburg the first American experiment in the museum-oriented preservation of a community. It also created, unintentionally, the first interdisciplinary training program for historic preservation professionals.

The only other single private investment in historic preservation to equal Rockefeller's was made by Henry Ford, but Ford's intent was radically different. His Greenfield Village at Dearborn, Michigan, was meant to be, in Ford's own words, an "animated textbook" conceived as a teaching tool. In the view of one curator who visited in 1938, it was "a mixed-up hodgepodge." Even though teaching was Ford's primary purpose, his twofold lesson of simple American life and the power of inventions to transform it was conveyed by real historic buildings and their artifacts. The fact that the buildings had been torn from their original sites renders their value dubious by today's standards of preservation, which recognize a structure's site as essential to its historical integrity. Impending demolition is usually considered today as the only justification for moving a building from its original location.

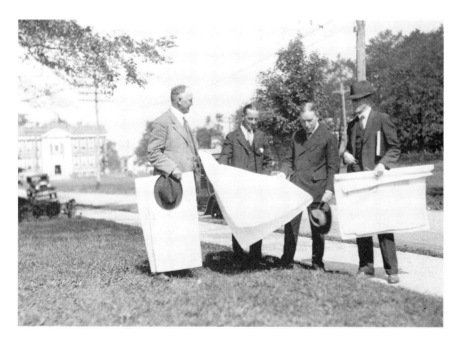

Figure 2-5   A prerestoration planning meeting in Williamsburg. Dr. W.A.R. Goodwin is at the far left; John D. Rockefeller, Jr., is third from left. They are shown consulting with restoration staff members Robert Trimble and Arthur Shurcliff. The Williamsburg High School in the background stands on the site of the eighteenth-century Governors' Palace, which has since been reconstructed at its original location. Note the overhead utility wires, which were sunk underground during restoration.

Despite this, Greenfield Village remains a pioneering experiment in the use of historic buildings for educational purposes. As one of only two major privately funded schemes of the period to create historic outdoor museum environments, it brought an awareness of preservation to a large public. It also stimulated professional discussion of historic preservation practice, and helped to establish the idea of outdoor museums (which had been initiated in Stockholm, Sweden, in the late nineteenth century) as a major form of preservation in America. Further, Greenfield Village helped to bridge the development of the preservation movement from house museum to historic district.

Millions of visitors to Colonial Williamsburg and Greenfield Village returned home with changed attitudes about the meanings of American history. Whether those attitudes were compatible with the intentions of John D. Rockefeller and Henry Ford is difficult to say. One thing is certain, however. Historic buildings, "villages," sites, and monuments were still experienced by the majority of Americans as momentary detours from everyday life, not as integral to it. Visitors might perceive such buildings and sites as celebratory, educational, commemorative, or patriotic, but they were singular—rarely part of the workplace of the familiar neighborhood. Even such powerful phenomena as Colonial Williamsburg and Greenfield Village did not seem able to elicit in American preservationists an understanding of environmental management in those communities and neighborhoods where Americans worked and lived. It took the action of the citizens and local government of Charleston, South Carolina, to do that, by designating the first Old and Historic District in 1931 (see Chapter 4).

In reviewing the early years of the preservation movement in the United States, several things strike one most clearly. First, from the very beginning, women like Ann Pamela Cunningham and Mrs. William Holstein were highly visible in their preservation efforts and in most cases exercised the leadership that men seemed loath to employ. Second, patriotism was the most obvious motivation, a patriotism that approached religious zeal at times. These patriotic moving forces sustained themselves and became intertwined with educational motives in the minds of such early twentieth-century proponents as Rockefeller and Ford. It was William Sumner Appleton at the SPNEA in Boston, however, who launched interest in the aesthetics of architecture as a basic criterion for preservation in addition to the associative values of history. Interest in the monument for the monument's sake, rather than for what happened at it, laid the basis for an easy acceptance of the developments in preservation planning that would occur in the second half of the twentieth century.

Finally, one must remember that early leadership in the preservation movement was characterized by its reliance on private citizens, not on government, and especially not federal government. Government's contributions to preservation have been made primarily in the twentieth century. It should be further noted that most, if not all, of this private concern for our national patrimony came from such affluent Americans as Appleton, who, throughout his career, volunteered his services to the SPNEA which he had founded. Therein lies yet another distinction of the

American preservation movement. Outside the United States, government agencies have exercised responsibility for preservation leadership since the 1840s.

Throughout the decades of the 1930s and 1940s, the initiative of women continued to characterize the active preservation movement at the local level even as the focus of that movement broadened from its traditional house-museum form. The name of Katherine Warren has thus become synonymous with the success of the Preservation Society of Newport County in Newport, Rhode Island, as has that of Dr. Mary Wingfield Scott with the William Burd Branch of the Association for the Preservation of Virginia Antiquities in Richmond, Katherine Miller with the Natchez and Pilgrimage Garden Clubs in Natchez, Mississippi, and Emily Edwards with the San Antonio Conservation Society in San Antonio, Texas. These were just a few of the early leaders in their respective communities.

The interests of these female pioneers in the preservation movement were often linked to saving specific buildings, and their organizational affiliation was often the local garden club. Their collective vision can be characterized as broad and their attitudes and actions, tenacious. They are among those private leaders of American society who guided the transition of preservation from a preoccupation with isolated house museums to a neighborhood concern for the environments in which particularly notable buildings stood. In doing this they not only continued the quality of leadership in the private sector so characteristic of America, but they maintained the prominence of women in the movement as well.

CHAPTER 3

The Preservation Movement and the National Trust for Historic Preservation

B Y THE END of the Second World War, preservationists had come to realize the need for a national, private, nonprofit organization to unite expertise and
leadership with the preservation movement's growing
popular support. There was also a need seen for an organizational entity which could take on the problems of
property stewardship that the federal government could
not. At the time, there was simply no nationwide organization which could respond to controversial preservation
issues with greater alacrity and freedom than could
government. The establishment in 1947 of the National
Council for Historic Sites and Buildings was a first step toward securing a congressionally chartered National Trust
for Historic Preservation in the United States.
Unlike the American conservation movement,
which has created a spate of national organizations devoted to the various aspects of conservationists' interests,
the American historic preservation movement has developed only one major organization—the National Trust. A

number of national organizations, such as the American Institute of Architects, the American Society of Civil Engineers, the Society of Architectural Historians, and the Victorian Society in America, have operative preservation committees as part of their overall enterprises. More recently, special-interest preservation organizations have developed, including Preservation Action, the Association for Preservation Technology, the Center for Preservation Law, and the National Conference of State Historic Preservation Officers. The National Trust, however, remains the largest single national organization representing the private citizen or a broad spectrum of preservation issues. Thus the history of the National Trust, and its growth, tend to mirror the growth of the preservation movement in America. To study the changes in the Trust as it has developed is, indeed, to study the course of preservation in America since the Second World War.

The National Park Service was instrumental in the creation of the National Trust, for among the earliest advocates for a private national preservation organization was Horace M. Albright, the former NPS director. And Ronald F. Lee, who became the northeast regional director of the Park Service, was a catalyst in unifying the diverse interests of individual promoters of such a national organization, among them George A. McAneny and David F. Finley. McAneny was president of New York's American Scenic and Historic Preservation Society, which had been founded in 1895 with the express intent of saving a row of Greek-Revival houses on Washington Square. Finley, director of the National Gallery of Art, was particularly interested in preserving Oak Hill, President James Monroe's house near Leesburg, Virginia, perhaps because of its proximity to Oatlands, which was then owned by Finley's mother-in-law, Mrs. William Corcoran Eustis. (Oatlands is today a National Trust property.) Other early proponents of a national organization were Fiske Kimball, director of the Philadelphia Museum of Art, and Newton B. Drury, director of the National Park Service.

In October 1946, in an address to the American Association for State and Local History, Ronald F. Lee portrayed the changing nature of postwar technological America and warned that the preservation movement must emerge as a unified national private and public constituency with a clear program of action. He stressed the urgency of surveys to identify resources worthy of preservation, of cooperation among national, state, and local organizations, of active community involvement, and of advocacy on the part of preservationists across the country.

Lee's remarks brought into clearer focus the notion of a national preservation organization. About the same time, he, George McAneny, and Christopher Crittenden, a founder of the American Association for State and Local History, and eventually a trustee of the National Trust, met with David Finley at the National Gallery of Art in Washington, D.C. They decided to convene a preorganizational meeting to explore the kind of group that might be created and to follow it with a larger conference in the spring of 1947.

The preorganizational meeting was held on February 5, 1947. It brought together ten selected representatives of key interests and re-

sulted in further endorsement of the idea of a new organization. The conferees produced an invitation list for an organizational conference to be
held by mid-April that would establish the National Council for Historic
Sites and Buildings.

On April 15 that conference was held at the National Gallery of Art.
George McAneny presented the concept of a National Trust that would
receive contributions of property and funds and administer properties—a
concept patterned on the British National Trust and the San Antonio Conservation Society in Texas, both of which were already established organizations that had been carefully studied. The conferees included Mc-
Aneny's proposal in the bylaws they adopted. Thus the National Council
came into being. Ronald Lee of the National Park Service had the daunt-
ing job of secretary, with no budget, no office, and no support staff.

A significant feature of the April meeting was the dominance of the
grass-roots leaders of the preservation movement. For the first time, local
preservationists from around the country heard what was happening in
other localities and saw clear evidence that they were not alone in what
they were attempting to achieve.

Once the council's establishment was announced, the need for a central office to handle the overwhelming flood of correspondence its formation generated was recognized. Once again Ronald Lee exercised leadership in recommending the appointment of Frederick L. Rath, Jr., an
historian then serving at the Franklin D. Roosevelt National Historic Site
at Hyde Park, New York. Rath became the council's first executive secretary, working from offices on the third floor of Ford's Theatre in Washington, D.C. (See Figure 3-1.)

Figure 3-1
Four men, each of
whom served as
chief executive offi-
cer of the National
Trust, compare
notes during a re-
ception at the
Smithsonian Institu-
tion. From right to
left: Frederick Rath,
first director; Dr.
Richard Howland,
first president;
Robert Garvey, sec-
ond director; and
James Biddle, second
president.

When they convened at the National Gallery for their annual meeting in November, 1948, the delegates of the council recognized that their organization had already become an established entity and no longer seemed an appendage of the National Park Service. This meeting was seen as the forum for discussing the formation and goals of the proposed National Trust. Rath had previously secured the services of an assistant, Betty Walsh, with whose help he had prepared a budget for the council for 1949. He also started exploring the possibilities of garnering support and assistance from philanthropic organizations such as the Avalon Foundation, a Mellon family trust. Rath further aided in preparing a National Trust charter bill for submission to Congress. The council leaders had already appointed a committee on the organization of a National Trust, and that committee's report had convinced the council's executive board to launch on all-out campaign to obtain a congressional charter within the following year. The perceived need for such a charter and the appointment of the attorney general of the United States as one of the three ex-officio members of the board of trustees (along with the secretary of the interior and the director of the National Gallery) gave the new organization immediate national status. It also guaranteed the enterprise's public identity as a separate but government-allied organization, a guarantee that would prove important in the Trust's subsequent involvement in controversial issues and give authority to its statements and positions.

At the November meeting, the charter was formally presented by H. Alexander Smith, son of the United States senator from New Jersey, whose interests, legal background, and political connections had given him a major part in drafting it. The conferees officially endorsed the report of the Committee for the Organization of a National Trust. Smith and his associates continued to refine a charter that would give the Trust a quasi-public status, comparable to that of the Smithsonian Institution, with which preservationists in the private sector could identify.

In February 1949, the committee met for a final review of the charter bill before its introduction in Congress. Congressman J. Hardin Peterson of Florida was the principal proponent of the measure in the House of Representatives. There was no Senate leader to champion the bill at the time, and preservation leaders adopted the tactic of urging individual members of the Senate to report the bill to the floor. The *New York Times* became a strong ally in this effort, and on October 17, 1949, the bill passed unanimously and went to President Truman for signature. The president signed it on October 26, and on October 31, Major General U. S. Grant III, president of the National Council, announced the creation of the National Trust for Historic Preservation in the United States. The council and the Trust coexisted for a short time, and then the parent organization was dissolved in favor of the newly established Trust. In May 1950, the Trust moved its headquarters from the third floor of Ford's Theatre to the upper floors of the Octagon at the invitation of the American Institute of Architects, which owned the building. This distinguished structure, scene of the signing of the treaty that concluded the War of 1812, served only until 1951, when growth took the Trust to an upper floor of a building on Lafayette Square. By this time, the staff had been enlarged to include his-

torian Helen Bullock, formerly of Colonial Williamsburg and author of
The Williamsburg Art of Cookery.

Woodlawn Plantation in nearby Mount Vernon, Virginia, first preserved as a residence by Senator and Mrs. Oscar Underwood of Alabama
and subsequently rescued from destruction by a local citizens' action
group, became the first National Trust property in 1951 (Figure 3-2). Its
acquisition triggered a debate within the Trust about stewardship of
property. Rath felt that all Trust properties should be centrally administered; some of the trustees wanted all properties to be self-sufficient. Because of the disagreement, Rath gave up his position as the organization's
first director, a post to which he had been appointed after the Trust was
created.

In 1956, the Trust realigned itself, abolishing the title of director and
securing its first president, Richard H. Howland, a native of Rhode Island
and holder of a doctorate in classical studies from Harvard. He had
launched the art history program at Johns Hopkins University and had
been a force in the American School of Classical Studies in Athens.

Dispensing advice by letter, telephone, and personal field trip to an
ever-enlarging and changing constituency, the organization took on an
increasingly educational and informational role. The preservation movement was evolving. Its composition had changed, no longer dominated
by informed, affluent amateurs who were the champions of individual
house museums, but now increasingly composed of more knowledgeable
individuals whose concern was the overall planning and protection of

Figure 3-2
Woodlawn Planta-
tion, Mount Vernon,
Virginia: the first
property acquired by
the National Trust
was accepted with
no endowment.

entire historic districts. In the process, volunteers gradually began to be replaced by paid staff. In the less litigious era of its early years, the Trust had little or no reason to call upon the potential powers inherent in its charter through the inclusion of such ex-officio board members as the attorney general of the United States. Its stewardship of property continued to expand.

In 1958, the Trust moved from Lafayette Square to offices that it rented in a contemporary high rise at 2000 K Street. Terry Brust (later Morton) joined the staff and, under the guidance of Helen Bullock, became assistant editor of the Trust's newsletter and, later, assistant editor of the Trust's magazine, *Historic Preservation*. By the time Terry Morton left the organization twenty-six years later, she had become vice president and publisher of the Preservation Press, the publishing subsidiary of the National Trust.

In retirement, Hardinge Scholle, at one time curator of the Art Institute of Chicago and then director of the Museum of the City of New York, assisted the Trust on a part-time basis. In 1958, William Murtagh, trained as an architect and architectural historian, left the directorship of Pennsylvania's Historic Bethlehem, Inc., to accept an appointment as assistant to the president of the Trust. At that time, therefore, there was a staff of five professionals, aided by several assistants, in its attempts to handle an ever-growing volume of correspondence. Requests for assistance relating to museum curatorship, interpretation of historic resources, and the postwar urban renewal and interstate highway programs came from a growing membership (then numbering about 2,200), as well as from the general public.

In 1959, when Richard M. Howland left the Trust to become assistant to the secretary of the Smithsonian Institution, the office of president was abolished by the board of trustees and that of executive director was reinstated. Robert R. Garvey, Jr. came to the post from the presidency of Old Salem, Inc. William Murtagh then became director of education, and Terry Brust—now Mrs. M. Hamilton Morton—continued in her publishing capacities under the direction of Helen Bullock. The offices were moved to the third floor of the Stephen Decatur House on Lafayette Square, which had been left to the Trust by the late Mrs. Truxtun Beale. This proved to be a relocation of some permanence: the offices remained at Decatur House through the 1960s and well into the 1970s, expanding into adjacent town houses that had been reconstructed during the Kennedy administration.

As the Trust's membership continued to grow, so did its property holdings. In addition to Woodlawn Plantation and Decatur House, in 1954 the organization acquired Casa Amesti in Monterey, California (known locally as the Old Capital Club). In 1958, it acquired Shadows-on-the-Teche (Figure 3-3) in New Iberia, Louisiana, and in 1961, the Woodrow Wilson House in Washington, D.C. The Louisiana property was secured through the generosity of William Weeks Hall; the Wilson house, through the benevolence of Edith Bolling Galt Wilson, widow of the president. Most of these holdings came to the Trust with endowments considered sufficient at the time to operate them as historic house museums. Subse-

Figure 3-3
The Shadows-on-
the-Teche, New
Iberia, Louisiana:
William Weeks Hall,
who donated the
plantation to the
Trust, included an
endowment for its
maintenance. His ac-
tion set a pattern for
future Trust acquisi-
tions.

quently, inflation has proven these endowments to have been woefully inadequate.

The sixties proved to be a decade of creative change for the Trust, specifically, and for the preservation movement as a whole. With passage of the National Historic Preservation Act of 1966, the Trust, which was the only private organization in the country cited by name in the law, became the recipient of federal funds through a matching grant program. This put the Trust in a position to embark on development to an extent previously undreamt of, and brought it closer in organizational identity to a national institution like the Smithsonian that uses private philanthropy and income from memberships, as well as monies appropriated by Congress, to carry forward its programs. As of 1998, the Trust is no longer budgeted to receive federal funds as it once was and returned to the private nonprofit organization it was prior to 1966.

Further, as a result of direct mail campaigns, the Trust's membership, which had barely reached 20,000 before 1966, exploded to well over 100,000 in a short time. Russell V. Keune, who had been assistant keeper of the Department of the Interior's National Register of Historic Places, became the Trust's vice president for preservation services. Through his energy and inventiveness, the Trust's ability to educate the public was enlarged considerably with the establishment, among other facilities, of regional offices across the country, beginning in 1971, which apply professional skills to local preservation problems formerly handled out of headquarters in Washington, D.C. A board of advisors, consisting of two representatives from each state and territory, helps the Trust bring its expertise closer to the grass-roots level.

Visits of field representatives from the regional offices give affiliated member organizations a sense of mission which helps them see their local work as part of a national effort. The representatives help provide access to specific resources not necessarily available to the local individual member or member organization, while keeping the Trust aware of the diversity of preservation issues nationwide. The relationship between headquarters and the regional offices and advisors not only reflects a complex preservation network, but enables the Trust to develop practical programs responding to the emerging needs of special-interest constituencies. Among these are such projects as the Main Street, Rural Conservation, and Neighborhood Conservation programs launched in the 1970s. (See Chapter 11.) The former has since become the National Main Street Center. With termination of the tall ships program which had been part of the Bicentennial celebration, the Trust received that effort's assets and, in response to Senator Edward Kennedy's proposal that a separate, new maritime organization be set up, established the Maritime Preservation program, effectively defeating Kennedy's plan. The Maritime Preservation Program ceased to operate in 1995 after its assets had been dispersed through grants.

After the passage of the 1966 Historic Preservation Act, Robert Garvey left the executive directorship to become director of the Advisory Council on Historic Preservation called for in the new law, and James Biddle, a Philadelphian who was then curator of the American Wing of the Metropolitan Museum of Art in New York, became president of the National Trust, a title reinstituted by the board of trustees. For approximately twelve years, under Biddle's leadership and with the assistance of grants from the Department of the Interior, the Trust continued to expand its programs and its network.

When Biddle left in 1980, his post was assumed by Michael L. Ainslie, who was engaged for his fund-raising capabilities and experience in the corporate world. During Ainslie's tenure, the headquarters continued to develop as the corporate center of the organization, the regional offices came to reflect an ever-enlarging spectrum of Trust programs, and the board of advisors became more involved in the implementation of Trust programs at the state level.

Seeing preservation as an "ethic for the eighties"—a conference in Williamsburg in the late 1970s having resulted in the publication of a book by that title—the board of trustees approved a five-year plan that was adopted in 1983. The plan defined the Trust's mission as fostering preservation of the nation's diverse architectural and cultural heritage for all Americans and its fundamental role as advocating the ethic of property stewardship; strengthening local, state, and national preservation interests; and influencing public policy in shaping the values and methods of preservation. Through a broad collegial process, the Trust set as its objectives to:

1. Identify and act on important national preservation issues;
2. Support, broaden, and strengthen organized preservation efforts;
3. Target communications to those who affect the future of historic resources; and
4. Expand private and public financial resources for preservation activities.

In the Trust's effort to become more service-oriented and responsive to the preservation community, more innovative in program development, and stronger in its advocacy of preservation issues, the process of strategic planning continued. A major outcome of this process was the establishment of a program council, comprised of staff, members, advisors, and trustees, to systematize new proposals and maximize value in dollar expenditures in the face of ever-broadening involvement and needs.

The National Historic Preservation Act of 1966 called for the establishment of grants to support the activities of the National Trust and the states. Efforts to change the program were begun in the Carter administration and continued during the Reagan administration. There have been severe reductions in the grants-in-aid to the states and to the Trust, and attempts to eliminate those grants entirely.

The more generous government grants of previous administrations had caused the Trust to overextend itself in critical areas which felt the pinch of subsequent cutbacks: programming, enhanced administration, and the direct-mail costs of membership. Further, the inflationary impact on previously adequate property endowments and the departure of Ainslie prior to the launching of the fund-raising campaign projected upon his arrival also had their negative impact on the organization. All of these developments placed J. Jackson Walter, Ainslie's successor, in the position of streamlining the Trust's programs and organization. Since 1993, Richard Moe has been president.

The National Trust was begun in the late 1940s as an organization for the stewardship of property. Under the rubric of education, it has since attempted to take on a great diversity of programs in the name of preservation. As a result, the preservation movement and the Trust, reflective of the preservation movement in general, now stand in a crosscurrent of change. The Trust attempts to give meaningful service to an increasingly diversified constituency, using resources of capital and personnel that fail to keep up with demand, and as a result it thus appears to be changing from the professional, humanistic organization its founders envisaged. Indeed, those founders might never have foreseen the diversity of operations that engage the organization today nor the needs that are generated as a result. (See Figure 3-4.)

The current beaux-arts home of the Trust, at 1785 Massachusetts Avenue, was erected as an apartment structure that at one time housed Andrew Mellon and his family as well as Lord Duveen, from whom Mellon acquired many of the great canvases that became the nucleus of the National Gallery of Art's collection. This association and the first major philanthropic initiatives for the Trust—through the Avalon and Old Dominion Foundations of the children of Andrew Mellon—have cemented the continuing connection between the Trust and the Mellon family through the years.

The organizational growth of the National Trust through the establishment of a board of advisors and regional offices, reflects the growth and broadening of the preservation movement since the Second World War. At the local level, such long-established preservation organizations as the San Antonio Conservation Society and the Historic Charleston

Figure 3-4   The National Trust has developed a broad spectrum of activities and programs to stimulate discussion and the interchange of ideas. Trust properties are often the sites of such meetings: this is a training conference at Woodlawn Plantation.

Foundation have been joined by similar organizations in all parts of the country. These have come into existence to provide a unified voice for local residents who are concerned by the rapidity of change taking place at the grass-roots level. Historic Denver, the Hartford Architectural Conservancy, Preservation Tulsa, Friends of Wheeling, Pasadena Heritage, Billings Preservation Society, the Blue Grass Trust for Historic Preservation—all are representative examples of private preservation activity at the local level and are usually member organizations of the Trust. (See Figure 3-5.)

A similar development can be observed at the state level: as state government preservation offices have been established and/or activated through the stimulus of the National Historic Preservation Act of 1966, so, too, has the national Trust stimulated private organizations statewide. Thus the Historic Preservation League of Oregon, Inherit New Hampshire, the Historic Hawaii Foundation, the Heritage Foundation of Arizona, and the Louisiana Preservation Alliance, to name but a few, have joined such long-established statewide preservation organizations as the Association for the Preservation of Tennessee Antiquities and the Association for the Preservation of Virginia Antiquities.

With modest financial support which has never reached its potential, the staffs of the state historic preservation offices have struggled to carry

Figure 3-5   In the early 1960s the Trust acquired Lyndhurst, at Tarrytown, New York, from the Duchess de Tallyrand-Perigord. The responsibility was a great one: in addition to the main house, seen in this original drawing by architect Alexander Jackson Davis, the multiacre property carried with it approximately twelve other buildings.

out their responsibilities. At the same time, the strength and activity of private organizations in the various states and of state preservation offices have become increasingly vital in carrying on the work of preservation. America thus seems to have greater strength in preservation at the state and local levels today, in both the public and private sectors, than at any time in the past.

CHAPTER 4

Government and the Preservation Movement

U NLIKE ENGLAND, whose organizational concern for the natural environment has been accompanied by a concern for the built environment, America has tended to keep her interests in natural conservation distinct from those of preservation. The federal government entered both of these fields, however, in the late nineteenth century. In 1872, it established itself as a conservationist by setting aside Yellowstone National Park (Figure 4-1) to protect the "curiosities" and "wonders" sighted and reported by early hunters and trappers in the area. In 1889, to protect the prehistoric ruins from looters, Congress authorized the acquisition of Casa Grande in Arizona (Figure 4-2). The following year, Chickamauga Battlefield in Georgia was authorized as the first military park. This came about shortly after national cemeteries were authorized because of pressure from veterans' groups.

As we have already noted, state and local governments had made intermittent forays into the preservation field at least as early as 1816, when Independence Hall was purchased and subsequently restored. The tradition of strong private support, however, typified by such figures as Cunningham and Appleton and culminating in the major philanthropy of Rockefeller and Ford in the 1930s, established preservation as a stronghold of American private entrepreneurship. State legislatures could

Figure 4-1
Yellowstone was the first National Park established in the United States. It and other similarly vast lands subsequently acquired by the federal government secured America's world leadership in the conservation of open space.

Figure 4-2
Arizona's Casa Grande was the first prehistoric ruin acquired by the United States government. The huge structural canopy was added in an attempt to protect the ruins from erosion by the elements.

sometimes be persuaded to appropriate monies in the cause of preservation. Thus, in 1850, New York purchased Hasbrouck House, George
Washington's headquarters in Newburgh, to be developed into the nation's first historic house museum, and Tennessee purchased Andrew
Jackson's Hermitage for a similar purpose in 1856. Such rare benefactions
from a state or local government as the 1908 gift of $5,000 to the Ladies'
Hermitage Association were extraordinary for their time and reflected no
policy of financial assistance at the federal level of the type put in place
with the passage of the National Historic Preservation Act in 1966.

The upheaval of the Great Depression transformed government
structure, and the posture of federal nonintervention began to change
rapidly. Before the 1930s, two important government actions were taken
that, though still defined in tightly circumscribed terms, set the stage for
modern preservation. These were the Antiquities Act of 1906 and the creation of the National Park Service in 1916.

The Antiquities Act of 1906 was the legal response to pressure
from educational and scientific groups concerned about the wholesale
destruction of prehistoric remains in the Southwest by pilferers and
looters, either for their personal collections or for resale. Vandalism and
trafficking in Amerindian artifacts were explicitly enjoined by this legislation, which sought to prevent the unlicensed excavation, removal or
injury of " . . . any historic or prehistoric ruin or monument, or any
object of antiquity, situated on lands owned or controlled by the Government of the United States." It further provided that the president
might " . . . declare by public proclamation historic landmarks, historic
and prehistoric structures, and other objects of historic or scientific
interest to be national monuments." All of the foregoing provisions
applied only to federally owned lands, but their impact was potentially
far-reaching nonetheless.

A decade later, in 1916, the earlier work of John Muir and the Sierra
Club culminated in the creation of the National Park Service to " . . . promote and regulate the use of the federal areas known as national parks,
monuments, and reservations." As early as 1892, John Muir had founded
the Sierra Club to promote the establishment of national parks and to
protect them as national resources. The Antiquities Act of 1906 signified
the government's growing concern for land conservation and for the protection of native American cultures.

Today, the National Park Service ranks as one of the largest managers of public lands within the bureaus of the Department of the Interior. To carry out its responsibilities for the almost 84 million acres of
land within its various jurisdictions, it is responsible for a budget of
approximately $2.3 billion with a staff of over 23,000 people and 120,000
volunteers.

It was not always so. The beginnings of the National Park Service
were indeed modest. The act that authorized the Park Service called for a
total budget of $19,500, out of which came the $4,500 annual salary of a
director, the $2,500 salary of an assistant, and the $2,000 salary of a chief
clerk. Such was its growth a year later that the fledgling service was
managing fourteen national parks and twenty-one national monuments,

spending approximately half a million dollars to develop facilities for almost half a million visitors.

The genius behind this rapid growth was Stephen Mather, the first director, who was assisted by Horace M. Albright, former superintendent of Yellowstone National Park, and ultimately Mather's successor (Figure 4-3). Mather was a dynamic, wealthy industrialist from Chicago who was responsible not only for establishing the organizational framework of the Park Service, with its superintendents and rangers, but also for the essential spirit of the Park Service as well. Advantageously connected, he indulged in private fund raising to establish the new effort quickly, in addition to using his own money to attain certain things he felt important to achieve. In this respect, he is firmly placed within the established preservation tradition of private leadership and private capital, albeit exercised in this instance within a governmental framework.

The creation of the Park Service and its placement under the aegis of the Department of the Interior shifted attention from the traditionally historic East and South to vast areas of the West and Southwest. Initially, it was thought by many preservationists that the inclusion of natural areas, aboriginal sites, and archaeologically significant properties would threaten to dilute the old Eastern emphasis on buildings. As events devel-

Figure 4-3   Shown at a meeting in Yellowstone National Park in 1923 are, from left to right, President Warren G. Harding, Stephen Mather, first director of the National Park Service, Secretary of the Interior Hubert Work, and Mather's assistant, Horace Albright, wearing the official Park Service uniform.

oped, however, it was this framework of environmental conservation-*cum*-preservation that, in the final analysis, helped historic preservation to achieve new prominence and brought it into the planning mode by which it is often categorized today.

Two events of 1933 proved decisive in the maturing climate of twentieth-century preservation. The founding of the Historic American Buildings Survey established federal interest and involvement in buildings owned by private parties; and the work of the new Civilian Conservation Corps, also directed by the National Park Service, helped legitimize government management of the built environment.

The genesis of the Historic American Buildings Survey (HABS) is often recounted as an example of how New Deal emergency measures cut through federal red tape. Charles Peterson, restoration architect for the National Park Service, recognized the need for a national architectural archive. He also knew how many architects and draftsmen had been thrown out of work by the Great Depression. His master stroke was in combining the need for historical documentation with human exigency. Peterson's proposal to create nationwide survey teams of professionals who would prepare measured drawings and photographs of historic buildings was presented to the Park Service on November 13, 1933. It called for less than half a million dollars to employ roughly one thousand out-of-work architects through February, 1934. Four days later, Secretary of the Interior Harold Ickes authorized the necessary funds.

HABS did not survive for long under its emergency funding authorization, but by 1935 it was back in business, thanks to the initiative of local chapters of the American Institute of Architects, which cooperated with the Park Service and the Library of Congress, where the documentation would be catalogued, stored, and made available to the public. HABS was not meant to save buildings, and its early priorities of structures to be recorded were uneven because worthwhile historic buildings and unemployed architects were not always distributed equally. The agency did, however, create an incomparable national archive, quickly put to use for practical and scholarly purposes. It established consistent recording techniques that contributed to high professional standards and broadened the scope of preservation, since Peterson's guidelines included many types of nonresidential architecture often ignored by local preservationists, among them mills, barns, churches, lighthouses, and public buildings. By 1941, HABS had recorded 693 structures on 23,000 sheets of drawings, with photographic documentation covering each building. In 1969, the Historic American Engineering Record (HAER) was established to document American engineering and industrial structures. In 2000, the Historic American Landscapes Survey (HALS) was added to address the recording of landscapes important to our heritage. As of 2003, the HABS and HAER programs together covered 35,885 documented structures of which 28,824 represent those covered by HABS and 7,061 by HAER. As a new program, HALS is sufficiently new as to have no contributions at this writing. Coverage of the 35,885 documented structures of HABS and HAER consists of 55,439 drawings, 235,251 photographs, and 163,085 pages of written data. All of these materials, and the fruit of the agency's documentations are on file at the Library of Congress in the Department of Prints and Photographs.

Even before HABS was established, the Park Service had put the Civilian Conservation Corps (CCC) to work developing National Park sites. Two of the earliest projects where CCC labor was used extensively were Colonial National Historical Park at Yorktown, Virginia, and Morristown National Historical Park in northern New Jersey. According to the late Charles B. Hosmer, Jr., historian, teacher, and chronicler of the historic preservation movement in the United States:

> The CCC (which was sometimes referred to as the Emergency Conservation Work) had a tremendous impact on Yorktown. By mid-fall 1933 four companies totalling eight hundred men were available as a labor force. The supervisory personnel divided the work into six major projects: forestry rehabilitation, development of the terrain of the battlefield, construction of educational models, archaeological work, and the restoration and reconstruction of colonial buildings.

The CCC's (Figures 4-4 and 4-5) work categories illustrate the fact that environmental and cultural resources were being brought into direct relationship on a large scale for the first time. Such coordination emphasized the Park Service's growing concern with historic preservation and interpretation and began to justify the executive order of President Franklin D. Roosevelt on June 10, 1933, to transfer to the Interior Department all battlefields, parks, monuments, and cemeteries administered by

Figure 4-4   A crew of CCC workers reconstructs a portion of California's La Purisima Mission in 1938.

Figure 4-5
A view of the same
section of La
Purisima pho-
tographed in 1953.
Age and repeated
damage by earth-
quakes has made
such reconstruction
and heavy restora-
tion necessary in
many buildings of
the important His-
panic chain of mis-
sions along the
West Coast. The in-
tervening years since
the reconstruction
have laid a patina of
authenticity on the
"modern" work.
.

the War Department (which had enjoyed complete control over battlefield monuments) and the Forest Service. The combination of Roosevelt's order and his administration's willingness to spend emergency relief funding on cultural resources that had suddenly fallen within the purview of the Park Service gave new logic to government support for historic preservation. The New Deal was turning out to be a good deal for historic preservation.

The success of HABS and the impact of the Park Service's new involvement in preservation did not escape administrative notice. Even though restarting the economy was the New Deal's first order of business, the energetic and dedicated staff of the Park Service was already looking to the future. Everyone involved realized that existing programs and laws could never meet the task of preserving and interpreting the national heritage. Private organizations, encouraged by fresh federal interest, agitated for even greater governmental involvement. Prominent in the private sector was the staff at Colonial Williamsburg, which had become the most concentrated pool of preservation expertise in the country, frequently consulted by other private groups and by the Park Service itself.

The case for preservation was aided further by the personal interests of Secretary Ickes and President Roosevelt. In a very short period, a complicated series of meetings, memos, conferences, and debates (including an Interior Department study of European legislation and, finally, a Congressional hearing) culminated in a draft bill that proclaimed " . . . a national policy to preserve for public use historic sites, buildings, and objects of national significance for the inspiration and benefit of the people of the United States." Roosevelt signed the seminal Historic Sites Act into law on August 21, 1935, and it heralded the real coming of age of American preservation. Its greatest achievement was the wide latitude it gave the secretary of the interior to act in three ways: first, to establish an information base for preservation by conducting surveys and engaging in research; second, to implement preservation by acquiring, restoring, maintaining, and operating historic properties and by entering into cooperative agreements with like-minded private organizations; and third, to interpret the heritage thus identified with historic markers or by other educational means. With the Historic Sites Act the federal government finally possessed enabling legislation that could lead to coherent planning. Available at last was a coordinated policy that recognized the documentary value of buildings and sites which often combined patriotic, associative, and aesthetic content.

Between 1933 and 1935 preservation in the public sector made and consolidated more gains than in all previous years. Because of the Great Depression, the federal government was able to commit unprecedented resources to a multitude of needs, including historic preservation, resources that included not only money, but the increasing professionalism of the Park Service and, equally important, the muscle of the CCC. Although it is usually considered the great turning point in the history of preservation in America, the Historic Sites Act never achieved its maximum potential in its first years. The resources the New Deal was able to pour into economic recovery were preempted for the war effort before policy could be translated into the type of action needed at all levels of the federal bureaucracy.

At the local level, however, important actions had already been taken which were to change the preservation movement, redirect its energies, and make it the planning force it is today. These began in Charleston, South Carolina, in 1931, when the city council zoned a neighborhood known as the Battery as an "Old and Historic District." (See Figure 4-6.) Today such selectively zoned neighborhoods, usually known simply as historic districts, are ubiquitous, their establishment spurred by the passage of the National Historic Preservation Act in 1966.

A concerned citizenry and a sympathetic local government, stimulated by the construction of gas stations in what was essentially a residential neighborhood, and by the raids of museum directors and curators on the interior detailing of some of the best structures in the area for installation in other parts of the country, were receptive to Charleston's seminal zoning law. With the Battery's establishment as an historic district, the concept of preservation was to broaden, encompassing neighborhoods where average American citizens lived. Five years later, in 1936, the Louisiana state legislature authorized the Vieux Carré Commission in New Orleans to monitor development, in a fashion similar to that of Charleston, in the unique neighborhood that gave the commission its name.

Charleston's concept was manifold in impact. It created a major divergence in the path of the preservation movement and laid the basis for the mainstream planning position that exists in America today. With every citizen's house, environment, and neighborhood the prime focus of concern and action, it helped lay the groundwork for increased government interest and involvement at all levels. As a result, the historic preservation movement drew away from its preoccupation with house museums, and government, organizations, and private citizens began considering buildings of less than national significance as worthy of attention.

Concern for local vernacular structures, considered collectively in their neighborhood environments, would thenceforth mystify the unin-

formed. Americans had, after all, been used to limiting their perceptions of preservation to landmarks of national significance. A more rigorous evaluation and application of architectural knowledge would be needed to recognize the validity of preserving locally significant vernacular architecture within the context of its neighborhood. Given the variable humanistic values involved in all judgments relating to preservation, these new concerns tended to intensify the conflict which differences of opinion create. They also broadened the number of players on the preservation scene, bringing into the dialogue disparate segments of American society that had heretofore no common ground on which to discuss preservation.

The period from the beginning of the twentieth century to the advent of the Second World War was, then, a time of ever-increasing involvement and professionalism in federal preservation activities. Three basic legislative building blocks had been put in place: the Antiquities Act of 1906, the National Park Service of 1916, and the Historic Sites Act of 1935. The boom-bust economic cataclysms of the late 1920s and early 1930s were to prove highly beneficial to preservation efforts, especially through the make-work programs of the depression. In retrospect, it almost seems that there was an historical flash fire of action and creativity in the private sector as well as in government.

Figure 4-6
An aerial view of the core of Charleston, South Carolina's historic district, the first in the country. The neighborhood contains a high concentration of National Historic Landmarks, so designated by the office of the secretary of the interior.

As late as 1926, there were no historians, no architects, no archaeologists in the National Park Service. Historic properties consisted of some ruins and some Civil War battlefields. Neither Rockefeller's Williamsburg nor Ford's Greenfield Village had opened. The Historic Sites Act was a decade in the offing. By 1936, however, the picture was totally different. The Historic Sites Act had been made law the year before. An eager young staff of professional historians, architects, and archaeologists was at work in the federal government as well as in Rockefeller's massive privately funded project at Williamsburg. Both groups of professionals—in the Park Service and at Williamsburg—became the only major resources available to increasing multitudes of local preservation groups seeking help for their projects. The staff of the Park Service proved especially important to the history of preservation. Not only did some of the employees play a part in creating the National Trust for Historic Preservation in 1949, but a few of the younger ones even helped in the creation of the National Historic Preservation Act of 1966, thus providing a continuity of knowledge and purpose to the preservation movement of the time that is all too often overlooked today.

The government's involvement with preservation, even as it increased in professionalism, was predominantly male, a sharp contrast with the highly visible role of women in the private sector throughout the decades leading up to the founding of the National Trust. Indeed, if the creation of the Trust did nothing more, it provided a platform on which the private sector and government could interact, bringing the monied interests of one into closer interaction with the professionalism of the other. (See Figure 4-7.)

Figure 4-7
An 1834 engraving of Hasbrouck House, which overlooks the Hudson River at Newburgh, New York. The building served as Washington's headquarters for the last two years of the Revolutionary War. Predating Mount Vernon as a house museum by a matter of months, it is today the flagship property in a highly professional network of state-run house museums.

CHAPTER 5

Government and Preservation Since World War II

THE LATE Ronald F. Lee, regional director of the National Park Service and secretary of the board of the National Trust, often observed that significant developments relating to preservation in government seem to occur approximately every generation. He was referring to the creation of the Park Service in 1916, the Depression-related preservation activities of the 1930s (especially through HABS), the congressional charter of the National Trust in the late 1940s, and the passage of the National Historic Preservation Act in 1966. Indeed, the frenzy of activity that the 1966 federal legislation unleashed makes the years leading up to its passage seem tranquil by comparison, despite the catalytic quality of some of the earlier events.

After World War II, government and the private sector became more interwoven than ever in dealing with preservation. This symbiosis was stimulated by the collective impact on the environment of two major well-intended but environmentally disruptive federal programs. These were the interstate road program within the new Department of Transportation and the urban renewal program of the Department of Housing and Urban Development. These well-funded government programs were causing major social displacement and widespread obliteration of visual landmarks in most parts of the country, especially in cities. Peter Blake's highly pictorial book, *God's Own Junkyard* (1964), which graphically illustrates automobile graveyards, overhead utility lines, and uncoordinated, cluttered signs, brought home to a thinking public the trashing of America which the throw-away mentality of the twentieth century seemed to foster. (See Figures 5-1 and 5-2.)

By the early 1960s, Williamsburg was the popular tourist destination of an increasingly informed and discriminating public. In the same period, the National Trust boasted a membership of over 15,000, published a magazine and a monthly newspaper, and administered half a dozen properties of national distinction. For sheer size and breadth of impact, no other preservation programs came close to the national stature of these two institutions—government and Trust. It was natural, therefore, for the two organizations to convene a three-day conference at Williamsburg in September of 1963 to review the history of preservation in America, to analyzc its philosophical basis, discuss its effectiveness, and determine ways of shaping its future. The result was a "Report on Principles and Guidelines for Historic Preservation in the United States." The conclusion of this report was published with the conference proceedings as *Historic Preservation Today*, a landmark publication that called for the equivalent of what eventually became the National Register of Historic Places and

Figure 5-1 Following World War II, Hartford, Connecticut, was among the cities substantially changed by the bulldozers of urban renewal and the interstate highway program.

Figure 5-2   Demolition erased much of the urban fabric of America after the Second World War and caused the irreparable loss of local landmarks such as the Chapin-Logan House in Tampa, Florida.

the Advisory Council on Historic Preservation, and the possibility of tax incentives to encourage preservation; all ideas that were implemented through congressional action in the fall of 1966 and in the years that followed.

The progressive programs of the Lyndon Johnson administration, known collectively as the Great Society, had their basis in the idealism of the short-lived Kennedy presidency. Lady Bird Johnson's interest in national beautification and preservation's role in improving the cityscape bore fruit in February, 1965, when President Johnson, in his annual message to Congress, made direct reference to preservation and the need to encourage and support the National Trust.

In May of the same year, the White House Conference on Natural Beauty, opened by Mrs. Johnson, was held. Out of it came a special committee on historic preservation under the auspices of the United States Conference of Mayors. With the National Trust providing staff support, this committee, consisting of representatives of both the public and private sectors, published *With Heritage So Rich*, a book so evocative that it was used as a major instrument in the introduction of congressional legislation leading to passage, on October 15, 1966, of the National Historic Preservation Act. (See Figure 5-3.)

The "Conclusions to the Findings" of *With Heritage So Rich* provided guidelines for the philosophy of preservation planning deemed necessary at the time. These conclusions, translated into the language of the law,

Figure 5-3 Philadelphia's twentieth-century Museum of Art and the adjacent nineteenth-century Water Works are good examples of the "aesthetic quality of the townscape" Americans were urged to consider for preservation in *With Heritage So Rich.*

were to have major impact and change the course of preservation in our time. They read:

The pace of urbanization is accelerating and the threat to our environmental heritage is mounting; it will take more than the sounding of periodic alarms to stem the tide.

The United States is a nation and a people on the move. It is in an era of mobility and change. Every year 20 percent of the population moves from its place of residence. The result is a feeling of rootlessness combined with a longing for those landmarks of the past which give us a sense of stability and belonging.

If the preservation movement is to be successful, it must go beyond saving bricks and mortar. It must go beyond saving occasional historic houses and opening museums. It must be more than a cult of antiquarians. It must do more than revere a few precious national shrines. It must attempt to give a sense of orientation to our society, using structures and objects of the past to establish values of time and place.

This means a reorientation of outlook and effort in several ways.

First, the preservation movement must recognize the importance of architecture, design, and esthetics as well as historic and cultural values. Those who treasure a building for its pleasing appearance or local sentiment do not find it less important because it lacks "proper" historic credentials.

Second, the new preservation must look beyond the individual building and individual landmark and concern itself with the historic and architecturally valued areas and districts that contain a special meaning for the community. A historic neighborhood, a fine old street of houses, a village green, a colorful marketplace, a courthouse square, an esthetic quality of the townscape—all must fall within the concern of the preservation movement. It makes little sense to fight for the preservation of a historic house set between two service stations, and at the same time to ignore an entire area of special charm or importance in the community which is being nibbled away by incompatible uses or slow decay.

Third, if the effort to preserve historic and architecturally significant areas as well as individual buildings is to succeed, intensive thought and study must be given to economic conditions and tax policies which will affect our efforts to preserve such areas as living parts of the community.

In sum, if we wish to have a future with greater meaning, we must concern ourselves not only with the historic highlights, but we must be concerned with the total heritage of the nation and all that is worth preserving from our past as a living part of the present.

The National Historic Preservation Act (Public Law 89-665) set up the system of checks and balances for evaluating sites, buildings, objects, districts, and structures which should be taken into account in the planning process. (See Figure 5-4.) The United States government has operated under this system ever since its adoption. The act broadened the federal government's traditional concept of preservation, taking it beyond entities of national historical significance to include those of state and local importance and architectural value as well. It therefore established legal guidelines for the preservation of cultural artifacts on many levels, encompassing prime examples of buildings and sites important for their time and place regardless of their significance from an associative or historical point of view.

By Title I of this legislation, the secretary of the interior was directed to create a list of those sites and properties of the past worth keeping. Called the National Register of Historic Places, the list was to include "sites, buildings, objects, districts, and structures significant in American history, architecture, archaeology, and culture." These could be of national, state, or local significance.

Of prime importance is the inclusion of the word *district* in this directive from Congress. First used in the establishment of Charleston's "Old and Historic District" in 1931, the term by 1966 was part of the established lexicon by which preservationists talked about neighborhoods and their potential for preservation. Thus, when advised by concerned individuals in the private sector and by historians of the Park Service as to how to include neighborhoods in a preservation-oriented bill, Congress adopted the word *district*. The political world accepted the term to justify grants made through the secretary of the interior for rehabilitation and exterior restoration in historic districts. Such grants were not to be confused with housing grants in order to avoid conflict with the existing programs of the secretary of housing and urban development. (Government precludes budget expenditures from more than one secretariat for the

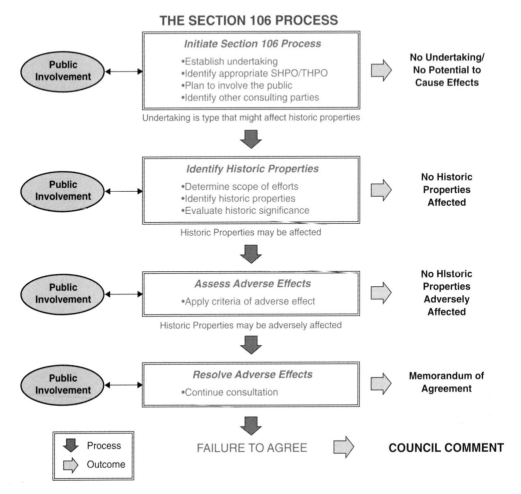

ADVISORY COUNCIL ON HISTORIC PRESERVATION

THE SECTION 106 PROCESS

Initiate Section 106 Process
•Establish undertaking
•Identify appropriate SHPO/THPO
•Plan to involve the public
•Identify other consulting parties

Public Involvement

No Undertaking/ No Potential to Cause Effects

Undertaking is type that might affect historic properties

Identify Historic Properties
•Determine scope of efforts
•Identify historic properties
•Evaluate historic significance

Public Involvement

No Historic Properties Affected

Historic Properties may be affected

Assess Adverse Effects
•Apply criteria of adverse effect

Public Involvement

No Historic Properties Adversely Affected

Historic Properties may be adversely affected

Resolve Adverse Effects
•Continue consultation

Public Involvement

Memorandum of Agreement

Process
Outcome

FAILURE TO AGREE

COUNCIL COMMENT

Figure 5-4 Section 106 of the National Historic Preservation Act serves as a system of checks and balances which governs the relationship between all agencies using federal dollars or issuing federal licenses and the Advisory Council on Historic Preservation in the identification and evaluation of historic properties. This flow chart illustrates the procedures used in the evaluation process.

same activity.) As a result, the 1966 law guided the Department of the Interior towards a responsibility for planning and rehabilitation in historic districts, a responsibility distinct from that of the Department of Housing and Urban Development. Further, the law created an acceptable public alternative for improved housing. At the same time, it helped to eliminate the indiscriminate destruction of urban renewal as the only choice to secure better housing at the state and local levels. For the first time, local jurisdictions could not only secure financial assistance from the secretary of housing and urban development to *replace* existing housing stock, but funds could also be secured through the secretary of the interior to *rehabilitate* instead. There was a choice.

Title II of the act set up the Advisory Council on Historic Preservation, consisting of certain members of the president's cabinet and a selected number of private citizens. The duty of this body was and is to discuss how to treat cultural property when it is affected by federal tax dollars or federal licenses.

The relationship between the advisory council and the office of the secretary of the interior, responsible for creating a list of what is worth keeping, was spelled out in Section 106 of the law. This section indicates that after the effective date of the act, no federally funded or licensed program could have an effect (direct or environmental) on a site, building, object, district, or structure on the secretary of the interior's list (National Register) without the advisory council's being given an opportunity to comment. Prior to this law, preservationists had no legal basis by which their voices could be heard when federal dollars or licenses were being invoked to make a change in the built environment. As far as federal law was concerned, preservation was legally a rear-guard brush-fire action in all American communities. The National Historic Preservation Act of 1966 was meant to change that. For example, it required the advisory council to comment before the secretary of housing and urban development could fund the destruction of certain buildings in local urban-renewal areas identified for clearance. Such buildings could be identified by the secretary of the interior as cultural property of national, state, or local significance worthy of being listed on the National Register. Cultural property, then, was to be taken into account *before* expenditures of tax dollars and *before* a federal license was issued which would make changes to the built environment.

The National Historic Preservation Act of 1966 has been described as environmental legislation, concerned with what one might call the cultural ecology of America's built environment. Its thrust is to put limitations on government's use of tax dollars to alter the environment. Thus, it is a restriction on the federal government and not on what the private citizen can do to his own property with his own money. The common misconception is that the act prevents the private citizen from changing his property in any way. This false assumption usually grows out of a reading of stricter local laws, which may indeed restrict the private citizen's ability to make structural alterations at will.

The Eighty-ninth Congress became known among preservationists as "the Preservation Congress" not only because of the National Historic Preservation Act but also for two other pieces of legislation also passed in 1966. The Department of Transportation Act created a policy of preserving natural and man-made sites along highway routes (Figure 5-5). The policy, spelled out in Section 4F of the act, delineates the preservation responsibilities of the secretary of transportation, and is referred to colloquially as "4F" for that reason. The Demonstration Cities Act made it a policy for the secretary of housing and urban development to recognize preservation and to fund preservation projects which, in essence, laid the basis for an entirely new potential direction for urban renewal through that agency. As a result, HUD has changed its philosophy on renewal considerably and encourages local authorities to retain and recycle existing

Figure 5-5
Visual pollution of the environment, as evinced in this photograph of Van Buren Street, Phoenix, Arizona, spurred the legislative activities of the Eighty-ninth Congress.

housing stock in urban centers rather than continuing to advocate its earlier posture of demolition and replacement.

In mid-summer of 1966, foreseeing that the passage of the National Historic Preservation Act would create new responsibilities, George B. Hartzog, Jr., director of the National Park Service, convened a special advisory committee, consisting of Ernest Allen Connally, J. O. Brew, and Ronald F. Lee. Connally was then teaching at the University of Illinois School of Architecture, Brew was director of the Peabody Institute in Massachusetts, and Lee was northeast regional director of the National Park Service. All three had had long-standing involvement with the Park Service as employees or advisors, and, of course, had been influential in creating the National Trust.

Out of their deliberations came the concept of the Office of Archaeology and Historic Preservation (OAHP) (Figure 5-6) which Connally agreed to head. Existing units of the Park Service concerned with architectural, historical, and archaeological programs were gathered into this new office, to which were added the new National Register and advisory council. William J. Murtagh, then director of program of the National Trust, became the first Keeper of the National Register and Robert R. Garvey, Jr., executive director of the National Trust, assumed the post of executive director of the advisory council, prompting the late Gordon

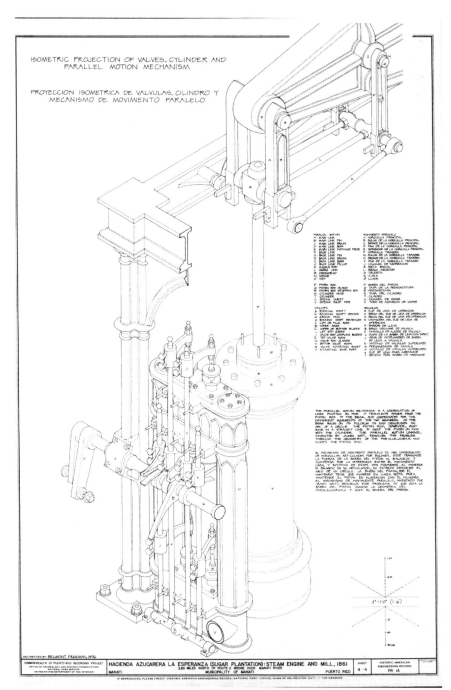

Figure 5-6
After the passage of the National Historic Preservation Act of 1966, the Office of Archaeology and Historic Preservation set up the Historic American Engineering Record (HAER) to document and record America's industrial legacy. This isometric drawing of machinery at the Hacienda Azucarera La Esperarnza in Manti, Puerto Rico, is illustrative of HAER's work.

Gray, chairman of the board of the Trust, to state publicly, "I regret that I have but one staff to give for my country."

The Office of Archaeology and Historic Preservation consolidated and implemented agency preservation programs within the National Park Service until abolished during the Carter administration, when a reorganization combining elements of the Bureau of Outdoor Recreation with the external preservation programs of the National Park Service resulted in the creation of the short-lived Heritage Conservation and Recreation Service (HCRS). During the Reagan administration, HCRS was in turn abolished when external preservation programs—those not concerned with government-owned property—were returned to the Park Service, programs now administered by the associate director for cultural resources. In due course, the advisory council became an independent agency, as it continues to be today.

Shortly after the National Historic Preservation Act was passed in October 1966, Secretary of the Interior Stewart L. Udall decided to decentralize his new responsibilities for preservation. A letter over his signature was sent to each of the governors of the fifty states and the territories asking for a state-level appointee to carry out the secretary's new congressional directives at the state and local levels. Thus came into being the State Liaison Officers (SLO), subsequently renamed the State Historic Preservation Officers (SHPO). Its members have since been organized into the National Conference of State Historic Preservation Officers, with headquarters in Washington, D.C.

The fifty states, the territories, and the National Trust, the only private organization named in the seminal 1966 act, became eligible for matching grants (50 percent of projected cost) under the act to help carry out the intent of the law. This was to bolster considerably the Trust's activities in education and stewardship of property. The states would use the grants to identify and survey the categories of resources named in the law, to develop comprehensive plans, and to acquire and develop (restore, rehabilitate, or stabilize) these resources directly or indirectly. Each state could apply to the federal government for fifty percent "bricks and mortar" (restoration and rehabilitation) money which, at its discretion, could be passed on to local public jurisdictions, private organizations, or individual citizens. These federal dollars could be used to match state and local dollar resources, in-kind services, or value in kind, to acquire and to restore and rehabilitate cultural property listed on the National Register. Available grants could be used by a private individual to rehabilitate an interior and restore an exterior or an entire building for private occupancy. The building does not have to function as a museum open daily to the public. If monies are used in a way that cannot be readily seen by the general public, as on the interior of a private dwelling, the grant recipient must agree to open his house twelve days a year on an equitably distributed basis determined by the state to satisfy the public benefit (i.e., the public's tax-dollar investment in the individual's house). If the expenditure can be seen from the public right of way—the street or the sidewalk—there is no requirement to open the house to the public. All such public investments are protected through convenants in the deeds to the property. These covenants apply to the land itself and are not affected by a change in the ownership of the building. They vary for periods of years, with length related to the size of the public investment in the building.

Federal funding for this program never reached any higher than $60 million in 1979; but by 1985, it stood at only $25 million for the states and the National Trust, most of which was applied by the states to do survey work. By 2001, funding had reached its highest at $94 million, but by that time, appropriations to the states had diminished by the introduction of grants out of the total appropriation to black colleges, Native American tribes, and the Save America's Treasures program introduced in 1999 as part of the millennium celebration. In 2003, the states' appropriation stood at approximately $34 million with $30 million more earmarked for the Save America's Treasures program administered internally by the National Park Service, $3 million to Native American tribes, and nothing to traditional black colleges.

Over the years, the status of the state historic preservation officers has changed and grown considerably in importance. Congress gave the responsibility to create a National Register to the secretary of the interior. It was the secretary who chose to decentralize the program, requesting that the governors appoint someone to carry out that responsibility in the secretary's name at the state level. Until 1980, these appointees existed at the discretion of the secretary, at which time they became legally part of the system by an amendment to the law.

The secretary of the interior's directive from Congress was threefold and became the basic charge of these state appointees. Their first responsibility was to survey the sites, buildings, objects, districts, and structures within their states. The lists which resulted became each state's contribution to the collective patrimony of the nation. Once properties were identified, each state was to develop a statewide plan so that it and the federal government could consider what actions to take concerning its resources. The third charge was to activate the restoration and rehabilitation of the resources identified in the survey. (To help them, the 50 percent matching grant program was provided.)

The National Register is essentially a humanistic program functioning in the nonhumanistic political and economic arenas of American society. At all levels, therefore, the value judgments of the professionals working in the program are extremely important. Anticipating inevitable differences of opinion over whether an entity should be considered cultural property worthy of inclusion in the National Register, the states were asked to hire professional historians, architects, archaeologists, and architectural historians. In addition, a second body of reviewers trained in the same disciplines was formed in each state to review the nominations from the professional staff to determine whether cultural property so identified should be forwarded, with the signature of the SHPO, to the Keeper of the National Register in the Department of the Interior.

At the federal level, each nomination is reviewed by staff with similar professional credentials. If there is agreement, the nomination is signed by the keeper of the National Register under authority delegated by the secretary of the interior. At that point, the entity in question is placed on the National Register, is officially considered part of America's collective patrimony, and becomes subject to review when threatened by federal programs. When funds are available, each property listed on the National Register is also eligible for assistance through the grant-in-aid program. From the National Register's beginnings in 1966, when 868 properties were catalogued, until 2003, almost 77,000 nominations have been accepted and listed, covering about 1.3 million properties. Historic Districts account for 12,000 of the 77,000 entries.

The National Register is thus essentially a state and local program in which the federal government reacts to those identifiable man-made resources that the states and localities recommend as worth preserving. In turn, the federal government gives the states and localities a degree of protection from threats to those resources by all federal expenditures and federal licenses through recourse to the Advisory Council on Historic Preservation. This group mediates conflicts of interest and attempts to bring about resolutions.

While the National Register remains the vehicle that is depended upon by both the public and private sectors to distinguish cultural property, government has continued to be creative in the name of preservation. In 1969, Congress enacted the National Environmental Policy Act, which stressed federal responsibility for preservation and required environmental impact studies to focus the attention of federal agencies on the effect their projects might have on their surroundings.

Yet another building block of preservation was put in place in 1971, when President Nixon issued Executive Order 11593. This directive required all federal agencies to survey all cultural property on the land they administer, to preserve such property when located, and to restore and maintain it. Agencies are directed to solicit the opinion of the secretary of the interior when in doubt about a property's cultural merits. Properties so identified do not have to be on the National Register to be considered by the advisory council when endangered, but only deemed eligible for inclusion. This order was a major achievement in securing the interest and cooperation of all other federal agencies.

In 1976, over ten years after the need had been first expressed at the Williamsburg/National Trust conference and documented in the book *Historic Preservation Today*, the Tax Reform Act was passed by Congress. This provided the first major preservation tax-incentive system for certified income-producing properties. Prior to this, tax incentives favored new construction, which encouraged the replacement of the existing building stock. The 1976 Tax Reform Act made the existing building stock of historic buildings economically attractive to developers and competitive with new construction.

The 1976 Tax Reform Act was replaced in 1981 by the Economic Recovery Tax Act, which provided significant new investment tax credits for rehabilitation. (See Figure 5-7.) This offered developers an allowable tax credit of 25 percent on certified historic structures, 20 percent on buildings forty years old and older, and 15 percent on those thirty years old and older. (A certified historic structure is an individual property or district certified by the secretary of the interior.)

According to the late Dr. Ernest Connally, first chief appeals officer, National Park Service, cumulative statistics concerning the use of the tax credit system for preservation reveal that 18,736 certified rehabilitation projects were approved by the Park Service from October 1, 1976 through September 30, 1987. The reported investment in such projects totaled $12 billion dollars ($12,102,200,000). This represents a combined level of activ-

Figure 5-7   Rehabilitation of prime examples of America's cultural legacy, such as the Mission Inn in Riverside, California, constructed between 1890 and 1901, were made economically feasible by the incentives included in the Economic Recovery Tax Act of 1981.

ity and investment resulting from the Tax Reform Act of 1976, the Economic Recovery Act of 1981, and the Tax Reform Act of 1986.

Prior to the Tax Reform Act of 1986, the Economic Recovery Tax Act had given the investor the incentive of allowing a tax reduction equal to his investment as well as tax relief for losses incurred early in a project. The 1986 act, however, lessened the economic incentives provided under the 1981 Economic Recovery Tax Act by allowing a tax credit of 20 percent for historic buildings and 10 percent for nonresidential buildings constructed before 1936, thus lessening the economic attractiveness of historic rehabilitation to developers. The justification for these changes was to cut abuses of the 1981 act on the part of large investors and developers. The 1986 act limited annual tax credits to an amount equal to tax liability on passive income from rental properties and limited partnerships.

And even this disappeared for individuals with incomes of $250,000 or more per annum. In 1988, rehabilitation tax-credit use was limited to $7,000 for taxpayers with incomes of less than $200,000.

According to statistics from the National Park Service, the National Trust, and the Internal Revenue Service, the 1981 Economic Recovery Tax Act alone produced an investment of almost $9.5 billion in 13,000 historic buildings between 1982 and 1986. Eighty percent of the projects were for less than $500,000. A National Trust study showed that of projects over $1 million, 62 percent were syndicated with fewer than thirty-five investors. Wealthy individual investors and corporations provided a high percentage of the capital involved.

Such large projects were most affected by the Tax Reform Act of 1986 and an increase in smaller investors was anticipated as a result, with a projected drop in the use of the tax act and a corresponding decline in investment in historic properties. On this score, it was reported that between 1983 and 1985, certified rehabilitations had been approved by the National Park Service at the rate of about 3,000 a year. For 1987, after changes brought about by the Tax Reform Act of 1986, these dropped to slightly less than 2,000. Current 2003 information on tax act use reports 30,198 projects completed and certified between 1997 and 2002 representing a private investment of $28.7 billion dollars. Since 1998, the Park Service reports that tax act projects have leveled off to approximately 1,000 per year representing a private investment of about $2 billion per annum. While the number of projects per year may have diminished, the value has risen indicating that large developers are syndicating projects and that developers of big projects, such as Rockefeller Center and Radio City Music Hall in New York, the Ferry Building in San Francisco, and the New Jersey Convention Hall, in Atlantic City, are taking advantage of the tax act as well as the so-called mom and pop operations of more modest projects.

To be eligible for a tax credit, a property must not only be certified historic, but the rehabilitations to which it is subjected must be certified as conforming to the secretary of the interior's standards (see Appendix C). These certifications are given by the National Park Service. It is the wise developer who procures provisional clearance for rehabilitation from the Park Service prior to the commencement of work. The Park Service has the final authority to assess whether or not the work has been achieved in conformance with the standards. Without both of Interior's necessary certifications, the Internal Revenue Service will disallow investment tax-credit claims. There is an appeal process for developers whose rehabilitation proposals have been denied by the National Park Service at the staff level; after appeal, decisions are binding.

Obviously, much has been achieved, great changes have taken place, and important legislative building blocks for preservation have been constructed at all levels of government during the past quarter of a century. Preservation activity has become so catholic in the forms it has taken in recent years as to give rise to myriad questions concerning the integrity of some of these forms and their validity as responsibilities of preservation. Were one to make a graph of preservation activity in the public and private sectors over the last 150 years, the vector of the private sector would rise at a gentle but constant rate. That of the public sector would be noted as commencing at a lower point, but climbing rapidly and steadily, especially through the early twentieth century, to a juncture with the private sector following the 1966 legislation. At the present time, governments at all levels have a greater involvement in preservation than ever before. And rehabilitated buildings, as a result of the application of the tax acts of 1976, 1981, and 1986, can be seen in most cities throughout the United States. The offices of the state historic preservation officers have grown in importance, stature, and workload as responsibilities redelegated from the federal level have increased. The equivalency of what Europeans would call a "monuments office" has thus been established in each of the states and territories in the form of the SHPO and his staff. This means that Americans may have finally accepted the validity of spending tax dollars not only for an environment that is safe and healthful, but also for one that is good to look at. We seem to have finally arrived at a true acceptance of the Supreme Court's *Berman vs. Parker* decision, delivered by Justice William O. Douglas in 1954: "It is within the power of the legislature to determine that the community should be beautiful, as well as healthy; spacious, as well as clean; well balanced, as well as carefully patrolled." Such a philosophy of planning is a far cry from the simply patriotic activities of Ann Pamela Cunningham to save a landmark in 1854—just 100 years earlier.

CHAPTER 6

The Historic Room
and House Museum

A HOUSE MUSEUM, according to the National Trust, is "a museum whose structure itself is of historical or architectural significance and whose interpretation relates primarily to the building's architecture, furnishings and history."

In the strictest sense of the term, a *house museum* can be considered an adaptive use, since the building to be exhibited is being put to a use different from that for which it was first erected, although it does represent its original function. Mount Vernon, once the private residence of George and Martha Washington, is a typical example. As a museum it no longer functions as a private house—the reason for which Washington used it. Open to the public, Mount Vernon is a three-dimensional teaching tool, instructing visitors about how our first president and his lady lived in the eighteenth century. The building differs from a history text about George and Martha Washington and their life at home only in dimension, but not in what it can teach. Thus, the visitor walks through the actual spaces of the Washington household, viewing furnishings documented as having belonged to the First Family.

A house and its contents, when maintained as a museum, teach how the original occupants lived and exhibit the objects of their everyday lives. When properly interpreted, often with a trained guide to explain various fixtures and furnishings or perhaps a well-researched printed brochure or leaflet, the house museum teaches a lesson in history about the occupants, their habits, their tastes, and their times.

The relatively recent commitment to environmental interests by preservationists has grown so quickly that the movement's roots in the historic house museum and historic room are often forgotten. Beginning in the 1850s, with the efforts of Ann Pamela Cunningham to save Mount Vernon, the house museum has developed as one answer to the question of how to keep buildings important to American history.

Our fascination with historic houses and rooms is easily understood. A passion for associative connections made early historic houses "shrines" to their revered occupants. Somewhat later, the historic room was judged worthy of attention in itself. Falling in scale somewhere between a single historic object (or a collection of objects) and an entire house, a room could be easily conceptualized as an artifact and was easy to manage physically.

In the early twentieth century, the idea of the historic room appealed to collectors of furniture, tools, and decorative objects. They recognized the logic of creating appropriate and authentic settings to display such artifacts. Almost simultaneously, historic rooms became the focus of attention by museums, whose specialists were recognizing the legitimacy of American decorative arts. At the same time, such specialists were becoming aware that relationships among objects, evident most clearly in historic room settings, were essential to the educational story such rooms could tell.

Looking to the recent past, we can identify two pioneering preservationists whose contributions were made through the medium of the historic house and the historic room. William Sumner Appleton (Figure 6-1) and Henry Francis du Pont, by their erudition and force of personality, helped to develop standards of contemporary preservation practice.

Almost single-handedly, Appleton dragged the historic house museum into the twentieth century and gave its existence a scholarly foundation. Without entirely negating the pietistic overtones of its origins (and thereby losing an influential constituency), Appleton promoted the historic house as an indispensable link in the chain of material culture, parallel in importance to written documentation. Equally important, his Society for the Preservation of New England Antiquities developed a network of historic house museums throughout New England, centrally administered from Boston. This created for the first time a critical mass of preserved architecture (or at least the perception of it) that testified to the serious purpose of the endeavor.

As an early American architectural historian, Appleton was instrumental in promoting the historic house museum as a pedagogical instrument and not merely a place where casual visitors might absorb some sense of their own past. He accomplished this by doggedly insisting on the analytical value of original architectural fabric. This, in fact, was how Appleton judged the importance of a house, regardless of whether or not it superficially expressed a coherent architectural style. By the end of his career, he had learned to study a house in the same manner a paleontolo-

Figure 6-1
William Sumner Appleton, founder of the Society for the Preservation of New England Antiquities (now known as Historic New England), pictured on the steps of the Harrison Grey Otis House in late 1929.

gist might study skeletal remains—a mode of examination now taken for granted by preservation professionals. Together with his insistence on the importance of "reading" a house, Appleton fought the impulse, which was shared by many of his supporters, to prettify or clean up an old building, in the process destroying its teaching potential.

A historic room, like a house museum, is essentially a three-dimensional historic document that exists (or has been re-created) to teach a history lesson. This history can be cultural history, such as one sees in the historic room settings of the Henry du Pont Winterthur Museum, the Metropolitan Museum of Art in New York, and the art museums in Philadelphia and Brooklyn, to name some of the leading installations. Or such rooms can reflect social or political history, such as the room installations in many historical society museums, the National Trust's Woodrow Wilson House in Washington, D.C., or the Alexander Ramsay House in St. Paul, Minnesota.

Today's broadly accepted standards of professionalism on how one treats such buildings in the restoration process owe their basis to Appleton, whose philosophy, in turn, was inspired by John Ruskin. Appleton was meticulous in keeping the old house as intact as he possibly could in the restoration process and aimed to preserve *in situ* at all costs. His main concern was the integrity of aesthetic quality. He would thus retain all original interior finishes and wallpapers where possible. If an earlier window or door which had been later covered or blocked was discovered in the investigative process, he would retain it and develop a method of

Figure 6-2
Villa Vizcaya in Miami is operated as a house museum by Dade County, which interprets in its contents and formal gardens the story of the development of the Florida peninsula during the early part of the twentieth century, a development led by wealthy Americans seeking a sunny haven from northern winters.

presenting it as an exhibit in the building. Sometimes he would glass it over, creating the effect of an exhibition case, to take maximum advantage of what the discovery could teach about the history of the building. He developed similar methods for revealing a building's structure. New materials would be identified in some manner so that later generations of investigators would not confuse with the original fabric those elements and materials that Appleton could not avoid replacing. He took maximum advantage of what he found for explanatory and teaching purposes, retaining original elements and minimizing changes to the building and its fabric. He clearly identified what he was forced to add. These are all cardinal dictates of his philosophy, strongly allied as they are to those of his English predecessor, John Ruskin. And these are the philosophical dictates which still guide the conscientious preservation professional today.

Over a career spanning thirty-seven years, Appleton fought and won innumerable preservation battles. The most notable, in 1917, was his protection of the Abraham Brown House in Watertown, Massachusetts. He established the historic house museum as the prime form of preservation. Even today, in the face of changing attitudes, our view of the historic house museum, the standards by which we measure it, and the uses to which we put it are essentially those formulated by William Sumner Appleton (See Figure 6-2.)

If the historic house museum is an entity that sometimes occupies surroundings bearing scant resemblance to its original environment, the historic (or period) room is, by definition, an entity torn from its original fabric. Because of this violent dislocation, the historic room has always generated controversy. Proponents argue that they saved irreplaceable examples of architecture and decorative arts which would otherwise have vanished. Detractors counter that the willingness of dealers and collectors to buy period rooms encourages the destruction, for lucrative piecemeal sale, of buildings that might otherwise survive intact.

The historic room began to reach maturity in 1924 when the Metropolitan Museum of Art opened its American Wing in the first large-scale attempt to display and interpret American interiors. This was followed shortly thereafter by the installation of period rooms in the Philadelphia Museum of Art. Despite the Metropolitan's leadership, perhaps the single most important flowering of the historic room was the development of the Henry Francis du Pont Winterthur Museum in Wilmington, Delaware.

As did many of his contemporaries, H. F. du Pont began paying serious attention to American furniture at about the time the Metropolitan Museum opened its new wing. Seeking suitable settings for his collections, du Pont began to remodel his ancestral home with paneling purchased from a number of historic houses. Beginning as an enthusiastic dilettante, he gradually became a knowledgeable connoisseur. His collection and his erudition grew apace until he was acquiring entire historic rooms.

Over a period of twenty-five years, du Pont abandoned the idea of limiting his now enormous collection to personal use and began to evolve the concept of a definitive museum of decorative arts in authentic settings, which would be open to the public on a limited basis. In 1951, that goal was realized when du Pont opened Winterthur, which was quickly recognized, by virtue of both quality and quantity, as the most prominent assemblage of American artifacts and historic interiors anywhere in the world.

Like William Sumner Appleton, du Pont had much to do with setting standards of scholarship and authenticity through his installations at Winterthur. These standards were later carried on in the publication of the *Winterthur Portfolio* and the establishment of the Louise du Pont Crowninshield Research Building, housing a laboratory, classrooms, and a reference library. Throughout the period of his museum's development, du Pont was sensitive about the rooms he bought, striving to avoid any controversy with local organizations over houses that could be saved *in situ*. This practice helped him to escape the charges of cultural vandalism leveled against Henry Ford, who apparently thought little of moving a local community's landmark to Greenfield Village, his outdoor museum in Dearborn, Michigan.

Despite du Pont's efforts to develop an ethically sound policy, his practice of stripping houses of interior architectural detail, sometimes leaving no more than a shell, did elicit criticism, and even a bit of soul-searching on his own part. His final word on the matter, however, was to suppose that without his intervention innumerable important houses would have been burned or scattered, with bits in different houses all over the country.

Since developments at the Metropolitan and at Winterthur, any large museum with aspirations to a representative display of decorative arts has included a number of historic room installations. The standards of H. F. du Pont included a meticulous concern for using only original materials, whether they be the furniture, the objects, the fabrics, or the wall coverings. Equally close attention was paid to the historical accuracy of how these elements were used and placed within the exhibition space and, most importantly, the levels of light under which the room could be observed by the museum visitor. The latter was usually achieved using specially devised electrified wax candles, bored through to receive wiring for specially made bulbs of correct candlepower. Above all else, heating and cooling systems were hidden, usually vented through fireplace openings and above window valences. All electric wiring was also hidden, as were fire detection systems. The final product was an historic room environment of credibility, its twentieth-century systems of comfort and protection successfully hidden so as not to spoil the illusion of historical accuracy.

The time periods interpreted by historic rooms have been extended beyond the original colonial and federal eras to include the Victorian age and, more recently, the early twentieth century. The latter and more "important" such rooms are, architecturally and culturally, the more controversial their acquisition and installation are likely to be. The living room of Frank Lloyd Wright's Robie House and the trading room of Adler and Sullivan's Chicago Stock Exchange are recent cases in point. The nature of the controversy has changed little since the 1920s. Does the eagerness of major museums to fight over artifacts like these create a climate detrimental to preservation *in situ*? And is there any way to overcome the appearance of a stage set that to some extent inevitably accompanies such rooms, despite diligent efforts to avoid it?

Recent market forces have intensified the problem. As in the automotive world, wherein certain makes the collective value of the individual parts often exceeds the value of the assembled automobile, the value of architectural fragments as *objets d'art* has increased the potential for destructive looting. A recent case in point concerns a house in southern California. Not only is the house in question a prize example of arts and crafts workmanship, but it is the work of an established and well-known firm. A recent purchaser from another part of the country, together with an art dealer in yet a third part of the country, bought the house with the intent to market as art objects such architectural details as lighting fixtures, door hinges and knobs, window glass, and casements. Once sold, the originals would be reproduced and replaced in the house.

This is not without earlier precedent. Anyone who knows that the ballroom of Gadsby's Tavern in Alexandria, Virginia, now graces the Metropolitan Museum of Art in New York or that the interiors of the Powel House in Philadelphia are divided between art museums in New York and Philadelphia understands that the interiors he sees in these actual eighteenth-century landmarks are twentieth-century reproductions. To see the authentic interiors, he must visit them in the museums in which they have been installed—art objects torn from their original functioning environment.

For today's preservationists, involved so often with neighborhoods, districts, and adaptive use, the historic room may appear to be an anachronism, or a phenomenon largely peripheral to their concerns. In actuality, when well executed, such a room functions as a reminder of the high ideals and standards that need guide all preservation undertakings, whether the purest of restorations or the most creative of free-form adaptations. The historic room will always have more direct relevance to curatorship and museum practice than to more economically oriented adaptive use and rehabilitation, but as a three-dimensional documentary source it will continue to offer preservationists needed instruction. (See Figures 6-3 and 6-4.)

Excluding museum curators, the professional group with perhaps the most direct connection with the historic room is the American Society of Interior Designers. Historically, the relationship between designers and preservationists has been an uneasy one at best. The designer's first task, in most cases, is to create a living environment that expresses the taste of a client—not always a goal compatible with scholarly treatment of historic interiors and period furniture, where the designer's personal taste must be sublimated to the taste of the person and period he is trying to recapture.

Since at least the end of the nineteenth century, designers have borrowed from many sources and periods to produce pastiche settings

Figure 6-3 The dining room of the Ximenez-Fatio house in St. Augustine, Florida (1797–1802), as interpreted by members of a house-museum committee who reflected the common tendency of early twentieth-century preservationists to "early up" a building and its interiors to demonstrate age.

Figure 6-4   Thorough documentary research has produced this historically accurate re-creation of how the same room might have looked in the nineteenth century. Note the punkah, which would have been employed by a servant to create a breeze during oppressive weather.

intended to reflect no particular time. Or they have created rooms pur-ported to convey the style of a given period that are, in reality, billboards of the often *nouveau riche* taste of their own era. To complicate matters, some of these same interiors have themselves become historically valid with the passage of time.

A landmark in the evolution of American interior design was the publication in 1897 of *The Decoration of Houses* by novelist Edith Whar-ton and architect Ogden Codman, Jr. Its importance to historic preserva-tion is twofold. Its canons of taste are based on an analysis of what the authors judged to be the best historical models—houses and rooms that expressed the finest aspirations of their own periods. In addition to bas-ing their practical handbook on rational historical precedent, Wharton and Codman argued that the best interior design resulted when the treat-ment of rooms was seen as a branch of architecture. This view was a strong reaction against the turn-of-the-century taste that had created inte-riors crammed with bric-a-brac and examples of the upholsterer's craft. By helping to sweep away this acquisitive philosophy of decoration and by emphasizing the organic unity that ought to link exterior and interior, *The Decoration of Houses* was crucial in paving the way for Frank Lloyd Wright's approach to the architect's total control of design, an approach that has remained a constant in the best twentieth-century architecture.

Even though *The Decoration of Houses* was enormously influential, its lessons have had to be learned over and over again, both by decora-tors, who are all too willing to furnish a room with no recognition of its historical identity, and by preservationists, who are too often content to restore an exterior with little thought to what goes on behind its four walls.

In recent years, both the historic room and the historic-house museum (as well as historic interiors in active use) have benefited from a greater application of scholarship on the part of preservationists and a greater sense of responsibility on the part of interior designers. The former change is best represented by two of William Seale's books, *The Tasteful Interlude* (1975) and *Recreating the Historic House Interior* (1979). In both, the historian's personal objectivity is brought to bear on the manifestations of physical culture, as opposed to the subjectivity to which the designer, as an aesthetic creator, is prone.

In the second book, Seale reiterates a point that cannot be made too often. The interpretive failure of most house museums, he asserts, results from treating furniture and objects as works of art or as curios, presented in a manner appealing to contemporary standards of taste. Far more difficult and far more rewarding, he argues, is the task of presenting such artifacts as incidental to daily life in a way that will shock the viewer into a vision of the past and its personalities. In commenting on the tendency for preservationists to unwittingly impose the ambience of their own time, Seale contrasts the 1932 appearance of a room in the Raleigh Tavern at Williamsburg (interpreted then as the ladies' drawing room) with its reinterpretation in 1976 as a billiard hall (Figures 6-5 and 6-6). Speaking of its earlier appearance, he observes that it bore "close resemblance to

Figure 6-5 The ladies' parlour in Raleigh Tavern, Williamsburg, Virginia, as it appeared for almost half a century after the tavern's reconstruction in 1932.

Figure 6-6   Documentation has proved that the ladies' parlour was actually employed as a billiard room in the eighteenth-century tavern. The Colonial Williamsburg Foundation refurnished and reinterpreted the room in 1976.

expensive suburban living rooms of the 1920s in Grosse Point, Michigan, and Larchmont, New York," although "its objects were all authentic to the eighteenth century." By contrast, the room as it now appears, "though bare and simple, is striking as a stage for the historical imagination. Previously a decorated scene, it now reflects human habitation and use."

Seale's insistence that the historic house and historic room should "reflect human habitation and use" is another way of emphasizing their value as more than documents of art and history. Returning to our earlier distinction between museum-quality restorations and the great mass of adaptively used buildings that make up the bulk of preservation's current efforts, it is easy to understand how an 1860s house treated according to Seale's standards could enrich the perceptions of a nonprofessional visitor familiar with similar houses treated adaptively. It is a question of high standards functioning as a benchmark against which less exacting efforts can be measured.

Interest in the house museum and the historic room represents the basic foundation of the preservation movement in the United States, and indeed, in other nations of the world as well. This is amply demonstrated by the legion of great houses operated as museums open to the public in England, Scotland, and Ireland. Indeed, the house museum is so entrenched as the basic preservation form that it is the *only* major form of preservation in many countries—especially in developing ones. The charter of the National Trust for Historic Preservation reveals that its primary reason for existence is that of the stewardship of property. The remainder of its programming, developed over the years of its existence, has been created under the educational rubric of its charter.

Perhaps the best established program of property stewardship in the world is that of the National Trust in Britain, where onerous death duties (inheritance taxes) have made it economically impractical for many of the British to inherit their ancestral seats. Since the Second World War, the English National Trust has received an increasing number of such properties, many of which are open to the public as historic-house museums. In reality, the British inheritance tax system has made the National Trust one of the two largest property owners in the United Kingdom, second only to the Crown.

Younger and without the stimulation of the British tax system, the National Trust in the United States currently owns and operates as house museums approximately two dozen properties. State and local organizations, many of which are member organizations of the National Trust, as well as state and local governments, administer hundreds of other house museums throughout the country which are open to the public as educational tools. These museums comprise the most traditional form that preservation has taken in the United States, yet the high visibility of more recent forms of preservation, such as the Main Street program and tax act projects, has sometimes made us forget them.

CHAPTER 7

Outdoor Museums

I F THE historic house museum is the most traditional solution to the problem of saving a historic building, the outdoor museum has stood for decades as the second major answer to the preservation question. Unlike the house museum, the outdoor museum in the United States is essentially a product of the twentieth century, the outgrowth of a movement that originated in nineteenth-century Sweden.

An outdoor museum is defined by the National Trust as "a restored, re-created or replica village site in which several or many structures have been restored, rebuilt, or moved and whose purpose is to interpret a historical or cultural setting, period, or activity." Outdoor museums essentially take three forms in America. They may consist of original buildings, on their original sites, preserved and operated as a museum for educational purposes. Or they may be buildings of historical or aesthetic interest moved to a new site for similar purposes. Or they may be composed of totally reconstructed buildings built with the same educational aim in mind. American outdoor museums range from those consisting mostly of original buildings, preserved on original sites, such as Old Salem, in Winston-Salem, North Carolina, to original buildings collected on nonhistorical sites, such as Greenfield Village in Michigan and Sturbridge Village in Massachusetts. The latter types can be broken down according to their organization, i.e., whether they are a collection of buildings unrelated to each other and interpreted individually, as at Greenfield Village, or whether they are sited in an organized manner to approximate a village, as at Sturbridge.

Those outdoor museums farthest removed from original buildings on original sites are total reconstructions. Perhaps one of the best but most obvious of this type is Plimoth Plantation in Plymouth, Massachusetts, reconstructed on a new site for the simple reason that the current city of Plymouth had grown up and been developed over the original location. When planning total reconstruction, preservationists and historians, if they are not careful, can create complexes that resemble amusement parks—existing with entertainment rather than education as a first priority. A good example of such an amusement park would be the Victorian street of Disney World's Hometown U.S.A., presented in molded plastic to an undiscriminating public at three-quarter life scale. One must never lose sight of the fact that the great distinction between outdoor museums and operations such as Florida's Disney World is the order of priority justifying their existence. Themes parks exist primarily to entertain and amuse. If they educate in the process, so much the better, but that is not the prime reason for their being. Outdoor museums exist primarily to educate. If they amuse and provide recreation, that is an unintentional but plausible side product.

Buildings in the outdoor museum should be thought of in the same manner in which one thinks of display cases in a museum gallery. (See Figure 7-1.) The collection of artifacts is displayed, albeit in a functional context, as the chief means of getting across to the visiting public the educational reason for the exercise. This is perhaps the greatest contribution outdoor museums make to the preservation movement. Thus the outdoor

Figure 7-1 Salem, North Carolina, now part of the city of Winston-Salem, was founded by Moravians from Bethlehem, Pennsylvania, in 1766. Now operated as an outdoor museum, Old Salem probably has more original buildings restored on their original sites than any other outdoor museum in the country.

museum is a collection of houses and other buildings, whether arranged in an historical context or not, that is used for teaching purposes. The objects are placed in relation to each other in such a way as to maximize their communication and educational potential in explaining to the visitor how they were used and perhaps why they were created. If one adds to this contextual arrangement interpreters or docents dressed in period costume, who at some museums carry out activity characteristic of the time, place, and social status being presented, the educational experience is intensified. By analogy, it is the process of taking a single violin, adding to it first and second violins, cellos, oboes, clarinets, drums, and other instruments to create an entire orchestra. The subsequent enriched end product exceeds the capabilities of the individual parts of the total ensemble to communicate and educate if those parts "play well" together.

Sweden's Artur Hazelius is considered the father of the outdoor museum movement, credited with having created the first outdoor museum for patriotic and educational reasons. This was the same motivation which led a number of affluent Americans to create similar institutions in the United States in the 1920s, 1930s, and 1940s.

Hazelius was born in Stockholm in 1833 into a family known for its patriotism. He first taught language and literature, but ceased to teach because he found it insufficiently challenging. He became conscious that the industrial revolution was bringing about drastic changes in his environment and culture and, in the early 1870s, decided to begin collecting artifacts of the common man (furnishings, tools, costumes) as well as of the culture they represented in music, dance, folklore, and other areas. Hazelius hoped that with those artifacts he could instill a new sense of patriotism in his country. He also hoped that with an understanding of past institutions a new tradition could be developed by his generation which would be suitable to its own day, thus avoiding the homogenizing effects of the industrial revolution.

Hazelius opened his museum of Scandinavian ethnography in 1873 in central Stockholm, emphasizing a naturalistic approach to exhibiting materials, rather than the accepted system of arranging labeled objects in glass cases. He utilized historical interior architecture and furnishings and accurately dressed mannequins to tell his story. These efforts grew into what was subsequently named the Nordiske Museet (Nordic Museum), consisting of sections devoted to peasant life, guilds, the higher classes of society, and pharmaceutical materials.

In the process, Hazelius's concept of a folk museum gradually evolved and expanded. He began collecting buildings from throughout Sweden and placing them on a hillside near Stockholm's harbor on a site that he had secured from the king in the 1870s. Hazelius's outdoor museum opened in October of 1891. His aim was to educate while entertaining, relying upon the various senses of smell, sight, sound, and touch to achieve it. When the museum opened in the suburb of Skansen, it consisted of a sixteenth-century log peasant dwelling, as well as a house used by stonecutters. There was also a turf-covered farmhouse, an elevated storehouse, and a Lapp settlement complete with reindeer. All of these structures were furnished with a respect for authenticity as to furnishings, textiles, and colors. To heighten the experience, Hazelius's guides were clothed in folk costumes authentic to the buildings in which they worked and carried out various characteristic activities within the buildings, such as baking in the farmhouse, or making candles, soap, and cheese. Sometimes, folk instruments would be played and folk dancing would take place. In short, Hazelius employed every possible method to present the casual visitor with a complete overview of the period and the particular building, its occupants, their ways of life, and the activity he was attempting to portray. Despite separate activities and types of buildings that were gathered on this open site, the one entity that gave uniformity to the effort was the methodology by which the subject matter was presented.

It is important to understand the pioneering quality of what Hazelius did, for it set the pattern for similar development in other Scandinavian countries as well as in the United States, and, subsequently, in other nations of the world. Hazelius thus can be considered a pioneer in the outdoor museum movement, as is Appleton in the American house-museum field. Thanks to Hazelius's efforts, the outdoor museum is the most common solution to the problem of preservation in the Scandinavian countries, where approximately 800 regional and local folk museums have since been established. The idea spread beyond Sweden into other sections of Scandinavia with ease. Having seen Hazelius's exhibits at the Paris exhibition of 1878, Bernhard Olsen, the chief designer at the Tivoli amusement park in Copenhagen, established a small open-air museum of buildings in the Rosenborg Castle gardens in Copenhagen in 1897. Four years later, he created the Frilandsmuseet on a ninety-acre tract not far from Copenhagen.

In Norway, Anders Sandvig, a young dentist, seeing historical artifacts shipped to Hazelius in Stockholm, felt that it was unfortunate that this folk material was leaving its native region. He began to collect objects himself and to move old buildings to his garden. This was the genesis of Norway's outdoor museum at Lillehammer.

A similar effort by Dr. Hans Aall created the Norsk Folkemuseum in Oslo, begun in 1894 and subsequently moved to nearby Bygdoy. This outdoor museum, containing 150 buildings on twenty-five acres, is arranged by province. Many of its old structures, taken from their original urban settings, have been arranged to simulate a city of the past. In 1909, at Aarhus, in Jutland, Den Gamle By was the first open-air museum dedicated to the exhibition of buildings of an urban, rather than a rural, nature. Finland joined the movement in the same year, when Professor Axel Heikel founded an open-air museum on the island of Suursaari near Helsinki.

Having taken root so successfully in the Scandinavian countries, the concept of a museum presenting a total environment, its buildings and artifacts preserved with as much authenticity as scholarship would allow, spread throughout the world. Almost 100 outdoor museums now exist east and west of the Iron Curtain. This movement did not develop nationally in Great Britain until after the Second World War. Since then, regional outdoor museums have been created at Saint Fagens, near Cardiff (the Welsh Folkmuseum), near Belfast (the Ulster Folk and Transport Museum), at Telford, in Shropshire (the Ironbridge Gorge Museum), and at several other locations throughout the British Isles. Perhaps it is because of the plethora of great British country houses open to visitors that these open-air museums are little known to the public. Or perhaps it is because many of Britain's outdoor museums are dedicated to exhibiting artifacts and buildings related to the industrial revolution—to the uninitiated, a dreary, unattractive period of history with little popular appeal when compared with the memorable architectural and decorative aesthetics of stately English homes—that outdoor museums have not received the same attention as the historic houses in that country.

Despite the National Trust's definition, debate has always existed about the precise meaning of an *outdoor museum*. In the strict sense of the term, if one defines such a museum as a collection of historic buildings existing for educational purposes, then one must include such entities as Mount Vernon, consisting as it does of a main residence and a collection of service buildings expressive of the way of life in an eighteenth-century slave economy. The Mount Vernons of our country, however, are usually thought of as house museums, not as outdoor museums, despite the argument to the contrary which can be made. Perhaps one can make the distinction that more than one pivotal building needs to exist in conjunction with other important buildings and subsidiary outbuildings as support for the main display in order for the complex to be termed an *outdoor museum*. Whatever the distinction one chooses to draw, there seems to be little argument that open-air museums in the United States are indeed an outgrowth of the house-museum movement initiated by Ann Pamela Cunningham at Mount Vernon.

There is equally no question that in 1926, the leadership and financial support of John D. Rockefeller, Jr., fired by the enthusiasm of the Reverend W.A.R. Goodwin, rector of Bruton Parish Church in Williamsburg, provided the establishment of the outdoor-museum movement in the United States through the establishment of Colonial Williamsburg. (See Figures 7-2 and 7-3.) When the two men met at a Phi Beta Kappa dinner, the Reverend Goodwin succeeded in conveying his enthusiasm for the eighteenth-century royal capital to Rockefeller, who instructed Goodwin to acquire, anonymously, as much property as he could for the project. In the intervening decades, approximately ninety historic buildings spread over 175 acres have been acquired and restored. There are today approximately thirty exhibition buildings and craft shops interpreting life in the Williamsburg of the 1700s. Costumed guides and interpreters such as those Hazelius espoused in Sweden are important contributors to the complex.

Like some of the other outdoor museums in this country, Williamsburg also functions as an historic district within an operating town. Colonial Williamsburg Foundation is the largest corporation in the city. To make necessary changes within the public rights of way, the administrators of the foundation must deal with the mayor, the city council, the planning board, the fire department, the police department—all of the bureaucracy necessary to a functioning city. The same may be said of Old

Figure 7-2   A prerestoration view of the Duke of Gloucester Street in Williamsburg, Virginia, shows the eighteenth-century Ludwell-Paradise house on the left and the more visually altered but essentially intact Prentis Store on the right. The nineteenth-century house in the center has been removed, as it was not part of the original eighteenth-century fabric of the royal capital.

Figure 7-3   Before Williamsburg's restoration began, the site of Raleigh Tavern on Duke of Gloucester Street had been employed for new construction in the late nineteenth century. The buildings illustrated here, dating from that era, were demolished and the eighteenth-century tavern was reconstructed.

Salem, the Moravian settlement at Winston-Salem, North Carolina, but does not apply to such operations as Sturbridge Village, created intentionally on open land that is privately owned.

In Williamsburg, two of the four visually pivotal buildings are total reconstructions—the Capitol and the Governor's Palace. Another—the so-called Wren building of the College of William and Mary— is what might be termed a *heavy restoration*. The fourth building—the privately owned Bruton Parish Church—has survived in the least changed condition, but has itself undergone some restoration.

Colonial Williamsburg is an excellent case study of all the solutions available to the preservationist, ranging from total reconstruction to rehabilitation, restoration, and adaptive use. As the 1920s recede into history, there seems to be little question of the importance and impact of this early effort on the course of preservation. Rockefeller, like Hazelius, was motivated by patriotism and a perception that this project should be used to transfer to future generations those yardsticks of freedom and democracy he held so dear. His inspiration continues today, as the Rockefeller family still plays a leading role in American preservation and conservation.

If Rockefeller's primary motivation was patriotism, certainly education was the moving force behind the actions of Henry Ford. In 1923, Ford initiated his acquisitions with the purchase of the Wayside Inn in Sudbury, Massachusetts, which had strong associations with the poet Longfellow. Ford had a church and a small schoolhouse moved to the grounds and operated a private school for boys on the premises. Before Rockefeller's interest was stimulated by the Reverend Goodwin in Williamsburg, Ford certainly appears to have had the idea of creating a complex of museum buildings.

As early as 1924, Ford turned his attention to the Botsford Tavern in Detroit, finding in it an opportunity to create a pleasant site for dancing, of which he was very fond. Because of the proximity of the Detroit project to his home and the ease with which he could visit the project during restoration, he decided in the fall of 1926 to create a museum complex near his office. The complex would consist of two parts, a large exhibition hall and a collection of appropriate buildings transported to the site to display examples of America's unlimited opportunities and the achievements of past generations. The main museum building, a replica of Independence Hall in Philadelphia, demonstrates that Ford's interests were not entirely devoid of patriotism. The omnivorous quality of his interests can be seen in the collections, the underlying theme of which is American industry and its development. The main exhibit hall, an immense room, houses collections of radios, typewriters, washing machines, and other manifestations of twentieth-century life.

Ford's outdoor museum at Dearborn, Michigan, known as Greenfield Village, opened to the public in 1933. The initial concept of the village was that of a New England townscape, not unlike the plan of Sturbridge Village in Massachusetts. To this open site, he moved first the Scotch Settlement school which he had attended as a child, and, shortly thereafter, he added a tavern from Clinton, Michigan. By 1929, his "American village" consisted of a courthouse, a railroad station from Michigan, a post office, a farmhouse, and a carding mill. Yet Ford also added nearby a couple of Cotswold cottages from the south of England, as well as a five-story London jewelry shop, moved from its urban site, reduced to three levels, and situated without any relation to other buildings. He had little compunction about taking buildings from their original sites and also changing their proportions. In the case of the jewelry shop, the modifications were made in the interest of housing his watch and clock collection.

The high point of the developmental years of Greenfield Village was the fiftieth anniversary celebration of the invention of the electric light by

Henry Ford's friend Thomas A. Edison. So highly did Ford think of Edison's invention that he had the laboratory buildings moved from Menlo Park, New Jersey, and re-erected within Greenfield Village, where, in late 1929, they were opened to the public. (See Figure 7-4.)

The announced acquisition of buildings by Ford sometimes stimulated preservation efforts at the local level. Such a case was the acquisition of the seventeenth-century Iron Master's House at Saugus, Massachusetts. This building had been sold to the alumni of the Henry Ford Trade School, who intended to give it to Ford as a birthday present and have it moved to Dearborn. Through a series of letters and intercession on the part of the governor of Massachusetts, the town of Saugus reimbursed the trade school for its purchase and a new organization, the First Iron Works Association, took over the property in 1944.

An effort similar to Ford's developed into the Farmer's Museum in Cooperstown, New York. This grew out of an attempt on the part of Stephen Clark, a resident of New York City who summered in the Cooperstown area, to bring in some sort of business to keep the town economically healthy while maintaining its rural ambiance. The project was initiated in 1939 with the founding of the Baseball Hall of Fame.

Not too long after, Clark met with Edward P. Alexander, director of the New York State Historical Association. Clark suggested that the association move from its headquarters at Ticonderoga to centrally located Cooperstown and offered to subsidize the move and to underwrite the association for five years. From his point of view, this would create a second museum of historical interest that would be an attraction for Cooperstown. Alexander and Dixon Ryan Fox, president of Union College and chairman of the association, were trained as historians. With their interest in folk culture, museum science, period rooms, and other forms of

Figure 7-4
Pictured in 1929 at the dedication of Thomas Edison's laboratory, newly moved to Greenfield Village, are, from left to right, Edison, President Herbert Hoover, and Henry Ford.

three-dimensional history, the two men must be considered mavericks for their time, since, as late as the beginning of the 1960s, historians still looked upon academe, rather than museums, as the primary valid application of their discipline.

Upon his arrival in Cooperstown, Alexander urged Clark to begin collecting agricultural and domestic implements to supplement the paintings and sculpture he was already gathering. Beginning with that suggestion and those activities, the collection grew, directors changed, and finally, in 1944, the first buildings were erected as part of a village street design which eventually included a blacksmith's forge, a law office, and a farmhouse. Unlike Henry Ford, who never seemed to want expert advice, Clark, like Rockefeller, sought guidance constantly as he developed the Farmer's Museum. Its interpretive and educational programs have led to the establishment of professional training programs, some leading to degrees, which for a number of years have placed many knowledgeable persons in the preservation field.

Like Cooperstown, Sturbridge Village in Sturbridge, Massachusetts, (Figure 7-5), consists of a collection of historical properties removed from their original sites and arranged on a formerly open site to approximate a New England village. Cooperstown originally had been planned to be arranged around a central bandstand; Sturbridge Village was originally

Figure 7-5
An early aerial view of Sturbridge Village at Sturbridge, Massachusetts.

conceived as a series of newly constructed neocolonial buildings which would house the collections.

Stephen Clark's interests initially were in the fine arts. On the other hand, his contemporary, Albert Wells, owner of the American Optical Company in Southbridge, Massachusetts, always envisaged the creation of a New England industrial community. His interest in collecting revolved around the artifacts of his forefathers and the devices they had developed to ply their trades. By 1935, his collection had burgeoned to the point where it was too large to contain in his home. With his two brothers, he therefore set up the Wells Historical Museum and hired a curator. By the middle of the 1930s, the effort at Williamsburg was very well established and thus it was that Arthur Shurcliff, landscape architect of Colonial Williamsburg, was called upon for his advice in planning the housing of the collection.

He arranged for a New England green or common to be laid out, around which buildings could either be constructed or brought in to house Wells's collection. From the very beginning, Wells envisaged that the operation would be self-supporting from the sale of artifacts created in on-site demonstrations, and that its primary reason for being was to educate.

By 1938, Quinebaug Village Corporation was established, its purpose to create a town along the nearby stream of the same name. It is interesting to note that most of the early buildings brought to Sturbridge came from Connecticut, including the first one to be reconstructed—the mill—followed shortly thereafter by the Stephen Fitch House and the general store.

This living museum was conceived by Wells as a place where the arts and industries of early New England would be preserved and taught. It was his aim that the entire collection and the entire village would exist not just to teach about the arts and crafts, but about conditions and ways of life—how the implements were made, how they were used and what influenced the various designs. It was hoped that this knowledge could be applied to contemporary life.

Wells continued to pay personal attention to his avocation throughout his entire life. His daughter, Ruth, took over the operation in 1945, continuing her father's philosophy, and the project was officially opened in 1946, with eighteen reconstructed or old buildings moved to the site. Wells's admonition to balance the effort economically through sales of products produced at the village, while educating visitors in the process, has continued to be the overriding basis of the operation.

With such large-scale operations as Sturbridge, Williamsburg, Greenfield Village, and the Farmer's Museum established as the touchstones of the outdoor museum movement in the United States, it is not surprising that other similar donor-inspired projects grew as results of the collector's instinct. One of the later but most notable of these efforts began in 1945, when New York lawyer Henry Flynt and his wife decided to turn their attention, energies, and capital to the preservation of Deerfield, Massachusetts. Their aims were very similar to Stephen Clark's efforts in Cooperstown to preserve the ambiance of an existing town.

Henry Flynt had attended school in Deerfield as a child and had known the town all his life. After World War I, Frank L. Boyden, the headmaster of Deerfield Academy, had begun restoring old houses to use as dormitories for the students and had reconstructed the Old Indian House by 1930. In 1936, the Flynts had entered their son in Deerfield Academy and their interest in the village presumably was rekindled at that time. As W.A.R. Goodwin convinced John D. Rockefeller to preserve Williamsburg, Boyden persuaded the Flynts, who were aware of the operation in Williamsburg, to concern themselves with the preservation of Deerfield. (See Figure 7-6.)

The Flynts intended Deerfield to remain a living community as well as to educate the public, much like Colonial Williamsburg. Thus, they formed the Heritage Foundation (now known as Historic Deerfield). Yet the Flynts developed their project in such a quiet way, without the publicity attendant upon the establishment of other outdoor museum efforts, that to this day Deerfield remains less known than most other outdoor museums in the United States. This has had a beneficial effect, in that Deerfield has seldom, if ever, had to cope with the congestion that the great influx of visitors creates at some of the other sites.

As the outdoor museum as a means of preservation has matured, its emphasis on an educational role has increased. Methods used to interpret the objects, buildings, and industries and the crafts they reflect have become more sophisticated. An increasing interest in the methods used to simulate the life of another time has brought the interpreter into focus as an educational resource. The outdoor museum and an increasingly sophisticated understanding of interpretation have also stimulated interest in what might be called "everyday" history, or the history of the common man, usually referred to as *material culture*. The concerns of material culture include an interest in vernacular architecture and the life of the average citizen, usually ignored by traditional historians.

Figure 7-6
Like North Carolina's Old Salem, Historic Deerfield is noteworthy for its original buildings on their original sites.

The Pioneer America Society, founded in the late 1960s in northern Virginia, gave this interest in the vernacular its first real organizational base. The Association for Living Historical Farms and Agricultural Museums, founded in 1970, has given further organizational identity to the concerns of material culture. The traditional practice of using costumed interpreters to demonstrate how traditional crafts and everyday tasks were carried out is an attempt to create a lasting educational experience for the visitor. Recent developments in this field often include an attempt to involve visitors personally in the interpretation, by having the docent engage them in a first-person dialogue with the hope of accentuating the reality of the experience. This type of first-person involvement is encouraged by many museums today.

Outdoor museums are found in most parts of the country today. Yet, as important as they are as educational vehicles, they have never become in this country the major form of preservation they are in the Scandinavian countries which introduced them.

The boundaries of the world of the collector, curator, and interpreter are expanded when the outdoor museum is created on an existing historic site which still functions within the confines of an operating town or city, as is the case in Williamsburg, Deerfield, and Winston-Salem. Because the museum does not exist as an entity unto itself, but as a corporate resident in a functioning municipality, it is subject to the restrictions of that municipality. Many actions that the museum personnel may recommend, therefore, such as the closing of a street to automobile traffic, affect the functioning of the city and are subject to municipal review. It is primarily because of this that museum operations on original historic sites in functioning towns can also be viewed as historic districts.

Once the preservation issue is seen as a planning matter and not strictly as the purview of a museum, an entirely different set of values about the treatment of historic buildings comes into play. A new group of people becomes involved. The legal and economic issues at stake and the processes and methodologies that need to be brought to bear on such planning issues of preservation have little or no relation to the museum world. It is this environmentally oriented concept of preservation planning that has fueled the preservation movement in America with increasing strength since 1931, when the Charleston, South Carolina, city council set a precedent by defining its Battery neighborhood as an "Old and Historic District."

CHAPTER 8

Historic Districts

THE NATIONAL REGISTER of Historic Places defines a district as "a geographically definable
area—urban or rural, large or small—possessing
a significant concentration, linkage, or continuity of sites,
buildings, structures, and/or objects united by past events
or aesthetically by plan or physical development." In
common parlance, a district is a neighborhood. If the
neighborhood is of sufficient distinctiveness because of
its history, its plan, or the quality of its buildings, the
term *district* is usually applied to it in an attempt to distinguish it from neighborhoods that do not have such
distinct qualities.

Identifying and protecting such neighborhoods is
usually effected through a process of local selective zoning. This process was initiated in 1931 in Charleston,
South Carolina, when the city council zoned a neighborhood in that city, known as the Battery, as what it then
called an "Old and Historic District." Both adjectives—*old*
and *historic*—have become increasingly less applicable as
preservation has metamorphosed over the last half century or so from its narrow base of house museums to a
broader issue heavily dependent on professional planning and land-use objectives.

The local public action in Charleston restricted, to
a then unknown degree, the rights of property owners
within the Battery, limiting what they might do to their
own buildings in the interest of the welfare and well being of everyone within the neighborhood. In law, this is
termed the *public benefit*. The action in Charleston
changed the course of preservation in the United States

and initiated the concept of preservation as a planning activity. This approach was intensified when the National Historic Preservation Act of 1966 included the word *district* among the entities the secretary of the interior was to identify as he developed the National Register of Historic Places—a comprehensive list of those sites, buildings, objects, districts, and structures significant in American history, architecture, archaeology, and culture and therefore worth keeping.

The antecedents of such preservation-oriented zoning lie in the concept of the outdoor museum. As we have seen, some outdoor museums, such as Williamsburg in Virginia and Old Salem in North Carolina, also function as living neighborhoods defined as historic districts. The designation of a neighborhood as a historic district is therefore nothing more or less than the creation of a zoning tool in which the usual restrictiveness of zoning is increased. How severe this restrictiveness becomes varies with local ordinances and what is thought necessary to retain the local historical sense visually. Architectural style can be a restriction, as in Alexandria, Virginia, or the colors of buildings can be limited, as they are in Santa Fe, New Mexico.

The local Charleston ordinance stimulated the idea of interior rehabilitation and exterior restoration with the aim of maintaining or recapturing the sense of neighborhood identity and locality. (See Figure 8-1.) With the years had come a loss of architectural integrity which placed the local sense of the neighborhood identity in potential jeopardy. With the need to think in terms of planning rather than in terms of a single landmark museum building, the potential for preservation of existing American

Figure 8-1
Rutledge Avenue, Charleston, South Carolina: part of the first historic district in the United States.

building stock in local neighborhoods was recognized. Aesthetics as well as history thus became the motivation for preservation in such a neighborhood concept.

In the period immediately following World War I, preservation in Charleston had been museum oriented. The activism of resident Susan Pringle Frost, who was concerned about preserving such landmark buildings as the Joseph Manigault House and the Heyward-Washington House, stimulated local interest within Charleston's neighborhoods.

As the first president of the Society for the Preservation of Old Dwelling Houses, Frost requested the city council to introduce legislation to protect old ironwork and woodwork, which were being raided by museums for installation in galleries in other areas of the country. The construction of gasoline stations by the Standard Oil Company in what was to become the historic district also stimulated local preservationists to apply pressure. In 1929, that pressure led to an ordinance regulating the placement of such stations as well as that of schools, industry, and commerce. All of this activity ultimately led to the ratification by the Charleston city council of regulations which set up a board of architectural review whose function it was to issue certificates of appropriateness for changes to structures in the "Old and Historic District." Charleston's actions became the precedent for similar local actions in other American localities.

Several important factors that led to the decision-making process established in Charleston still hold true for other municipalities. The first is a sympathetic local government, and, primarily, a sympathetic mayor: i.e., strong public leadership. A second factor is strong private leadership. The third involves the financial resources of government as well as the private citizenry. To this in recent years can be added legislative tools at the national, state, and local levels which have eased the process of creating historic districts for local communities.

The timing in launching local preservation efforts also is important. The observation has been made that it unfortunately often takes the loss of one major structure in a community to galvanize its citizens into taking action.

During the 1920s, similar actions and interests were generated in cities other than Charleston. As early as 1925, a Vieux Carré Commission had been created in New Orleans, but it was only advisory. An initial effort to write a local preservation ordinance there as early as 1926 was unsuccessful. Not until 1937 was a Vieux Carré Commission with legal powers created because of pressure from a determined local citizenry. This commission had the means to protect and control its unique neighborhood in the face of inevitable growth and change. (See Figure 8-2.)

Other actions in the 1920s include the founding of the San Antonio Conservation Society. Texan Emily Edwards, an author and art teacher, spearheaded its establishment because of the impending loss of a local market which subsequently was destroyed. The society has concerned itself with the total preservation of the city; at least two historic districts have grown out of its efforts, La Villita and the nearby King William area.

Figure 8-2   The town of Locke, listed on the National Register of Historic Places, is a Chinese community in an agricultural area of California. Locke's architecture is vernacular and its historicity derives from its ethnic quality. Even to the casual observer, it has a finite sense of locality and place.

In 1946, the government of Alexandria, Virginia, passed what it still calls the "Charleston ordinance," signifying its inspiration. Similar action was taken in the interests of preserving Beacon Hill in Boston in 1955 and Santa Fe, New Mexico, in 1957. Today almost all of the fifty states have enabling legislation that allows any local jurisdiction within the state to zone a neighborhood selectively for preservation. The National Alliance of Preservation Commissions fosters the interchange of information among the local regulatory bodies.

The usual administrative structure called for in zoning ordinances written for historic districts requires the creation of guidelines for design and a board of review to whom owners must submit plans for approval prior to beginning projected changes or additions to their property. Criteria are developed which control design; these vary considerably from one neighborhood to another, some being quite lax and others, quite strict. For example, in Washington, D.C., Georgetown's local ordinance for years required new buildings constructed within the historic district (known as *architectural infill*) to be of traditional design (Figure 8-3). The city council of Alexandria has similar legislation. Santa Fe has restricted the colors that may be applied to new or old buildings, as well as the number of openings along the street.

Such highly restrictive ordinances may appear to some to be less useful than ordinances that allow a wider latitude of interpretation. The Savannah ordinance, for instance, encourages contemporary infill much like that of the Society Hill area of Philadelphia, which allows for a continuum of stylistic creativity within the neighborhood rather than a strict homogeneous adherence to the styles of design indicated by adjacent his-

toric structures. The end result is usually considered successful, provided that the architect of the new building is sufficiently sensitive to the historical context, scale, and mass of the built environment in which he is working. The architect must have a very clear and thoroughly grounded understanding of the abstracts of composition, irrespective of the medium, in order for his newly designed building to fit compatibly within the existing context of its historical neighborhood. In the aesthetic composition of a neighborhood, those abstracts of composition that determine the scale and mass of the streetscape include, among other things, the heights of buildings, their width, their materials, their roof types and shapes, the window openings, and the setbacks from the street.

The preservation of a neighborhood should be seen as a heterogeneous product, the whole of which exceeds the value of the individual parts. By analogy, a pearl has value. A string of graduated pearls, however, has value that far exceeds the value of all the individual pearls which compose it. In any given neighborhood, the quality of the pearls—i.e., the buildings—may vary considerably. The preservability of a neighborhood stands in direct relationship not only to the individual buildings and their sum total, but how they relate to each other, side by side and across the width of the street. The paving materials that cover the public right of way, nonconforming intrusions (buildings which do not "fit"), street furniture (lighting fixtures, trees, signs, and other accoutrements of the man-made environment), as well as open space, are all elements that help weave the visual tapestry of the neighborhood.

Figure 8-3
Placing new construction (architectural infill) into the existing built environment of a historic district is difficult to achieve from the standpoint of design. The Trentman House in Georgetown (center) is a successful example of such infill: careful attention has been paid to proportion, materials, texture, and silhouette with the result that the house is a complementary visual addition to the district, rather than a nonconforming intrusion.

As with the architectural design of an individual building, the abstract concept of space becomes a positive element in the design of a neighborhood. Thus, the significance of a historic district depends upon a collection of buildings, sites, structures, objects, and spaces that have an integrity of location, design, materials, workmanship, feeling, and association (history). The history can be national, state, or local, but no matter its significance, all of these aspects of compatibility combine to create a product which can be judged as a district worthy of preserving.

In considering a neighborhood for potential designation as a historic district, it is important to have a combination of sites, buildings, objects, structures, and spaces, a majority of which have existed in the same relationship to each other, as one sees them, longer than the average human life span. This does not necessarily mean that all such elements of the neighborhood must have existed relatively untouched that long, but that a majority should have. The total design of the neighborhood—as a product of its spaces, its objects, its buildings and their style, its street furniture— must convey a sense of cohesiveness. This cohesiveness can have a very strict rhythm, such as one sees in the streetscapes of Baltimore, Philadelphia, or Beacon Hill row houses, or a disparity, such as one sees in Georgetown or Savannah. Despite the dissimilarity of design in these latter neighborhoods, the abstracts of aesthetic quality, such as building scale, height, materials, and proportions, are generally compatible. It is the odd building in such a neighborhood, out of mass and scale and constructed of incompatible materials, in the wrong color, with the wrong textures, that planners call a nonconforming intrusion.

There are always varying levels of workmanship in the various buildings in a given neighborhood. While some structures may be better than others, as long as they are collectively homogeneous, they will convey a sense of locality and place that helps to identify the neighborhood visually. Sometimes, one finds that the overall visual impact gives to the viewer an instinctive sense of locality and place. One finds this clearly in small Texas towns (Figure 8-4), or in New England communities clustered around village greens. Special elements create the great distinctive qualities of those individual villages or neighborhoods. Although history, as an associative value, cannot be overtly seen, it can be a very important aspect of neighborhood identity. Alexandria, Virginia, for example, is George Washington's home town and Robert E. Lee's boyhood home. The buildings associated with these two giants of American history are very important landmarks. Such buildings form the skeleton which helps give that community its sense of locality and place, in this instance one of national significance.

Finally, it is important to look at the potential historic district from the point of view of how well it is defined. Thus, boundaries become critical as an aid in definition. The District of Columbia's Georgetown, for example, is very neatly defined by natural and man-made boundaries. The natural boundaries are a creek on the eastern edge of the neighborhood and the Potomac River on the southern edge. The two man-made boundaries are Georgetown University and Hospital on the west and Dumbarton Oaks Estate and Montrose Park on the north. Because of these physi-

Figure 8-4
Strand Street in Galveston, Texas, is noted for its late-nineteenth-century buildings, many of which feature cast-iron façades. Attention by preservationists has resulted in the restoration of many of the finest buildings and a listing on the National Register for the district.

cal restrictions, Georgetown can never become larger, despite local realtors' efforts to name the adjacent Burleith neighborhood "Upper Georgetown" for the social cachet and increased value the latter name brings.

The "little" buildings of a neighborhood are of primary importance in its identification. Every historic district has a bone structure or framework of landmark buildings. These are sometimes public buildings, such as the courthouse, the local library, or the church, or they can be the mansions of the wealthy. Around these landmarks, and supporting them, are rows and blocks of less important buildings, sometimes separated by alleys and gardens, which create the sense of continuity in the neighborhood and give visual support to the landmarks. It is in this context that the width of streets and sidewalks and spatial relationships in general become an integral part of the interplay of solids (buildings) and voids (streets, alleys). Like the component parts of an orchestra, the lesser buildings and spaces create the symphonic sense of locality or neighborhood. Initially, the loss of a few of these small units may create no great problem for the sense of locality. It is the continuing process of destruction, like pulled teeth in a smile, that ultimately causes the loss of integrity to the neighborhood. If the landmarks of such a neglected neighborhood survive, they then survive in a changed environment where they no longer function as the framework that holds the community together visually. A good example of this can be found in lower Manhattan, where the escalations of the scale of twentieth-century construction have visually separated the residual landmarks that had once been focal points of the earlier eighteenth- and nineteenth-century neighborhoods.

The reasons for visual cohesiveness of a neighborhood are difficult to grasp, comprising as they do the abstract components of artistic expression (i.e., scale, height, material, color). This cohesive sense may be accentuated if the neighborhood has been created around a geographic feature, as in Boston's Beacon Hill, or if it has been the recipient of a distinctive plan, such as Annapolis or Savannah.

The materials of which the structures themselves are made contribute to a strong cohesive sense. Witness the adobe buildings of Monterey or Santa Fe or the wooden buildings of New England, as well as the brick structures of Virginia. Finally, the aforementioned man-made or natural boundaries contribute further to this strong sense of identity and locality.

No neighborhood is so totally pure that it does not have its share of nonconforming intrusions. The fewer the intrusions, however, the greater the sense of homogeneity and cohesiveness which create the sense of locality and place. The more the nonconforming intrusions, the weaker the sense of identity. When the intrusions pass an acceptable minor percentage of the buildings that comprise the neighborhood, a new neighborhood identity then emerges.

There is no question that a neighborhood selectively zoned as a historic district becomes subject to sociological changes and increased economic value, changes that probably would not happen if it were not so zoned. No American neighborhood zoned as an historic district has ever decreased in value. Quite the contrary, the work of the appraiser and the assessor, stimulated by the increased attention of realtors to such neighborhoods, tends to accelerate sociological change and escalate economic values. Preservation programs in Pittsburgh and in Savannah have attempted to solve displacement problems through public and private financial assistance programs. The by-product of historic district designation tends to be social homogeneity and economic stratification.

Different approaches to neighborhood renewal have taken place in various cities. Publicly funded urban renewal programs that totally demolished neighborhoods stimulated the private sector to increase its involvement in preservation. In the long run, the questionable impact of urban renewal on the built environment also stimulated government to practice policies of retention and rehabilitation.

Charleston played yet another leading role in the neighborhood preservation movement by initiating the Historic Charleston Foundation Revolving Fund, whereby a sum of money is raised to buy a property, restore its façades, and offer the building for sale, leaving to the purchaser the responsibility of rehabilitating the interior to personal tastes and standards of comfort. Then the same money is recaptured in the sale and applied to other properties. The concept of a revolving fund has now become established in the United States and has been quite successful in Savannah, Pittsburgh, and other cities.

In 1976, the first great change in United States tax laws to affect preservation occurred. The Tax Reform Act of that year balanced the scales of incentives and disincentives, allowing the rehabilitation of existing buildings to become as economically attractive to developers as new construction. This was replaced by the Economic Recovery Tax Act of 1981, which significantly revised the tax incentives authorized by Congress five years earlier, and which has now been replaced by the Tax Reform Act of 1986. The 1981 law provided for a 25 percent investment tax credit for rehabilitation of historic commercial, industrial, and rental residential buildings, either individually listed in the National Register of Historic Places or located in a registered historic district if the building was certified as contributing to the significance of the district. Such registered historic districts include those on the National Register of Historic Places and those designated by the state or locality, if the ordinance authorizing the district and the district itself are certified by the secretary of the interior. This law further allowed a 20 percent investment tax credit for buildings at least forty years old and a 15 percent investment tax credit for buildings at least thirty years old, neither of which needed to be on the National Register of Historic Places. These incentives were changed by the Tax Reform Act of 1986, which lessened the economic incentives by reducing available tax credits to 20 percent for historic buildings and 10 percent for nonresidential buildings constructed before 1936. These reductions have had such a dampening effect on the use of tax incentives for preservation that yet another change in the law—which would restore some of the incentives—is being discussed at this writing.

To take advantage of the maximum credit, the developer of a building must secure two certifications from the secretary of the interior. The first attests that the building is individually listed on the National Register, or is a contributing building to a National Register historic district. The second concerns the quality of the rehabilitation work. With these two certifications from the Department of the Interior in hand, the developer secures the tax credit from the Internal Revenue Service.

Using the definition that "rehabilitation is the process of returning a property to a state of utility, through repair or alteration, which makes possible an efficient contemporary use while preserving those portions and features of the property that are significant to its historic, architectural and cultural values," the office of the secretary of the interior has developed *Standards for Rehabilitation* against which a *certified rehabilitation* may be judged. These standards include making every effort to find a compatible use for a property, effecting minimal alteration to the building, and maintaining its distinguishing original qualities or character. They further include recognizing a building as a product of its own time and recognizing past changes, which are now part of its history and development, that may be of significance in their own right. Treating distinctive stylistic features sensitively and repairing deteriorated architectural features rather than replacing them wherever possible are also part of the standards. Where replacement is necessary, an effort must be made to match new materials with those being replaced.

Two specific programs of the National Trust bear mention in dealing with historic districts. These are the Main Street program and maritime preservation. Established in the late 1970s, both aim at rehabilitating and restoring specific areas of a neighborhood—the commercial area and any water-related area that might be part of the district.

The Main Street program, inspired by the efforts of the Civic Trust in England, applies the management approach of the modern shopping center to the commercial hearts of smaller urban centers. (See Figure 8-5.) The modern shopping center generally has one owner who hires a manager to oversee all the shops, regulating special promotions, hours open, and many other aspects of retailing. The Main Street concept brings together the city government, the chamber of commerce, and downtown businessmen to pay the salary of one person—the Main Street manager—who functions in a similar way. The manager controls activities, public re-

Figure 8-5
Main Street, Madison, Indiana, is a good example of the type of commercial hub that has benefited from the Main Street program. Restoration of its buildings' façades has increased the town's economic well being.

lations, shop types, and other factors in the collective interest of the shop-keepers on the main street by coordinating their business efforts.

There are four areas in which the Main Street program attempts to secure cooperation from shopkeepers to rehabilitate buildings and economically revitalize businesses. These are design, promotion, cooperation, and economics. The first is addressed by considering the visual quality of the buildings and their signs and window displays. Promotion is a large part of the comprehensive Main Street effort, in which the downtown area is publicized and advertised as a shopping center. Cooperation is sought by bringing together the various organizations such as the chamber of commerce, the businessmen's association, and the various service clubs, as well as the city governing body, in an effort to work together effectively in the interests of the downtown area. Banks and local preservation groups are also included. Finally, diversification of the downtown economy is sought to create an economically balanced retail mix, and unused upper floors are converted into housing and offices.

The Main Street program is carried forward through seminars and workshops that improve the management skills of the local merchants. The end product sought is restoration and rehabilitation of the existing building stock and the reestablishment of appropriately designed street furniture. Hopefully, renewed attention to these elements will reawaken local residents to the advantages of the local main street and its businesses. The Main Street program has been widely publicized throughout the United States, and the results of its efforts can be seen in many parts of the country.

While the Main Street program focuses on the commercial part of the community, maritime preservation focuses on the waterfront and water-oriented aspects of urban and rural areas. Interest in maritime preservation was stimulated in no small part by the tall ships celebration during the Bicentennial and by efforts of the National Trust in bringing together an interested constituency. An effort was made to develop maritime standards, criteria, and programs that have a major impact on the preservation of American waterfronts and waterways (Figure 8-6). One has only to look at tax credit rehabilitation along the waterfront in Boston or to witness the Inner Harbour development in Baltimore to understand the effect that maritime preservation can have.

The shift of the preservation movement from a concern for museum-quality landmarks, intellectually isolated from their environment, and groups of buildings in outdoor museum complexes, to neighborhoods that can encompass many hundreds of structures, has broadened the concept of how buildings should be treated. With the growth of interest in historic districts, rehabilitating and adapting old buildings to new uses have become increasing preoccupations of the preservation movement. Beginning in 1976 and in the decade since, revisions to the tax code have made rehabilitation and adaptive use economically attractive to developers and have stimulated government to set standards for rehabilitation. Government has likewise developed a process of review for projects whose developers intend to use investment tax

Figure 8-6   The town of Nantucket, situated on Nantucket Island off the coast of Massachusetts, is a historic district in which the interests of conservationists and preservationists are combined. Open countryside and such widely separated maritime manifestations as lighthouses, Coast-Guard stations, and docks are as important to preservationists as are the eighteenth- and nineteenth-century commercial and residential buildings that line the cobblestone streets of the town.

credits. The end result is that preservation has become more of a planning endeavor than ever. It has also become process-oriented as well as economics-minded. The traditional preservationist whose goals are the humanistic interests of history, aesthetics, and education has been joined by a new preservationist who uses the movement as the means to a new and different end—profit.

CHAPTER 9

Rehabilitation and Adaptive Use

A MERICANS have long made pilgrimages abroad to enjoy the rich quality that recycling of buildings gives to European cities. Only in recent years have we seen fit to apply recycling—adaptive use—to our own built environment. This has been accelerated recently through the economic incentives of tax reform.

The National Trust defines *adaptive use* as "the process of converting a building to a use other than that for which it was designed, e.g., changing a factory into housing. Such conversions are accomplished with varying alterations to the building."

The problem inherent in adaptive use is summed up in the latter part of this definition, "accomplished with varying alterations to the building." In the strictest sense of the term, the *house museum* is an adaptive use since it converts a building constructed as a private residence into a three-dimensional educational experience—a museum. Thus, the building no longer functions for the reason for which it was originally constructed. Alterations are kept to a minimum, and devices inserted to use, preserve, and protect the building, such as heating, cooling, and alarm systems, are introduced. This is perhaps the most basic challenge in the design of such adaptations. In such disparate adaptations as museum conversions and warehouses made into condominiums as housing for the elderly, there exist challenging decisions on how to successfully effect adaptations for economic viability and still preserve that quality of historicity for which the building is being kept. (See Figure 9-1.)

Prior to decisions about the project's design, a host of factors must be considered and evaluated, beginning with the potential market. For example, does a need exist for the proposed use? Will the local social and demographic characteristics of the area make the project feasible? What type of development is taking place locally and what is the competition? What is the sale or rental market?

Evaluation of the potential project's location is primary. What sort of services are available, such as transportation? What other uses exist in the area? What are being planned? What is the existing or potential environmental quality of the surroundings?

Having addressed questions such as these, a physical analysis of the building needs to be made. What are the requirements of the local building code? Does the zoning allow or potentially allow the proposed adaptive use? What is the structural stability of the building? In what condi-

Figure 9-1 The Carson Mansion, Eureka, California: built in 1884–86 for a leading citizen who had made his fortune in the lumber industry. This exuberant Victorian mansion today houses the Ingomar Club, a private group whose members take pride in maintaining the architectural integrity of their headquarters.

tion are the mechanical systems? Can they be used? Must they be replaced?

Finally, an architectural and historical evaluation must be made. Can
the building meet the criteria of the National Register? If not, is rehabilitation still economically feasible if investment tax credits are to be
claimed? How much of the historical fabric—the authentic materials and
workmanship that give the building its character or integrity—exists?

Can the existing integrity of the building be retained in the conversion process? If not all, how much? What elements must be preserved,
should be preserved, or can't be preserved to achieve an economically viable conversion? If historical integrity has been compromised by change
or even lost totally, can it be recaptured through repair or restoration?
Can the needs for space and circulation in the proposed use be accommodated without the destruction of the building's sense of history?

Integrity is at the heart of adaptive use. What is integrity? How is it
lost? How is it retained or recaptured? Unfortunately, neither the National
Trust nor the National Park Service has specifically defined the term from
the preservationist's point of view, although, in the final analysis, architectural integrity is what the secretary of the interior's standards are all
about. Defining *integrity* is the crux of preservation as a humanistic
endeavor.

The dictionary defines *integrity* as "the entire, unimpaired state of being or quality of anything; perfect condition, soundness."

The secretary of the interior's standards and guidelines were developed in 1977 by W. Brown Morton and Gary Hume of the National Park
Service. Morton, now a professor at Mary Washington College in Freder-
icksburg, Virginia, defines *architectural integrity* as "those qualities in a
building and its site that give it meaning and value."

Recognizing that meaning and value represent many things to many
people, Morton admits that integrity is as intangible as love but that a
successful preservationist can, and indeed must, develop a sense for it.
For a building to have integrity, Morton believes, it must have some or all
of the following attributes: (1) style, (2) workmanship, (3) setting or location, (4) materials, (5) building type or function, and (6) continuity.

To understand architectural style, the preservationist must understand historical styles, not only when seen in pristine examples of the various types, but in their vernacular versions as well. (See Figure 9-2.) If the
preservationist cannot recognize historical styles, he must ally himself
with an architectural historian who can. If an architectural historian is un-
available the National Trust's *What Style is It?* concisely outlines American architectural styles. Virginia and Lee McAlester's *Field Guide to
American Houses* covers architectural styles as recent as 1985.

An example of integrity of style would be the 1817 East Family
House at Shakertown at Pleasant Hill, Kentucky, which epitomizes the pu-
rity of expression of the Shaker creed. No later generations have changed
or added anything that detracts from the utter simplicity and integrity of
the original architectural conception.

While Hyde Hall (1817–35), outside of Cooperstown, New York,
may be questionable as to its proportions, the quality and integrity of its

Figure 9-2
The spectacular Moorish-style Tampa Bay Hotel was built in 1888–91 for railroad magnate Henry Plant. It has been handsomely adapted to serve as the centerpiece of the University of Tampa's campus and accommodates administrative offices, meeting rooms, and classrooms within its immense interior.

workmanship, especially in the craftmanship of its stone cutters, is memorable. Thus, the preservationist must add a sense of craftsmanship to his arsenal of knowledge in evaluating the historic building, especially in relation to adaptive use.

The question of the integrity of setting is essentially an environmental issue which takes into account the surroundings of the building or buildings in question. Thus, the project that converts a residence to office use and blacktops portions of the surrounding garden for necessary but ill-placed parking destroys the sense of integrity of setting. Efforts should be made to place parking in such a way as to intrude minimally on the area.

Lyndhurst (1838), the National Trust's property at Tarrytown, New York, is a prime example of a property with integrity not only of style and workmanship but of setting as well. The A.J. Downing-designed gardens retain the integrity of their designer's intent. Parking for visitors to Lyndhurst does no damage to this integrity, being tucked out of sight in the original carriage area and behind the greenhouses. Downing's original concept of undulating sun-drenched lawns and massed trees remains intact, with integrity of site preserved.

Buildings are constructed of many materials, but those of cast iron are relatively rare, even in such long-established eastern urban concentrations as Boston, New York, and Philadelphia. The 1859 Arsenal building at Watervliet, New York, has lost its integrity of setting because of later adjacent construction. Its style and workmanship can easily be called into question, but on the basis of its materials—it is totally constructed of cast iron, rather than having just a single cast-iron street façade—one can not deny it a strong sense of integrity.

Churches and theaters are difficult to use adaptively because the economics of conversion seldom allow for the survival of the large interior spaces found in such buildings. When a conversion takes place, all buildings of this nature lose their interior integrity when their unbroken spaces are divided in the interests of economic viability. The world-renowned Pantheon in Rome fared better, its immense interior spaces preserved when the fourth-century tomb of Hadrian was converted to a church during the Renaissance.

Perhaps the most difficult aspect of integrity to grasp is that of continuity, for the simple reason that on the surface it appears to work against some of the other attributes mentioned. Integrity of continuity can perhaps best be observed at the Taos Pueblo in New Mexico, which is maintained and lived in today by descendants of the same tribe of Indians who constructed it in the seventeenth century.

This is not to say that this intricate complex of mud adobe brick hasn't always changed and been modified, however. With the social stability that the Spaniards brought, an increased sense of security eventually permitted the introduction of doors and small windows, when before there had been none. A case can even be made for the current television antennae, expressions of contemporary life, as the most recent manifestation of this continuum. In none of these modifications, however, have the massing and the silhouette of the complex been seriously compromised. And the complex's integrity survives because the same Indian tribe continues to occupy it.

Once the concept of architectural integrity has been grasped, the goal is to formulate a course of action to plan and complete a successful rehabilitation. Such action will ensure that the building's character-defining features and materials are preserved in the process of producing a contemporary use that is not only efficient but economically sound. Identifying the form and detail of architectural materials and features that define the historic character of the building is the first step. Deciding how to retain and preserve them in the conversion process is the basic challenge. It is important to understand that the decision to make minor changes, which would, in themselves, appear to have little or no effect on the historic character of the building, may collectively result in a major loss of historic character. This can happen when a series of decisions to delete architectural features have a cumulative effect on the historic character of the building. Unfortunately, many decisions of this nature are not reversible. Once original fabric is lost, it is permanently lost. New replacements do not have the patina that only time can produce. Caution and conservative decision making are therefore mandatory. It is the total impact of the rehabilitation for adaptive use that is judged. (See Figure 9-3.)

Once the important historic character-defining features have been identified, protecting and maintaining them during the process of rehabilitation and adaptive use must be considered. This can include, but is not

Figure 9-3
The restoration and rehabilitation of the 1825 Quincy Market in Boston has been demonstrably successful: the complex has attracted many thousands of people to its restaurants and shops since its grand reopening (shown) in 1976.

limited to, how much existing paint is removed and what sort of new protective coatings are applied; how and what materials are cleaned, if needed; what should be caulked, how, and with what material; and how the fabric of the building should be generally protected (with fences and alarm systems) during the rehabilitation process. *Patina* is the evidence of wear and tear on architectural materials, and the settling of what is commonly referred to as dirt, which only time and use produce. To remove too much of the patina, resulting in a raw, new look, contributes to the perceived loss of historic character. A certain amount of dirt and imperfection caused by the knocks of time—sags, chips, etc.—constitute the irreplaceable quality that is patina. Once removed, no amount of effort can reproduce it. For some reason or other, it seems to be easier for the average person to grasp this concept with furnishings, commonly called antiques. Historic buildings are antiques and should be treated as such. It is with the concern for existing patina that an evaluation of the physical condition of an historic building should begin.

Having identified what makes the building historic and devised methods to protect and maintain it, the next step is deciding what needs to be repaired and how, and what cannot be repaired and therefore must be replaced. As with the entire process, caution and a conservative attitude are called for. In Europe, the common term for such repair and replacement is *intervention*. The less intervention, the more the historic character of the building will survive the rehabilitation process. Thus repair does not imply the all-too-common practice of total replacement of a wooden window sill, for example, when only one end of it is rotted, but piecing-in, patching, or splicing to retain as much of the original material as possible. Repair also implies the limited replacement of documented missing parts, such as dentils, brackets, or slates, when surviving prototypes exist as guiding documents. The same type of material as the original is always preferred in replacing missing or severely deteriorated parts which cannot be rescued, although substitute materials can be used if they convey a visual compatibility in form and design with the finish of existing parts being matched.

Replacements should always be based on as much documentation as possible. This may be in the form of historical photographs, written descriptions, existing physical evidence such as actual fragments, or "ghosts"—outlines on walls of features that no longer exist. The greater the amount of evidence (i.e., documentation), the higher the possibility for successful replacement. As the amount of documentary evidence decreases, so does the potential for an acceptable end product. Failing sufficient documentary evidence to permit a reasonably accurate replacement for a missing feature, such as a stair, a porch, or a cornice, a new design should be sought that is compatible in size, scale, and materials with the character-defining historic features of the building. The design should be sufficiently distinct in detail to give a clear message that it is nonhistorical in character but visually compatible with the existing authentic elements of the building.

During any alterations in the process of adaptive use necessary to make the historic building usable, every effort should be made to effect changes without radically altering or destroying existing historic characteristics such as materials, finishes, architectural features, and spaces. Scraping, sandblasting, and other extreme methods of intervention should be avoided. If the proposed needs for the building cannot be met without drastically altering those interior spaces that define the historic character, then an exterior addition should be considered. Alterations should be minimally visible from the public right of way if they can be seen at all. (See Figure 9-4.)

The secretary of the interior's *Standards for Rehabilitation* and *Guidelines for Rehabilitating Historic Buildings* have become the criteria against which the success or failure of rehabilitation and adaptive use are judged. To developers intending to use investment tax credits successfully, adherence to the secretary's standards and guidelines is basic. With them, the rehabilitator has a guide book to the do's and don'ts of the process. As these guidelines are recognized, learned, and applied more widely, appeals to the National Park Service by developers new to preservation should ultimately diminish in volume and may eventually become unnecessary.

The secretary of the interior's *Standards for Rehabilitation* has quickly become the yardstick of acceptable rehabilitation. The controversy that

Figure 9-4
Before its rehabilitation and adaptation as a creative arts center, Alexandria, Virginia's torpedo factory, loomed as a hulking gray mass along the Potomac River waterfront. This successful example of adaptive use, repainted to highlight its art deco façade, has become a focal point in the heart of the city's historic district.

often rages around the enforcement of these standards is brought about by the clash of two distinct groups with a single goal (rehabilitation), working in disparate worlds for disparate but justifiable reasons.

On one side are the professionals in state and federal government whose responsibility it is to see that the standards are heeded in the interest of protecting the historical fabric in question. They attempt to assure that a maximum of the integrity and historicity of the building survives the conversion process. As trained humanists (architects and architectural historians), their judgments will vary case by case, given a certain uniformity based on the standards. Because such judgments are not scientific, however, they do not lend themselves to absolutes.

On the other side are the developers, for whom time is money in the rehabilitation process. They are not humanists, but operate in the statistical world of economics. There is a point of diminishing returns beyond which they cannot go to achieve a successful, profitable rehabilitation. At times, the opinions of the humanists appear overzealous regarding preservation. And in the haste to turn a profit, the actions of developers may appear insensitive to the integrity and historicity of a building. Getting these two disparate voices to sing in concert is not easy. When investment tax credits are employed, compromise on both sides is essential to harmony.

CHAPTER 10

Landscape Preservation

F OR a movement that enjoyed important connections with natural conservation early in its history, historic preservation has suffered a curious disassociation from its sister movement in America during most of the twentieth century. This is not the situation in other countries. Many informed professionals in the United States agree that (natural) conservation and (historic) preservation are two sides of the same coin, but efforts to treat them integrally have proven difficult, as the Carter administration learned when it tried to combine certain elements of the Bureau of Outdoor Recreation with most of the historic preservation responsibilities of the National Park Service. Why should this be so? Exploring the issue of landscape preservation offers some clues.

The American Society of Landscape Architects' committee on historic preservation classifies landscapes into three broad groups. The first are *designed landscapes*, defined as being "altered under a plan by a professional or avid amateur with verifiable results." *Cultural landscapes* are seen as "those that are altered through human interaction on the vernacular level, often related to a desired function and with a discernible pattern." *Natural landscapes* are seen as "those that are relatively unchanged by human intervention."

Recognizing that designed and cultural landscapes can also be historic and worthy of recognition and preservation, an international gathering of professionals in Japan, in 1977, defined a historic landscape as " . . . one which has had associated with it an event or series of events of historical note. A historic landscape may also be the visual perception of a particular period of civilization, a way of life or patterns of living."

What makes a historic landscape? What constituent parts convince us that a certain land area is as much the province of the preservationist as the conservationist? Do those distinctions make logical sense any longer? At the heart of the issue is the relationship between natural forms and constructed objects occupying, or creating, the same environment. The great national parks of the Southwest, predominantly natural areas that achieved their significance in prehistoric times, are perceived in terms of conservation, not preservation, management.

Conversely, and for obvious reasons, urban environments have been preservation strongholds. But what about Ellis Island and Liberty Island, great man-made symbols rising out of a dominant natural setting (i.e., waterscape)? The definitions become increasingly difficult to sustain. How do we go about defining and managing such phenomena as mining and company towns; great estates and summer "camps" of the Gilded Age; California missions and midwestern agricultural communities; small seaports, New England mill complexes, and historic railroad rights-of-way? All derive their significance from an important interaction between natural and man-made features. All constitute parts of a historic landscape. Their preservation has often emphasized the built environment at the expense of the natural context. In thinking about historic landscapes per se, how can we best define them? Perhaps we can only maintain a flexible approach to this question. For argument's sake, let us propose that to fall into the category of preservation rather than that of conservation, a landscape must include a significant component of notable man-made structures or buildings that enjoy a special relationship with their natural setting. The logical corollary to this assumption, then, is that preservation of both natural and fabricated elements, along with the aspects of their critical interrelationship, is essential in such an environment.

Several examples can best illustrate this point. Within its boundaries, the National Seashore at Cape Cod, Massachusetts, includes important historic buildings and sites, like lighthouses and the Marconi Station. Obviously, these relatively few man-made features stand in secondary importance to the awesome sweep of beaches and dunes that makes the seashore a unique natural resource. Here, the number and importance of man-made elements relative to natural features clearly results in the seashore becoming essentially a conservation landscape.

Thousands of miles away is another kind of landscape characterized by the surrounding ocean—Hanalei Valley on the Hawaiian island of Kauai. In this lush green landscape, human habitation has left its mark from the earliest period of Polynesian settlement to the ethnic taro farmers of today. The spectacular mountains, beaches, and fertile valley floor of Hanalei are dotted with simple buildings that recall various stages of its history: sugar cane and coffee plantations, cattle ranches, missions, and the villages of fisherman and farmers of Chinese, Japanese, Portuguese, Filipino, Korean, and Spanish ancestry. (See Figures 10-1 and 10-2.)

Figure 10-1   The cultural landscape of the Hanalei Valley Federal Wildlife Refuge includes the long-established taro patches of the valley bordering the Hanalei River. The Haragutchi Rice Mill, the only remaining rice mill in Hawaii, is visible in the distance; the Hanalei Bridge, in the foreground.

Figure 10-2   These ancient Hawaiian fish ponds are a good example of a cultural landscape. Early Hawaiians piled stones across inlet entrances, permitting small salt-water fish to wash in with the tides, but hindering their return to the deep. The fish were allowed to grow to a proper size before they were "harvested." The landscape remains essentially natural despite man's intervention.

In Hanalei an enormous amount of open land, much of it worked by man, contrasts with a small number of built resources, but the history of human occupation has had a major impact, despite the absence of "important" architecture. Here, unlike the Cape Cod National Seashore, the balance and tension between man and nature over time have contributed to the valley's identity, making it primarily a historic rather than a conservation landscape.

A third example brings natural and built features into closer proximity. Block Island lies twelve miles off the Rhode Island coast. Thus its 6,000 acres have long remained isolated, although white settlers arrived in 1635. By the late nineteenth century, tourism was augmenting the island's fishing economy. By the summer of 1916, wooden boarding houses and fancier mansard-roofed hotels accommodated as many as 56,000 visitors annually. The island's delicate ecology, with its salt ponds, sheer bluffs, encircling beaches, and gently rolling hills nearly devoid of trees, survives today. Because of the interplay of nature and human history in such an intimate setting, Block Island invites the close cooperation of preservationists and conservationists. The same may be said of other islands, including Nantucket.

The interaction of man and nature is rarely so simple and benign as it is on Block Island. Even in places where the unique value of a landscape is recognized, consensus about its treatment is often lacking. Two radically dissimilar landscapes, lying 3,000 miles apart, illustrate most of the problems confronted by preservationists. One is the Adirondack Forest Preserve in New York State; the other, California's Napa Valley.

At first glance the Adirondack Forest Preserve seems to be a rather clear example of a conservation landscape. More than six million acres of forests, rivers, and lakes exist in a wilderness condition few believe can be found at this scale in the Northeast. This vast area is owned by the state of New York, under a constitutional charge that it be kept "forever wild." But the forest preserve also contains a unique architectural resource—more than thirty-five "great camps" dating from the last third of the nineteenth century and the beginning of the twentieth.

Although inspired by models as diverse as Swiss chalets and Russian dachas, these rustic vacation outposts for the very rich are peculiarly American phenomena. As architectural and cultural signposts they are vivid and irreplaceable, rooted in the very landscape that inspired them. While the camps represent an outstanding example of the close relationship between the assets of conservation and preservation, their continued existence is tenuous because of the interpretation the conservationists have given to the 1895 legislation that created the forest preserve. This requires the state to dispose of any buildings on acquired Adirondack lands in order to keep them "forever wild." In 1895, this interpretation posed no conflict because the camps were safely in private ownership. Even if proponents of legislation had been able to envision changed circumstances nearly a century in the future, they might not have been able to assess the significance of the camps, since they lacked the historical perspective which only the passage of time can bring.

Today, conserving the camps has pitted wilderness advocates against preservationists. If the camps are to be saved, uses need to be found for them, and proposals that might seem logical under different circumstances can easily compromise the strict interpretation of wilderness objectives sought here by conservation officers of the state.

The great wine country of California's Napa Valley is decidedly different from the Adirondacks, but here, too, a conflict exists between proponents of the natural and man-made environments. While evoking the centuries-old values of a wilderness, the valley nonetheless has a venerable history that evolved from agriculture. With one serious hiatus brought about by Prohibition, the valley has been America's premier wine producer since the middle of the nineteenth century.

The wine barons of the 1870s, 1880s, and 1890s introduced eclectic architectural styles throughout the length of the valley. Stone wineries with deep cellars for the aging of wine and commanding manor houses for the owners' families were typical of the period. A great number of these buildings remain, some returned to use only in recent decades, thanks to the revival of California's wine industry.

Like the camps of the Adirondacks, Napa Valley's architecture enjoys a special relationship with the land. Unlike the Adirondack camps, it has little consistency, except for the use of stone where available. The Christian Brothers Vineyards at Mount LaSalle are graced by a mission-style administrative building, while visitors to Beringer Vineyards can taste wines in the Rhine House, a building that owes its appearance to the founders' native Germany. The main house at Château Chevalier, with its red slates and pyramidal towers, defies easy stylistic categorization. Whatever style of architecture appears in the valley seems almost invariably to possess a natural affinity for the landscape, perhaps because the practical considerations of viticulture are paramount. The patina of age has only served to increase this sense of affinity with the land.

The tension between the advocates of architecture and natural resources in the Napa Valley landscape has nothing to do with wilderness advocacy. The threat, in fact, comes from prosperity. Now that California wine making is a multimillion-dollar business, history and practicality can be expected to meet head on. To date, vineyard owners have demonstrated an impressive respect for the architectural heritage of their industry. Winemaking is, after all, something of a romantic business. But as any vintner will confess, most old wineries don't answer very efficiently to the requirements of modern wine technology. How long the expanding industry can afford to leave its own architectural heritage intact is a troublesome question. It illustrates, dramatically, the unexpected conflicts that keep historic landscapes in jeopardy.

Some of the biggest controversies surrounding landscape preservation occur in places divorced from dramatic wildernesses or lush valleys. Disappearing farmland is a good example. Nowhere does that problem incite more controversy than in New Jersey, the nation's most densely populated state, where agricultural land is disappearing so fast that "the Garden State" may soon be nothing more than a nostalgic motto.

New Jersey has been a great supplier of produce since the eighteenth century. Before westward expansion, it even dominated American wheat production. Since the end of World War II, its location within the eastern megalopolis has sent land values skyrocketing. Industrial, commercial, and residential development continues to consume prime farmland at a dizzying pace. Not only does this change in land use wipe out an important food source, but it also destroys a historic landscape. The vernacular farmhouses of the eighteenth and nineteenth centuries, reflecting primarily Dutch, German, and English cultural roots, lose their historical resonance as their surrounding landscape is encroached upon by urban and suburban development. As we begin to see condominiums instead of potatoes growing in the flat fields of Middlesex County and corporate centers rather than sheep dotting the hills of Hunterdon County, we recognize how much a landscape contributes to the unique sense of place. Once again, it becomes obvious that both man-made and natural components of the historic landscape are inextricably bound together.

It is for reasons such as these that a preoccupation with what is now known as *sprawl* has gripped the attention of more than a few peer groups in American Society including that of the preservationist.

It is questionable to equate the word *sprawl* analytically with development, the term traditionally associated with growth in small and large man-made concentrations. In Philadelphia, for example, at one point in time, the town's eighteenth-century limits stopped four to six blocks from the shore of the Delaware River. By the end of the nineteenth century, it had extended from the Delaware to the Schuylkill River, twenty-plus blocks west, and beyond in a dense built-up urbanized character of new housing inherited from its British-based London land-use precedents. Stylistically, one can easily trace there the architectural design fashions of the eighteenth and nineteenth centuries from one river west to the other just as easily as one can observe the design changes in row house development along Rhode Island Avenue in Washington, D.C., from the city center northward in the later nineteenth through the early twentieth centuries. So what distinguishes sprawl from traditional development and what has caused it?

As one might suspect, there are multiple answers to both of these questions. Among the most obvious are the scale of American life and increased population pressures, coupled with ease of mobility via the automobile. These have all exacerbated traditional concepts and solutions to development making seemingly unlimited extensions from the urban core possible. Add to that the entrenched definition of "highest and best use" of land equated to maximum development usually in the form of malls, housing tracts, and office parks (NEVER retention of open land). Coupled with our equally entrenched system of taxation tagged to the commonly held highest and best use definition, the inevitable result is the land-chewing sprawl all thinking Americans deplore. Leap frog residential and commercial development have melded independent townscapes and ever-shrinking farms and other open space into megalopolis urban concentrations without borders. This has caused a fragmentation of land use power among smaller localities within such areas, making difficult, if not eradicating, any centralized planning and land-use control. Strip development and mega-malls have drained economic vitality from former town centers and past planning insistence on segregated land use in lieu of mixed land use have all contributed to the problem. One of the keys to defining the problem should be the recognition of the removal of housing from a walking distance to retail stores and the auto use it creates. So-called "smart growth" developments whose house-to-streetscape relationship and planning density hark back to the mixed-use base of the traditional town or city development, in order to preserve green open space, may likewise be a potential answer. Such proposals, however, run the risk of being shot down by vote of the local citizenry now married to their cars and their acre of suburban land.

The preservationists' response to this dilemma has been to enlarge their sights and accelerate their efforts by identifying ever larger segments of America as cultural or heritage corridors called National Heritage Areas by the National Park Service which administers this recently conceived program within the Department of the Interior. The Park Service defines a National Heritage Area as "a place where natural, cultural, and scenic resources combine to form a cohesive, naturally distinctive landscape arising from patterns of human activity shaped by geography." It is noteworthy to observe that this trend, under various titles in various countries, is developing globally in such diverse areas as Europe, China and South America.

The author recognizes that this program, discussed in greater detail in the Epilogue of this book, is not the usual approach to sprawl control and not the answer in itself. It primarily uses the preservationists' traditional reliance on associative values (history) and aesthetic/cultural values (architecture) married to conservation and recreation rather than on the usual tools of the land-use planning professional. Our problem is that American Society does not seem to be able to shift its sight from the individual trees in order to see the forest. When and if that shift takes place, sprawl control should become a reality.

Farming, anywhere you find it, is a practical business. Some farmers have little patience for such extra-agricultural considerations as the historical resonance of the landscape. The preservationists' task, in this context, is to help prevent farmland from being priced out of the farm market. Only then will any opportunity exist for preserving the man-made components of the agricultural landscape. Various schemes, in New Jersey and elsewhere, have been proposed, including subsidized land banks and complex tax incentives. However, little significant headway has been made to date and the reason is simple. Americans still see land as a commodity and land speculation as an inalienable right. Until land is recognized as a communal resource, landscape preservation of any kind will remain an uphill battle.

The varieties of landscape discussed so far have been large-scale land forms molded by nature and modified by man's development. Another kind of historic landscape, with its own special problems, demands attention as well. This is the intentionally designed landscape which in the twentieth century has increasingly become the province of the landscape architect.

In America, the self-conscious management and design of large-scale land areas did not become commonplace until the middle of the nineteenth century, when romantic architecture was promoted by men like Andrew Jackson Downing and Alexander Jackson Davis. New York City's Central Park launched the career of Frederick Law Olmsted, who pioneered the modern profession of landscape design, along with such lesser-known practitioners as Jens Jensen, associated with developing the Chicago parks system. Individuals like the writer, planner, and landscapist H. W. S. Cleveland, a contemporary of A. J. Downing's, were instrumental in developing Sea Island, Georgia, as a winter resort. R. M. Copeland was a partner of Cleveland's. The importance of his early work in the design of cemeteries, public squares, and pleasure gardens is just beginning to be realized among researchers.

In the space of a few decades, Central Park and a host of other great public areas planned by Olmsted and his colleagues and disciples established new standards for the relationship between natural and built forms. These early accomplishments set the stage for the alliance of architects, landscape architects, and urban planners who would create the City Beautiful movement and suburban communities that still serve as yardsticks for enlightened design.

Many surviving monuments of the nineteenth-century landscape movement have become landmarks, their importance matched only by their fragility. If it is true that a building begins to die the day it is completed, how much truer it is of a landscaped environment, a fact that has profound implications for preservationists. How does one go about conserving or restoring a "landmark" that by its very nature is organic, with constantly changing living parts?

Consider the lavish use of boxwood in the southern garden, often used to border formal parterres and to articulate overall design. (See Figure 10-3.) Because boxwood grows slowly, a premium is placed on established specimens. There is thus a general reluctance to clip the shrub to keep its defining qualities intact. The failure to do this, however, eventually blurs the crispness of the formal parterres it was planted to define. Eventually the garden restorationist is faced with the dilemma of destroying years of accumulated growth to recapture the form of the original garden or foregoing the clarity of the original garden design in the interest of retaining mature plant specimens. Recently, that difficult decision was made at the terraced formal gardens of Oatlands, a National Trust property in Leesburg, Virginia. Years of boxwood growth, which had not only obscured the parterres but also made passage along the garden paths almost impossible, were severely pruned back. The immediate results were essentially leafless branches which defined the parterres as badly as the overgrown plants had done before pruning. The growth that the pruning stimulated, however, soon appeared, and once more the boxwoods function in the crisp defining role originally intended. (See Figure 10-4.)

The restoration of Central Park serves as a laboratory where these questions can be subjected to experiment and public and professional debate. In one sense, the entire park is man-made, the basic land form hav-

ing been radically altered by Olmsted. The more patently man-made constituents—bridges, fountains, shelters, and promenades—are subject to restoration with relative ease, if not enormous expense. Infinitely more complex are questions of how to treat the park's natural features. Olmsted never envisioned his Sheep Meadow as the scene of rock concerts and nuclear protests—uses that can turn pasture into dust bowl. He did envision the Ramble as a place artistically wild, where picturesque plantings would give way to vistas beyond the park itself. Plans to restore his intent by moderating 100 years of untrammeled growth invited the rage of birdwatchers, who feared that any changes would destroy the sanctuary—qualities never imagined by the Ramble's designer.

Managing a historic landscape of this sort, an organic landmark, means grappling with questions of change in the larger social fabric as well as the artifact itself. Is it legitimate, for example, to treat a historic landscape to adaptive use in the same way that we treat a historic building? And if so, adaptive use for whose purpose? Can the beauty of Central Park as originally designed be made compatible with the needs of the city's poor and disenfranchised, who have adopted Olmsted's greensward with a fierce sense of territoriality?

Such philosophical questions have direct bearing on the practical management of most designed landscapes, not just monuments of Central Park's stature. Long Island and northern New Jersey are both places where turn-of-the-century estates abound, many with landscaping as significant as their architecture. Solutions calling for adaptive uses to keep such estates intact involve transforming historic landscapes created for a privileged class (and usually designed with scant regard for maintenance

Figure 10-3
The boxwood fronting the east façade of Woodlawn Plantation, Mount Vernon, Virginia (1800), had been allowed to grow until the defining role it played had been lost; the paths beside the plantings were overgrown and thus unusable, and the mansion was partially obscured. The plantings have been pruned to restore their defining characteristics.

Figure 10-4   The gardens at Oatlands (c. 1800) in Loudon County, Virginia, have been restored. Severe pruning of the aged boxwood has restored its geometric shape.

costs) into environments suitable for a more democratic and inflation-prone way of life. Most of the standard solutions to date (conference centers, arts centers, luxury hotels, condominium developments) imply the necessity for at least some diminution in maintenance and thus a decline in quality. How far can we stray from the original landscape designer's plan and still claim to be preserving his original intent?

All of the foregoing issues of historic landscape preservation bring into focus past failures involving the integration of cultural and natural resources. It is not so much the means that is lacking as the vision. To stimulate both vision and means, a stronger alliance is called for between preservationists and conservationists, and a stronger professional bond is needed between preservationists and landscape architects. (See Figures 10-5 and 10-6.)

Figure 10-5   In the twentieth century, the William Paca House and Gardens in Annapolis (1765) became part of a 200-room hotel complex complete with large parking lot. In this photo the modern addition, in the midst of demolition during the mid-1960s, still obscures the graceful outlines of the house.

Figure 10-6   This documentary photograph, taken during the restoration of the Paca House and its gardens, shows the gardens "sketched out" and partially planted. Restorers were guided by archaeological findings and written historical data.

CHAPTER 11

Rural and Small-Town Preservation

THOSE philosophical attitudes that guide solutions to preservation in urban neighborhoods identified as historic districts are equally applicable to the rural environment. As has been noted in the discussion on historic districts, open space is a major component among those elements which compose a neighborhood.

In the urban environment, open space is usually quite restricted and consciously organized by the configuration of streets and alleys. The buildings of the neighborhood generally define such spaces. In small towns, open space tends to be no less organized, but is a much larger part of the area's composition because the defining elements of the environment are much less densely compacted. In the rural environment, open space becomes the predominant component. Man's imprint on the rural landscape gives that landscape definition through such impositions as buildings, bridges, and hedgerows. Natural attributes such as streams, ponds, swamps, and forests combine with man-made components to help identify the sense of locality of the rural landscape. Thus, the primary difference between the rural historical landscape and the historic district of an urban area is generally the greater distance between identifiable historic components in the rural landscape. The discussion that follows, therefore, does not dwell as much on the theory of area preservation, since the basics have already been

discussed in defining historic districts, as it does on the mechanics of applying preservation philosophies to rural areas and small towns.

There is very little agreement among those involved in rural and
small-town preservation as to what is indeed "rural" and what is indeed
"small." For the purposes of this discussion, the classification of the U.S.
Bureau of the Census has been followed. The bureau defines an urban
population as being composed of everyone who lives in an urbanized
area (which it considers as a closely settled territory of at least 50,000
population) and any place else with at least 2,500 inhabitants. It follows,
therefore, that any place else that lies beyond the density of a city/
suburban population and is relatively sparsely settled with small towns
can be considered rural. While the Main Street program is also germane
to a discussion of historic districts, the "small-town thrust" of its interests
seems to ally it even more closely with the rural preservation question.

The National Trust defines rural preservation, which it terms *rural
conservation*, as "the protection of the countryside including the preservation of buildings and villages of cultural significance, the protection of
their surroundings and the enhancement of the local economy and social
institutions."

Concern for open countryside, farmland, and small villages joins the
efforts of the American conservationist and preservationist as does no
other interest. The harmonious balance of historic resources with their
setting is nowhere more obvious than in the rural environment, where
the relationship of man-made elements to nature is a product of evolution
over time. So inextricably intertwined are the diverse elements of the rural scene that the subject is often referred to as *rural conservation* as often
as it is called *rural preservation*. (See Figure 11-1.)

Conservation of the rural environment can become as valid a concern of the preservationist as it is of the conservationist, for while rural
preservation necessitates attention to individual buildings and villages of
cultural significance within a given area, it also encompasses the husbanding and maintenance of the surrounding open space, which en-
hances the significance of those villages and helps to maintain the local
economy and social institutions. Thus, to preserve the harmonious relationship between the buildings and villages of the rural environment, as
well as their setting, rural inhabitants need to be equally attuned to all
component parts of their environment as are their urban cousins. The
preservationist can assist them in preparing for the change which economic pressure inevitably brings. Rural preservation therefore becomes a
very sensitive interdisciplinary effort, consisting as it does of agricultural,
economic, environmental, social, political, and historical factors.

The most crucial step in developing a concern for rural preservation
is to overcome the natural attitude of rural communities to look upon the
preservation of their environment as impeding economic development
and the growth of employment.

Traditional land-use development in America has created the
"doughnut" effect, wherein the socioeconomic structure of society has
tended to reach toward open countryside, suburban development blur-
ring the clear division between the city and the countryside so often ob-

servable in Europe. Such restricted land masses as Manhattan would, of course, be an exception to this observation. Thus, as the economic pressure for development of land reaches out to rural areas surrounding urban concentrations, the speculator, working with the appraiser and the assessor, paves the way for the developer to make inroads in the rural environment. Rural landowners tend to succumb to attractive real estate offers or are eventually forced out by increased tax levies. This chain of events not only tends to ruin the economic fabric of rural agriculture but destroys the beauty of the countryside as well. Coupled with the city dweller's recent flight to open countryside and small towns, these actions have exacerbated the problem of maintaining the rural landscape.

Retention of the agricultural economy is in many instances the key to rural preservation, since farming is usually the predominant land use, economic base, and visual feature of the countryside. The concerns of rural preservation, therefore, become more than protection of open space. Development reduces the total number of acres available for farming. When this number goes below a minimal level, the entire farming and local business economy becomes jeopardized and tends to disintegrate. At that point in many parts of the country, farmers tend to cease investing in new equipment and a subtle but important sociological and economic shift begins to take place. The working farmer is eventually replaced by the gentleman farmer with other sources of income or the need for tax shelters. Gentrification can have as serious a long-term impact on the agricultural economy and cultural qualities of the small community as it does on the city.

Figure 11-1
In many rural areas, covered bridges like the Hammond Bridge near Marysville, Iowa, are integral parts of the landscape and are thus prime candidates for preservation.

If sufficient incentives are to be maintained to encourage the rural society to remain in place, rural preservation must concern itself not only with the physical and economic concerns of the area in question but also with the social fabric. The rural village or town becomes a very important focal point for rural preservation since it is usually the central meeting place for the surrounding area. The village is the central point for schools, churches, grain dealers, other small businesses, and government, however limited, which constitute the service infrastructure satisfying a broad spectrum of needs in the rural community. Subdivisions and shopping malls thus become a threat to the economic well-being of not only the village but the entire rural area. (See Figure 11-2.)

A well-conceived program of rural preservation should be concerned not only with the existing environment, built and natural, but also with the siting and design of new buildings deemed necessary to serve the needs of the community as well as what needs these new buildings will serve, and what buildings, if any, they will replace. A study of traditional building practices and materials is necessary, as well as the siting of existing buildings in the area to provide guidelines for siting new buildings, use of materials, form, silhouette, and all of the abstracts of compatibility

Figure 11-2
This aerial view of the Kehlbeck Farmstead near Cass City, Nebraska, illustrates how critical open land is to the overall identity of a rural property.

that help ensure the successful integration of new construction into the existing environment.

Rural preservationists need to be aware of all of the land-use laws which may be called upon, whether federal, state, or local. Further, they need to understand the workings of the various agencies responsible for implementing and enforcing these laws and who the key officials are within those agencies as well as the importance of licenses and permits and the requirement of public notices for hearings. They also need to be apprised of those private organizations which deal with land use, conservation, historic preservation, and protection of open space.

Citizens' participation is as basic to a successful rural preservation program as it is to a successful urban one. This is often difficult because of the stringent demands of rural life and the lack of leisure time. As in the city, there is often a paucity of individuals in the rural community with sufficient time to give to further volunteer service or with sufficient perspective to understand the importance of involvement. Without the full participation of as many people as possible, rural preservation is unlikely to meet the needs of the community and therefore will fail to gain crucial financial and political support.

As is the case in the city, it is crucial to locate residents willing to take a leading role in establishing a conscientious preservation program in the rural community. Publicizing the perceived need for preservation through conversation and inquiries will indicate how much interest and support and/or opposition there may be to the notion. The county rural electrification co-op, the county fair board, the regional water district office, the local school boards, the local newspaper editor, and the county historical society are typical of the types of organizations with which the preservation question should be explored. Preserving a local one-room schoolhouse may be a convenient vehicle to rouse interest among those in the local community who may not readily identify themselves as preservationists, but who value a building made redundant by state orders to consolidate educational systems. (See Figure 11-3.) If there is an existing organization in the community, such as a local historical society, that might be interested in allying itself with a new preservationist group, so much the better—there is strength in unity. Especially in rural areas, however, such an alliance is not always possible. If the new group of preservationists must act alone, the creation of local private, nonprofit preservation organization is desirable. Such a group, able to act more quickly than government, can then work with local officials toward the common conservation/preservation goal. A cooperative group can divide the necessary tasks among its members to monitor governmental actions and changes in land use and to organize the community when crises occur.

Regardless of whether a preservation organization is concerned with preserving an urban or a rural environment, certain initial steps must be taken. The first is to initiate a process of information gathering, beginning with identifying the area in question, establishing its boundaries, and collecting data about indigenous cultural and natural resources. The

Figure 11-3   Rustic buildings such as this log grocery store in rural North Carolina, though not architecturally significant, are important parts of the rural scene, as are local one-room schoolhouses.

information collected will serve as a basis for developing local planning controls and incentives to husband the identified resources.

Boundaries can be established political lines, such as the boundary of the town or community; geographic lines, such as waterfronts or the ridge lines of hills; property lines; or more arbitrary lines based on a combination of the above. Only a thorough assessment of local issues and needs will determine which of these factors becomes primary. Boundaries must be established in order to determine where the preservation group's responsibilities begin and end, and are mandatory should a decision be made to submit the resulting district for listing on the National Register.

A thorough database is essential. This should include all known information on the history, environment, culture, economy, politics, and society of the community necessary to implement a broad program of preservation activity. The gathering of portions of the needed information can be meted out to volunteers within the local organization, provided that proper outside guidance is secured. Volunteers interested in history, for example, can be assigned to research the questions as to why people settled in the area and why they built the way they did. Others might address the architectural quality of the buildings of the area and the relationships among the various outbuildings on a given farm.

Other needed information includes the composition of the local economic base and the unusual features of the area, and its socioeconomic structure over and above agriculture. Environmental data—relating to the flora, fauna, streams, and wetlands—should be collected. Once all the information is at hand, it will provide a proper blueprint to guide the rural community in making intelligent decisions as to whether change can and should take place as pressures for development increase.

Much of this information usually already exists at the local, state, and federal levels and can be gathered there to avoid wasting time and energy. Such information may exist at disparate—sometimes widely separated—locations, however, and must be gathered and summarized by the preservation organization. Once assembled, all of the information will be used as a source of reference which will aid the organization in issuing guidelines for future preservation activity.

Among the agencies to be consulted are the county agent, the county home extension agent, the departments of archaeology and rural sociology at the state land-grant university, and that university's school of agriculture. The state historical society is usually a rich source and its director may also function as the state government's historic preservation officer. At the federal level, the Farmers Home Administration and the U.S. Bureau of the Census are prime agencies which should be consulted. Once collected, the information needs to be assembled in a form that is useful in identifying the cultural and natural resources of the area.

A cultural survey is necessary to identify architectural, archaeological, historical, and other data and thus help establish preservation goals for the area. The process of conducting such a survey, assessing it, and developing goals that lead to local protective ordinances, easement programs, land-use planning, and outdoor recreation employs the same techniques as assessments of the urban built environment. Goals should include educating the public about the area's resources, identifying properties that need to be protected, developing a local ordinance, and nominating such properties and/or districts to the National Register of Historic Places. Acceptance will give some degree of protection from the potentially negative effects of proposals for development made by agencies using federal dollars or licenses.

Considering that commercial agriculture is one of the more heavily regulated American businesses at both the state and federal levels, placement of rural resources on the National Register becomes a major vehicle by which to protect such resources against future rulings by the federal government. (See Figure 11-4.) Regulations in the interest of health, for example, may negatively affect existing built resources. In recent years such rulings have made small brooder and henhouses redundant in many states and the structures thus tend to disappear for lack of utility. A state board of health ruling in Wisconsin now requires any farm marketing Grade A milk to oil and blacktop its graveled roads to reduce the dust levels in the air, forcing a change in the look of the rural landscape. In these ways, systems for health protection affect existing built resources.

In order to establish proper survey techniques to achieve the preservation of rural areas, professional guidance is necessary. The local organization's aims should be discussed with the state historic preservation officer, who should be able to provide assistance for surveys.

Figure 11-4
These nineteenth-century coke ovens in Basalt County, Colorado, were abandoned in the 1880s, yet as rare and relatively early industrial remnants they deserve attention from preservationists.

Properties in the area must be visually examined, public documents and research publications consulted, and knowledgeable residents interviewed. All this information should then be placed on forms, with a photograph of each building or feature that contributes to the significance of the area. These features might include, among others, outbuildings, hedgerows, and mill races—collectively significant in determining the sense of locality and place of the rural area. All this data should then be mapped and color coded with different maps shaded according to subject—style, land use, age, and other factors. The resulting information should then be evaluated to assess the importance of each building's environmental setting, in addition to its architectural quality or age. Archaeological resources and topographical features should not be overlooked. The latter are especially important in making an assessment of the landscape and a systematic analysis of the open space and its scenic qualities.

Like information on the man-made evidence of the area and the results of surveying, the natural physical environment should be evaluated and the data and conclusions mapped. All of this will help provide town or county officials with the necessary information to help establish properties and policies for land development and guidelines as to where growth and change can take place without undue negative impact on the area.

Once the assessing process is completed, it is important for the local governing body to begin effective planning and to institute controls and incentives to regulate the environment in the interests of its preservation. This is often difficult because of the conservative attitudes of self-reliance which are at the center of rural life.

After the educational processes of preservation have been initiated and the organizational survey established, a number of existing techniques such as zoning, use-value assessment (the value of the resources involved), easements, transfer of development rights, land trusts, revolving funds, and other legal and economic processes should be explored and a combination of these processes employed. The local preservation organization and local government should work together to involve as many of the residents as possible.

Final action should be coordinated with the state government and the state historic preservation officer to devise a nomination of the area to the National Register of Historic Places. Until recently, a register listing gave access to federal grants-in-aid for preservation, in addition to the protection it offers. Currently most of the grant money for this program has dried up, but the capability remains.

Listing in the National Register by the secretary of the interior cannot be overstressed as a key step in the protection of the rural area. The Advisory Council on Historic Preservation has established a working relationship with all other federal agencies, and the register and the council remain the most positive direct force for preservation at the federal level. They provide a process to assess the potential effect when proposals are made that can be deemed deleterious to the rural area, such as a high tension line or an interstate highway right of way. Properties can be listed individually or in groups as historic districts. They are nominated to the secretary of the interior by the state historic preservation officers, and while the National Register does not include the natural environment per se, that environment is considered when submitted as part of the man-made environment of buildings, trials, roadways, hedgerows, and other evidences of human imprint upon the land.

In an attempt to focus on the rural environment, the National Trust experimented for several years with a pilot program in Oley, Pennsylvania and in Cazenovia, New York, applying the guidelines outlined in this chapter with considerable success. *Saving America's Countryside: The Rural Conservation Handbook,* which details the results of the effort, was published by the National Trust Press. Failing the reinstitution of a national program specifically directed at rural America, interested members of the rural public could certainly apply many of the methods and policies of the Main Street program discussed in Chapter 8 to their own small towns. The restoration and revitalization of villages improve the economic vitality and civic pride of the communities involved, deter the development of shopping malls that use up valuable land, and frequently have a positive effect on the outlying areas as well.

In 1980, the Trust established a National Main Street Center (NMSC) at its Washington headquarters to disseminate more widely the lessons learned from the original three pilot towns which had launched the Main Street program in 1977. (While the Trust houses the NMSC, the latter maintains itself financially through contracts with states and municipalities. The center's services are advisory, operated through workshops, publishing, educational films, and the liaison of its staff with the Main Street managers in the individual communities.) To expand the Main

Street program, a competition was held among the states so that a second level of development could be achieved. Georgia, Massachusetts, Colorado, Texas, North Carolina, and Pennsylvania were the winners, and the effort was expanded to thirty towns in those states. By 1984, eight additional states (Arkansas, Florida, Michigan, Minnesota, Oregon, South Carolina, Tennessee, and Washington) had started similar programs of training and technical assistance. At this writing, innumerable small towns have launched their own efforts, unilaterally based on the Trust's model, and the Main Street program has grown to include more than 100 communities. (See Figure 11-5.)

With its production of video-tape cassettes, conferences led by members of the Main Street staff for groups in various parts of the country,

Figure 11-5 Hot Springs, South Dakota, maintains a distinct identity due in no small part to the rock-faced sandstone of which most of the commercial buildings were constructed in the late nineteenth and early twentieth centuries. One of the communities selected for inclusion in the Main Street program, Hot Springs has been able to capitalize on its existing built resources by utilizing the Main Street system of organization, promotion, design, and economic restructuring.

and the capability to hold national video conferences, the center dissemi-
nates its work to many parts of the country, and its heavy public relations
efforts have made the Main Street program perhaps the widest known response to downtown renewal in small town and rural America.

While the success of the Main Street program seems to be having
positive results in many rural villages, agricultural consolidation will continue to have a major effect on the landscape that surrounds these villages. The consolidation of small farms of sixty or so acres into enterprises four to five times as large is having a visual effect on the land
similar to the collectivizing of farmland in Eastern European bloc countries. Seen from the air, the crazy-quilt-like pattern of small plots of land
gives way to vast blankets of one color and one crop as the rural areas of
Western Europe give way to those of the Iron Curtain countries. It has
been estimated that such consolidation will jeopardize over half of the
built resources of the rural environment in our country. In addition,
larger acreage requires larger equipment, which in turn raises the question of the viability of existing barn structures and their ability to accommodate the machinery of mass production. From the preservationist's
viewpoint, the rural picture is far from bright and deserves timely critical
attention before these rural resources disappear entirely.

CHAPTER 12

Archaeology

U NTIL the passage of the National Historic Preservation Act of 1966, archaeology had not been seen by a majority of Americans as a prime concern of the preservationist. The exception was in the Southwest, where the abundance of prehistoric remains has traditionally made archaeology a primary moving force. Concern for archaeological remains in all parts of the United States has been a major development of government's involvement in preservation. Because the 1966 legislation cited archaeology as one of the three disciplines to be taken into account (along with history and architecture), there is now an observable concern for historic and prehistoric archaeology nationwide among preservationists in private, as well as government, practice. Indeed, to the uninitiated, archaeology holds an enviable fascination and its language cloaks it in a mystique that only heightens this public perception.

A dictionary definition of *archaeology* explains it as "the scientific study of life and culture of ancient peoples, as by excavation of ancient cities, relics, artifacts, etc."

The National Trust defines it as "the study of past human lifeways through evidence found in the ground."

To the National Park Service, archaeology is "the scientific study, interpretation and reconstruction of past human cultures from an anthropological perspective based on the investigation of the surviving physical evidence of human activity and the reconstruction of related past environments. Historic archaeology proceeds upon the same basis but uses historical documentation as additional sources of information."

Whatever the wording, it is abundantly clear that archaeology concerns itself with evidences of man's past, rather than his present (known as *anthropology*). Thus, archaeologists are seen fundamentally as anthropologists who excavate for artifacts and other evidences which will help piece together the picture of earlier cultures, how people lived and evolved. As such, therefore, archaeology is a vital part of the preservationist's concern.

The archaeologist is concerned with time and change, "reading" evidence through the deposit of artifacts in the soil and assessing the effects of cumulative change and environmental adaptation. The position of soil deposits and artifacts in those deposits tell archaeologists about the passage of time. Unless there is evidence that soil has been disturbed, archaeologists date artifacts or objects back in time, beginning with the most recent at the top or closest to the existing surface of the earth, and moving back in time, the deeper they dig, until they reach a depth where no artifacts exist, indicating that the site was not then occupied. This layering of human clutter is referred to as *stratigraphy* or *sequence* (Figure 12-1). Objects can then be dated, though not necessarily precisely, in relation to one another. There are times, however, when evidences of different periods of the past are found within the same stratum, making the usefulness of the sequential method much more questionable.

The language of archaeology continues to expand in direct relationship to the involvement of archaeology in everyday life. Thus, the neophyte is faced not only with an arsenal of terms concerning the methodologies of archaeology but with the forms it takes as well. Modifiers to

Figure 12-1   This cross section of an archaeological excavation of a trash pit and its immediate environs at one time was once on display in the Visitors Information Center at Colonial Williamsburg, Virginia. An excellent teaching device, it is indicative of the wealth of information archaeologists can provide to the restoration process.

the term *archaeology* include *prehistoric, historic, underwater, industrial, commercial, rescue, salvage, urban, landscape,* and *conservation.* Each has been devised to clarify some aspect of the basic generic term. To understand their distinctions is to understand the forms archaeology takes.

The layman's preconceived idea of archaeology is more than likely what the professional refers to as *prehistoric archaeology.* This concerns itself with the scientific study of cultures that existed before recorded history, as opposed to *historical archaeology,* which deals with the remains of literate societies. In America, historical archaeology is seen to include not only artifacts dug up out of the ground, but above-ground evidence as well, such as buildings and furnishings. Indeed, the study of such evidence is often referred to as *above-ground archaeology.*

Within these broad parameters of prehistoric and historic concerns, many special interests have developed. The *underwater* or *marine archaeologist* (Figure 12-2), for example, limits his investigations to submerged property of all types. He works in such inundated areas as those created by dams, but most frequently on historic shipwrecks such as the Civil War *Monitor* or the *Titanic,* in rivers, bays, and surrounding seas. Underwater archaeologists come to their work with basic field and laboratory training and skills, to which they add the special knowledge and equipment needed to work in their underwater environment on objects of a specialized nature.

The marine archaeologist plays a pivotal role in maritime preservation projects. The archaeological advantage a shipwreck has over a building site is that the instant loss of the ship at sea provides a time capsule

Figure 12-2   Marine archaeologists usually confine their activities to submerged property. On a relatively rare occasion when its remains were exposed by a winter storm, the wreck of the 1856 *King Philip* in San Francisco could be measured and documented.

and unquestionable terminal date for the wreck and all of its recoverable artifacts. The continuous occupation of land-locked resources often makes dating more difficult, but processes such as radiocarbon dating are helpful if the artifacts concerned are of sufficiently ancient age.

Landscape archaeology deals with the attempt to find clues to original or historic land uses by concentration on vegetative evidence and evidence of human occupation, such as path and road outlines, earth mounds, and building sites.

There are two terms in common acceptance that use the word *archaeology* in the generic sense. The first is *industrial archaeology,* applied to a concern for industrial structures of technological and engineering interest. The second is *commercial archaeology,* which refers to an interest in very recent roadside architecture of above-average quality and unique or unusual form. The professional preservationist conversant with these terms finds no problem with them, but the layman may have difficulty in understanding their meaning. The word *archaeology* is used in these two terms to connote a scholarly interest in a specific subject, without using the processes (carbon dating, digging) necessary to the study of older civilizations. By extension, people interested in the preservation of historic residential and commercial buildings might therefore be termed *building archaeologists* rather than preservationists. Established as the terms *industrial* and *commercial archaeology* are, the neophyte needs to understand that these two particular modifiers of the word *archaeology* do not necessarily imply the same type of activity inherent in other archaeological forms.

With the development of increasingly more scientific approaches to preservation in general, a new type of archaeology—referred to as *conservation archaeology*—has come into focus. In essence, conservation archaeologists recognize that traditional excavation is costly and cannot always be financed. More importantly, however, they recognize that excavation is a systematic method of digging that can destroy a site in the process of trying to retrieve artifacts and gain information. Such archaeologists limit excavations to a minimum consistent with the objectives of research and preservation. They limit excavation in order to keep sites intact for future scientific investigation, in adherence to the "let-it-alone" philosophy first proposed by John Ruskin and William Sumner Appleton which has become dominant in current preservationist thinking. Conservation archaeology thus forces the archaeologist to explore alternative but equally productive methods of learning about a site, such as remote and magnetic sensing, which may be less destructive than digging. (Remote sensing utilizes sound-wave techniques or aerial photography to see patterns of disturbed soil from above far more easily than they can be detected on the ground. Magnetic sensing is a ground-level technique which uses sensitive machinery to locate such things as coins, metallic buttons, and other man-made metal objects.)

There are other terms which refer more to relationships than to methodologies or specific activities of archaeological interest. One of these is *salvage* or *rescue archaeology,* which refers to the retrieval of archaeological materials and data threatened by damage or destruction, often through proposed development. For the archaeologist, salvage archaeology can be a frustrating experience, since the time limit for retrieval is usually dictated by nonarchaeological interests, such as a building developer's schedule. In instances of this nature, the archaeologist "rescues" as many artifacts and records as much data as he can in the allotted time available, which is usually quite short. Such salvage archaeology may take place after construction of a new building has begun and archaeological evidence has been uncovered in the process. To investigate the site at that point necessitates stopping construction, a decision costly to the contractor. Hence sites are often lost, unknown to the archaeologist. Sometimes only a photographic record of the site can be made, given the brief time available.

Like rescue archaeology, *public archaeology* is a term which describes relationships. This term refers to archaeological programs and projects funded by government. For example, the city of Alexandria, Virginia, has a well-established archaeological program which is considered to be part of the local government's responsibility and which is concerned with almost 250 years of historic archaeology. The federal government has included a concern for archaeology in at least eight to ten major pieces of legislation written in the twentieth century. Such legislation has been strong at the state level as well, especially in the archaeologically rich Southwest. This legislation has given rise to major new archaeological concepts: management of cultural resources, preparation of archaeological reports, certification of professionals, and communication of the importance of archaeology to the public.

The importance of archaeology is that it verifies what man has achieved through actual evidence—that which he has left behind. Rather than relying on historical interpretation through the written record or the unreliability of human memory, surviving artifacts speak for themselves. As is true with restoration architects, the better educated and more experienced an archaeologist is, the better positioned he is to recognize valid evidence and its meaning.

Before taking any action at a site, any professional archaeologist will develop a carefully constructed written plan which documents the intent of the project from beginning to end. This plan includes the reason for the project and the questions or hypotheses for which answers are sought. No archaeological work is done without a reason. It follows that indiscriminate digging and treasure hunting does not constitute archaeology. This is a basic distinction the layman must keep in mind.

First, a survey of the area in question must be developed. This is usually done on foot, locating, noting, and recording all visible historic and prehistoric evidences for eventual evaluation. Such a survey should locate potential nonarchaeological sites in the study area as well, sites that may have some associative or aesthetic importance. A more sophisticated method of survey, especially for difficult surface sites, is by aerial photography, sometimes with the use of infrared and remote sensing methods. Survey methods and capabilities developed by the military for space and aerial photography have valid applications to archaeology.

The human animal clutters by nature. Therefore, whether the site is an open field, a riverbank, or a privy or outbuilding that is part of a historical complex, evidence of previous occupation can usually be noted on the surface or uncovered easily. Clues may include shards and flint chips at a prehistoric site, or nails, bits of glass, brick, and the like at historic sites. (See Figure 12-3.)

If the research strategy and planning objectives call for excavation, it is initiated with the clear understanding of its usual expense and potential for destruction of the site.

The disposition of artifacts taken from the site is as important as finding them. In the laboratory where such data is collected, it must be accessioned, cleaned, and catalogued. It is important to record the provenance (specific information on where the object was found), which is crucial in piecing together the information the site potentially can yield. Equally as important is the analysis of the object. (See Figure 12-4.) There are a number of techniques used at this point. These can include weighing, measuring, sketching, replicating, and comparing and contrasting with other objects. More sophisticated methods include microscopic examination, radiocarbon dating (in the case of shell, bone, wood, and char-

Figure 12-3 Much of the romance of archaeology can easily be dissipated by the reality of long, back-breaking hours of excavation carried out under conditions which are often less than ideal. Such difficulties quickly evaporate, however, in the excitement generated by a "find." Here, National Park Service archaeologists are at work at Tumacacori National Monument, Arizona, where Jesuits first established a mission on the site of a Pima village in 1691.

Figure 12-4   Retrieving artifacts from an archaeological excavation is only the first step in the archaeological process. In a laboratory such as this one, found materials are accessioned, cleaned, and catalogued. The position where each artifact was found is noted and the object is carefully analyzed, adding to the total body of information available to restoration experts.

coal fragments), as well as the use of dendrochronology—the science of tree-ring dating—for more recent specimens. The radiocarbon method of interpretation allows for such a wide latitude of time that its effective use can only be applied to objects of venerable age.

The archaeologist's final step is to prepare a scientific report of his findings which explains everything about the project, including how, where, and why it was conducted as well as the conclusions that have been drawn. Along with archival documentary research and the physical examination and study performed by the restoration architect, archaeology uncovers the unseen to add invaluable information to the total process of restoration.

CHAPTER 13

Preservation Values in Oral-based Cultures

A S WE have noted in previous chapters, the National Historic Preservation Act congressionally mandated the creation and development of the National Register of Historic Places to include sites, buildings, objects, districts and structures significant in American history, architecture, archaeology and culture. It is the problem of defining culture which is at the root of the difference between societies that write their history and those Americans, native and otherwise, who pass on their history orally.

According to Webster's Dictionary, *culture* is defined as "the concepts, habits, skills, art, instruments, institutions, etc., of a given people in a given period of civilization." In National Register terms, *culture* is defined primarily as "traditions, practices, lifeways and beliefs, as well as arts, crafts, and social institutions." Internally, the National Park Service Cultural Resource Management Guidelines are much more detailed but seem to sum up the preservation priorities of such cultures. "Culture is a system of behaviors, values, ideologies, and social arrangements. These features, in addition to tools and expressive elements such as graphic arts, help humans interpret their universe as well as deal with features of their environments, natural and social. (See Figure 13-1.) Culture is learned, transmitted in a social context, and modifiable. Synonyms for culture include: *lifeways, customs, traditions, social practices*, and *folkways*. The terms

Figure 13-1   Native Americans quarrying the easily carved pipestone in traditional fashion at Pipestone National Monument, Minnesota. This soft red claystone is used to make ceremonial pipes which are an integral part of their religious and civic ceremonies. The pipes are considered sacred as the pipestone is thought to have formed from the blood of ancestors who perished in a great flood brought on by the water monster *Unktehi*.

"folk culture" and "folk life" might be used to describe aspects of the system that are unwritten, learned without formal instruction and deal with expressive elements such as dance, song, music and graphic arts as well as storytelling.

In the writer's considered opinion, written cultures can be most conveniently conceptualized as linear, that is, they usually identify those aspects of their culture important to them by date and the more ancient the date, the more revered the item in question becomes. Thus, "this is the oldest house in the village" or "this is the oldest documented barn of its type in this state" is the type of distinction age holds for such societies. To make that ideology work, such societies must also be product-oriented in order to identify and revere a given object, structure, site, district, or building as valid components of their society.

Oral-dominated cultures, by contrast, that do not record their culture in writing, pass it on by practice or verbally through identified leaders who are keepers of traditional knowledge, since knowledge is equated to power in such societies. In the writer's unanthropologically trained mind, such societies can be likened to the salamander, entwined in the elaborate first letter of a medieval manuscript, circular in form, with its tail in its mouth devouring itself and reinventing itself as its method of continuity.

In oral societies, traditions and beliefs evolve, change, go out of fashion and come into fashion, are modified and are reinterpreted. Further, unlike written culture product-oriented peoples who put a premium on what their society has crafted, oral societies can be said to be process-oriented. Such societies put a lesser premium on what they produce as opposed to how they create, and value the human cycle of passing on knowledge held by the identified traditional bearers of knowledge within their society. Thus, preserving an old outrigger canoe among the Pacific peoples is less important to them than perpetuating the knowledge of how such a canoe is lashed together with palm fiber in intricate joints where patterns have proven stable and dependable by tradition over time.

This is not to say that societies who record their history by writing do not have oral traditions. Quite the contrary: they do have oral traditions, and they usually refer to them as "folklore." The major difference is that oral traditions, that is, folklore, remain a relatively small part of written societies' culture. By comparison, traditions, customs, and the spoken word are the basic foundation and essence of oral societies. These are the channels through which history is passed from generation to generation orally. And like the whispered message game wherein the message is whispered from person to person only to be announced aloud at the end of the line in surprisingly changed form, slight or major, oral cultures have a degree of fluidity to them less possible in the written world because of the verbal transmission rather than written communication.

It is important to understand the difference between written and oral-based cultures to clearly comprehend what is important in their respective societies to preserve and why. There are hundreds of recognized Native American nations in the lower forty-eight of the United States and Alaska, as well as the native Hawaiians and the peoples of Micronesia in the Pacific. These are all oral culture societies that exist within the predominately written-based Eurocentric culture of the United States.

In an American society that centers its preservation energies on the products of its culture, there is often a mystified reaction on how to deal with places regarded as special or sacred to oral culture societies within our country. Such sites seldom have anything built upon them and may consist simply of: a natural formation of rocks, an open field, a grove of trees, a range of mountains, or a combination thereof (Figure 13-2). Yet, such sites have as much validity for peoples of oral cultures as the constructed products (buildings, bridges, etc.) have for cultural groups with written traditions. The San Francisco Peaks in Arizona are well-documented and widely recognized as places of exceptional cultural importance to the Hopi, Navajo, and other Native Americans of our Southwest. Such sites, wherever they are, may be believed to be the dwelling place of spirits, the potential sites for Vision Quests sought by young men for life guidance in which the spirits may come to them in the guise of animals. Sites may be special also where certain medicinal plants, herbs, and other elements may be found that are important to the health of a given group. In addition to the potential loss of such sites when development is proposed by outside interests in the form of buildings, logging, excavation for minerals, pipelines, etc., there is the basic question of

Figure 13-2
Holy Bird offering prayer on top of Bear Butte, South Dakota, in 1939. Called *Nowohaus* in the Cheyenne language, it means "where the people were taught." The most revered Cheyenne prophet, *Matsiiuiv*, meaning "Sweet Medicine," came here to learn how the Cheyenne should live and act from Sacred All Father.

disturbing the spirits important to the life of a tribe or tribes which such intrusions create. (See Figure 13-3.)

By way of example of the type of problems that can arise when oral and written cultures interact, a distant island campus of a university in the Pacific proposed to introduce a course in celestial navigation—the type of traditional knowledge that is at the core of local Pacific island culture. Individuals with the traditional knowledge of how to successfully sail from one island to another distant enough to be out of sight, by scanning the skies, listening to the waves slapping the side of the dugout outrigger sailboat, and noting how frequently the waves hit the boat and from what direction, were few and far between and getting rarer to the point that the knowledge might be lost. Hence, there was every justification for such a course offering but the proposal was initially rejected by the administration. Why? A university is an institution that grew out of the educational needs of written societies. The ideal person to teach the course, however, had never been to school and was an elder. The university, representative of a written society concept, could not expect accreditation and respect among its peers were it to admit it was offering a course taught by someone who not only was not certified to teach but who had never been to school at all. The solution was to team the knowledgeable native seafarer with a certified faculty member who handled the course organization, including the necessary exam requirements and any

Figure 13-3   Native Chignit Aleut drying salmon along the North Shore of Aniakchak Bay, Alaska. This practice was discontinued by the natives early in the twentieth century when nonnative commercial fishing operations began in the area.

other needs of an acceptable course offering. There was ample student demand for the course, and the course was offered preserving this information vital to the history of the local society.

Little thought was initially given to the question of the identity, definition, and impact of the word *culture* included in the text of the National Historic Preservation Act. This changed with the authorization in the 1980 amendments to the act when Congress, for the first time, appropriated funds for direct grants to Indian tribes. Pivotal to the understanding and dissemination of the differences in the thought processes and actions relating to preservation between native oral cultural societies and the predominate Euro-American culture that writes its history was the publication of *National Register Bulletin* No. 38 in 1990, entitled "Guidelines for Evaluating and Documenting Traditional Cultural Properties," by Patricia L. Parker, cultural anthropologist and archaeologist, National Park Service and Thomas F. King, consultant, archaeologist, and historic preservationist. By that time, five preservation-related federal laws between federal agencies and Indian tribes had been prompted not only by the National Historic Preservation Act (1966) and the National Environmental Policy Act (1969) but by the American Indian Religious Freedom Act (1978), the Archaeological Resources Protection Act (1979) and the American Graves Protection and Repatriation Act (1990).

The Park Service's *National Register Bulletin* No. 38 was a milestone in the evolution of the National Register and a much-needed clarification of the understanding of what is important to Native American oral culture societies within the United States from a preservation point of view and why.

Taking the aforementioned laws into consideration, the 1992 amendments to the National Historic Preservation Act clarified that Native American sacred sites, which are a type of traditional cultural property, could be determined eligible for the National Register despite the fact that traditional cultural properties have been included since the inception of the National Register. (See Figure 13-4.) Thus, *Bulletin* No. 38 does not make a case for a new class of property, but like the 1992 amendment, simply attempts to make clear how to recognize and evaluate such property.

An Australian archaeologist, speaking at a meeting of the International Council on Monuments and Sites some years back, pinpointed the basic philosophical question when one culture tries to evaluate another culture's values in terms of their own culture. The case revolved around the cave paintings executed by an aboriginal group in the Outback of Australia. The aborigines traditionally painted extensive murals in local caves in their area, illustrative of their lives, nature, and their environ-

Figure 13-4
Totem and whale housefront at Son-I-Hat's Whale House and Totems Historic District on the east side of Prince of Wales Island about 30 miles north of Ketchikan, Alaska, in the village of New Kassan. The whale house was built in the 1880s and moved to its current site before 1904. The totem is probably a replacement carved by native carvers in the 1930s as part of a Civilian Conservation Corps (CCC) work project during the Great Depression.

ment. These were deemed by government officials as exceptionally fine examples of native traditional art. The government officials reacting out of the same Euro-based culture as ours in the United States, upon seeing them were anxious that they be preserved. The cultural tradition of the natives who had created them, however, dictated that they be painted over every several years. As the speaker summed up the impasse, it raised the question of preservation by whom and for whom. This is the basic question that one must never lose sight of, if the heritage laws and systems of one culture are to work successfully with a second culture whose preservation values diverge from their own.

CHAPTER 14

International Preservation

THE United Nations (UN), headquartered in New York City, came into being at the close of World War II as the international tribunal that provides the platform to discuss questions of international concern potentially affecting the nations of the world.

The United Nations Educational, Scientific and Cultural Organization (UNESCO) headquartered in Paris, is that arm of the UN that handles a large menu of educational, scientific, and cultural duties, including the broad charge of fostering international cooperation for the protection of cultural and natural heritage. Five major legal instruments, referred to as conventions internationally, which are part of international law, have been adopted by the member nations of the UN and form the basis for UNESCO's broad programs of preserving cultural heritage. These are the 1954 Convention for the Protection of Cultural Property in the Event of Armed Conflict (also known as the Hague Convention), the 1970 Convention on the Means of Prohibiting and Preventing the Illicit Import, Export and Transfer of Ownership of Cultural Property, the 1972 Convention concerning the Protection of the World Cultural and Natural Property (also known as the World Heritage Convention), the 2001 Convention on the Protection of the Underwater Cultural Heritage, and the 2003 Convention for the Protection of the Intangible Cultural Heritage. Under the 1972 World Heritage Convention, UNESCO encourages the identification, protection, and preservation of cultural and natural heritage in the world that is considered to be of outstanding value to all humanity, such as the Great Pyramids of Egypt in Africa, the Great Wall of China, and Ankor Wat in Cambodia. (See Figure 14-1.) By way of comparison, in the United States, the Department of the Interior National Historic Landmarks program identifies entities whose importance is thought to exceed the community in which they are located thereby, indicating that they are of value to all Americans, not just those citizens within the state and locality where the landmark is located. While the World Heritage Convention contains a number of capabilities, such as the World Heritage Fund, the most visible and best known is the World Heritage List.

UNESCO defines *cultural heritage* as "monuments, groups of buildings and sites of historical, aesthetic, archaeological, scientific, ethnological or anthropological value." It defines *natural heritage* as "places of outstanding physical, biological and geological formation, habitats of threatened species of animals and plants and areas with scientific conservation or aesthetic value."

One should note that the language of preservation internationally is usually used slightly different than it is in the United States. *Conservation* is preferred over the word *preservation* and includes concern not only for the natural environment but for the man-made environment as

Figure 14-1   Ankor in northwestern Cambodia was the capitol of the Khmer Empire from the ninth to the fifteenth centuries. It was abandoned in 1431, after being sacked by forces from Thailand. Its period of importance produced numerous temple complexes constructed around Ankor Wat, the centerpiece temple complex. Many teams of archaeologists from various countries continue to work on stabilizing, restoring, and reconstructing complexes at this site—the size of which can be measured in miles.

well. For example, the word *inventory* is used for what we usually refer to as *survey* or *register*, and there are other differences that the American preservationist should be on the lookout for.

As a result of UNESCO's work, all countries now are aware of and create inventories through surveys of their cultural and natural attributes. This is usually done through governmental programs, as opposed to the United States where it usually began within the private sector, prior to 1966, before the National Historic Preservation Act was passed. Early steps toward international action concerning these interests resulted in the founding of the International Council of Museums (ICOM) in 1946, based on the museum office of the League of Nations, followed in 1948 by the establishment of the International Union for the Conservation of Nature (IUCN). Both of these organizations were facilitated by UNESCO.

In the late 1950s, UNESCO launched the International Centre for the Study of Preservation and Restoration of Cultural Property in Rome, known as ICCROM. It gathered an international faculty of architects, art and architectural historians, and scientists, among other disciplines, developing a program that married the traditional knowledge of architectural expertise with that of the scientific world. Out of that combined training and knowledge came a group of preservation professionals soon known in this country as architectural scientific conservators. Their scientific diagnostic training positioned them to deal primarily with the illnesses of building materials and approaches to stabilizing existing building fabric in the interest of saving as much original historic building fabric as possible in the restoration process. This knowledge and approach to such problems has had a major impact in our country on the restoration process, replacing, as it has, the massive introduction of new materials approach that often has led to what has been called "creeping reconstruction." The Association for Preservation Technology (APT) is the international membership organization around which such specialist interests revolve.

The proposal of the Egyptian government in the late 1950s to construct the Aswan High Dam, which would flood the valley containing the Temple of Abu Simbel and the Philae Temple, galvanized world attention on the potential loss of these internationally recognized landmarks. Upon appeals from the Egyptian and Sudanese governments, UNESCO launched an international campaign to save them and accelerated the archaeological research of the area. Half of the cost of the project was donated by approximately fifty countries demonstrating the national sense of responsibility felt internationally for the preservation and conservation of a site identified by the participating nations as being of outstanding cultural value to all peoples and cultures of the world.

In the case of the Rameses complex (Figure 14-2), not only were the four monumental seated figures of the pharaoh moved hundreds of feet higher than the projected flood waters level, but the rock mountain, out of which they were carved and against which they sit, was moved to preserve the site relationship integrity of the carved rock figures with their background. The inside of the moved natural rock background has become the interpretation center explaining the tomb and the phenomenal engineering feat of the massive relocation.

Figure 14-2   King Rameses II built this temple complex at Abu Simbel, Egypt in the thirteenth century B.C. It was salvaged from the flood waters of the new Aswan High Dam in the 1960s. Through the leadership of UNESCO and the financial support of 50 contributing countries, the four 67-foot-high statues as well as three 185-foot-long interior chambers were disassembled and moved 200 feet above the dam.

To comprehend the difficulty and magnitude of what was achieved in the move, one must remind oneself of the immense scale by which the Ancient Egyptians conceived of their monuments. A human individual standing in front of the seated figures of Rameses II, for example, is dwarfed by the big toe of the seated pharaoh above the visitor's head.

So successful was their campaign that UNESCO subsequently launched similar safeguarding campaigns in such centers as Venice in Italy, Moenjodaro in Pakistan, and Borobodur in Indonesia, among others.

The 1965 White House Conference on Natural Beauty, referred to in Chapter 5, inspired the concept of *combining* the preservation of cultural sites with the conservation of natural areas to encourage international co-operation in protecting such outstanding buildings, sites, and areas for all mankind. The White House Conference followed by a year the Second International Congress of Architects and Technicians of Historical Monuments which met in Venice (The first such meeting had been held in Athens in 1931). Assembled delegates to this Second Congress came up with a statement of principles titled "The International Charter for the Conservation and Restoration of Monuments and Sites." The Venice Charter responded to a perceived need to provide unified international guidance as to what good preservation entails. It is interesting to note American involvement in this effort in the person of the late Carl Feiss,

AIP, a planner who had taught at Columbia University and who was also a planning and design consultant, and, at the time of the conference, a trustee of the National Trust. In addition to being the secretary of the Historic Preservation Committee of the International Union of Architects, Feiss was also one of the authors of *With Heritage So Rich,* the report of the Special Committee on Historic Preservation that resulted from the White House Conference on Natural Beauty. The book *With Heritage So Rich*, with its "Conclusion to the Findings," documenting where preservation should proceed, was the basic document distributed to the American Congress urging them to ratify passage of the National Historic Preservation Act, which they did on October 15, 1966.

Perhaps one of the most important developments growing out of the Venice Charter, as it became referred to, was the creation of the International Council on Monuments and Sites (ICOMOS). It exists basically to promote the doctrine and techniques of preservation and has developed a world network of national committees whose countries adhere to this World Heritage Treaty. As of 2005, there are 24 international scientific committees, plus national committees in approximately 120 countries who identify sites, and who advise their governments to nominate such sites within their respective countries to UNESCO for inclusion on the World Heritage List, including information as to how the site in question is protected and what sort of management plan is in place for its maintenance. Nations are expected to protect the World Heritage values of their sites and to report on their condition.

For Americans familiar with our National Trust, ICOMOS can be best thought of a world version of it, that is, as an international nongovernmental organization relating to the world and its cultural sites as our National Trust relates to us nationally.

Issues concerning natural sites are handled by the International Union for the Conservation of Nature (IUCN), which functions in the same advisory and monitoring capacity as does ICOMOS concerning cultural sites. Together they create the type of World Heritage Trust discussed during the White House Conference on Natural Beauty in 1965 in Washington, D.C.

The benefits to a country signing the treaty grants it the right to nominate cultural and natural properties for potential inclusion in the World Heritage List, the world prestige that comes with the process when nominations are accepted, access to international technical and monetary assistance, and the international recognition that comes to a nation as a result of signing the treaty.

ICOMOS plays a major role in the evaluation of nominations to the World Heritage List which, as of 2003, includes 563 properties, 144 natural properties, and 23 involving both culture and nature for a total of 730 properties worldwide.

France has the largest ICOMOS committee and, with 600 members, the United States is the second largest among the 120 countries with national committees. Among its activities relating to the man-made environment, ICOMOS tries to assure the highest professional standards, where sites and monuments concerning architecture, archaeology, and urban

concentrations are identified. Through its network of specialized committees, it tries to stimulate the exchange of information in fields as diverse
as underwater archaeology, cultural tourism, and the economics of preservation, especially as it relates to historic towns and cultural landscapes.

Figure 14-3
Bath, England, was
founded as a Ro-
man outpost and
flourished through
the Middle Ages. It
reached its peak of
architectural distinc-
tion, however, in
the eighteenth cen-
tury, primarily
through the work of
John Wood the El-
der and John Wood
the Younger whose
Palladian style im-
printed the town
with approximately
140 terraces of
buildings. Perhaps
the most well-
known of these is
the Royal Crescent,
a terrace of town-
houses executed be-
tween 1767 and
1775.

In synchronization with professional development of what should be
included within the preservationist's sights, the World Heritage List has
been enriched with the inclusion of cityscapes and landscapes based on
UNESCO recommendations that "Historic areas are part of the daily environment of human beings everywhere. . . . Their safeguarding and their
integration into the life of contemporary society is a basic factor in town
planning and land development." This focus aims to preserve not only the
physical elements of a neighborhood, village, or town but also those human activities which it includes that make it vital. The concept is that the
human face of the town is preserved as well as its physical elements, thus
connecting the past with contemporary life and intensifying identity of
place and civic pride.

Approximately seventy-five countries have had nominations of historic towns and cultural landscapes accepted to the World Heritage List
from 1978 to 2003. Among the total 194 such nominations are the city of
Bath, England (Figure 14-3), the historic center of Bukhara in Uzbekistan,
the city of Cuzco in Peru, Mont Saint-Michel and its bay in France, Tim-
buktu in Mali, and the ancient monuments of Kyoto, Japan.

Despite myriad historic district designations on the National Register
of Historic Places, as of 2003, only the governor's mansion known as La
Fortaleza and those portions of the San Juan fortifications administered

by the National Park Service in Puerto Rico appear on the World Heritage List of cities and towns. This is due to a short-sighted and misguided point of view on the owner consent issue for such areas by the United States government. It requires 100 percent property owner consent before it will accept such areas for consideration. This effectively precludes our country from adding most properties, save those in public ownership, to the list.

This restriction notwithstanding, the USICOMOS committee is active in functioning as our country's major window on the world in preservation. Primary among the missions of all ICOMOS committees worldwide is the development of international preservation standards and the adoption of such in each country, as well as promoting international cooperation in heritage conservation through exchange programs, publications, model projects, etc. In addition to its special publications, USICOMOS newsletters and active specialized committees, it offers a spring symposium and has offered foreign study tours. It is perhaps best known for its summer exchange program which sends approximately thirty Americans abroad each summer to work on preservation projects and receives an equal number of foreign students to work on projects in this country, often as part of the Historic American Building Survey and the Historic American Engineering Record summer-work teams within these two National Park Service programs.

The New York-based World Monuments Fund (WMF) was created in 1965 in the wake of the devastating floods that had ravaged Venice, Italy. It was founded to champion the preservation and restoration of the major monuments of that city. It has subsequently developed into an international membership organization of stature, offering various publications, lectures, seminars, and international tours. In addition, it offers financial support on a project by project basis. Most visible of its programs is its World Monuments Watch, which publishes the world's most endangered sites list.

The Getty Conservation Institute, headquartered in Los Angeles, has been a major international force in preservation. It has developed training programs and an important publication program. Of great import are the research programs it has developed in material conservation, heritage site management, and philosophical issues and values inherent in heritage in general.

In the Asian-Pacific part of the world, the most visible preservation linked organization is the Pacific Asia Travel Association (PATA), which brings together hotel chains, cruise ship lines, government tourism agencies, travel agencies, etc., in a commitment to international preservation in that part of the world. The American Express, already supportive of the work of USICOMOS and the WMF, has played a major role in launching and nurturing the development of this effort with strong American support and leadership through our National Trust.

In the arena of American philanthropy, the J. Paul Getty Trusts' Grant program, a development distinct from its conservation institute, has also been very active internationally, as has the Kress Foundation in the support it has given to USICOMOS programs, for example.

CHAPTER 15

Preservation in Practice

D URING THE COURSE of the twentieth century, preservation has moved from a preoccupation with only nationally significant landmarks to buildings and sites of local value. Preservationists have broadened their sights to include neighborhoods and the towns and rural areas where we live, and have expanded their motivations from patriotism, education, and history to aesthetics, planning, and economics.

The Great Depression of the 1930s not only produced major federal legislation in the Historic Sites Act of 1935, but also the first major compilation of America's built resources through the establishment of the Historic American Buildings Survey. At the local level, the pivotal action of the Charleston, South Carolina, city council to zone the Battery neighborhood as an "Old and Historic District" brought to the preservation movement an emphasis on planning which was to forever change its course.

These are but some of the major building blocks of preservation which had been put in place at the national and local levels prior to the Second World War. After World War II, events and circumstance conspired to accelerate change and create further progress in the practice of preservation. In 1949, in the face of continuing changes spurred by the war, the private sector received a national vehicle for preservation with the creation of the National Trust.

If the American preservation movement in the nineteenth and early twentieth centuries can be characterized as a house-museum movement led by volunteers from the general public, certainly the 1920s can be associated with the rise of the outdoor museum and the 1930s and '40s with the development of the concept of historic districts. The decade of the 1950s saw the fruition of the change from a preoccupation with historic house museums to preservation planning, a change stimulated by the global conflict of World War II and fueled by new government programs in transportation and housing. War had brought a great upheaval in the social fabric of society: great demographic changes had taken place and were to continue. The lingering effects of the Great Depression had been swept away and Americans were beginning to experience an ease of communication and mobility previously undreamed of because of the invention of television and improvements in commercial air transportation. The nuclear age had introduced a psychological dimension of unease. New government-assisted programs, notably urban renewal and the fledgling interstate highway program of the Department of Transportation, were decimating America's cities and countryside to provide urban housing and a network of interstate routes, both of which eradicated major visual landmarks previously taken for granted. The 1960s saw a reaction to this with the passage of the National Historic Preservation Act, which established what we now know as the National Register of Historic Places and the Advisory Council on Historic Preservation. State historic preservation officers were granted official status through a later (1980) amendment to the act.

These developments have given the public a greater role to play in the husbanding of preservation resources at all levels of government. They have also given government visibility and leadership in preservation that was long overdue, strengthening the private citizen's concern for his heritage. The explosive character of this change is attested by the fact that as late as 1960, no comprehensive book on preservation was in print, despite an increasing body of ephemera on the subject. Government regulations on preservation, now taken for granted, did not exist, nor did the grant money subsequently appropriated by Congress. Most of the jobs available in preservation were with museums and historical agencies, which continued to be served primarily in a volunteer capacity by the private citizen. Any tax assistance for preservation was, of course, unheard of.

Government has now produced regulations to formalize how preservation works in the public sector. A grants program has established a strong relationship among the federal, state, and private sectors. Such things as the secretary of the interior's *Standards for Rehabilitation* and certified local governments recognized by the National Park Service to carry out national preservation programs at the local level are manifestations of the evolving methodologies by which government attempts to carry out its now highly visible and pivotal role in preservation. Further, today's concept of preservation has broadened so indiscriminately in so relatively short a period as to sometimes raise questions in the minds of thinking preservationists. Are all the multifarious activities of current preservation indeed the responsibility of the preservation movement? Whatever the answer, preservation continues to be essentially a humanistic activity exercised primarily in arenas of law and economics. It is indeed important for preservationists to know the costs of what they do, but, at the same time, they must never lose sight of the *value* of what they do.

In the public sector, perhaps the greatest result of the National Historic Preservation Act of 1966 has been establishment of preservation offices in each of the fifty states, the territories, and the District of Columbia. Irrespective of how successfully (or not) they operate, they now exist as an important function of government at the state level and loom as the indispensable contact point between federal and local governments, especially as more municipalities begin to establish offices of city conservators or their equivalents.

In the private sector, the National Trust has nurtured the growth of local preservation organizations, including statewide private organizations. These groups work in tandem at the state and local levels with the public infrastructure. This cooperative effort places preservation at those levels where it can be most effective and of greatest everyday impact in the state and especially in the cities, towns, and rural villages.

Perhaps the best way to illustrate preservation in practice today is to examine, by way of example, a successful state-level public agency and an equally successful private organization at the local level. Two excellent paradigms, public and private respectively, are the programs of the Maryland Historical Trust, a state-level public agency, and Historic Savannah, Inc., a local, private preservation organization.

Although founded in 1961 as a quasi-public organization, the Maryland Historical Trust became part of the State Department of Economic and Community Development in 1970. In 1987, the organization was incorporated into the Division of Historical and Cultural Programs of the newly reorganized State Department of Housing and Community Development. As of 2003, the Maryland Trust operates with a staff of 105 and a budget of about $9.9 million. In it are concentrated not only the state preservation programs, but also those activities that the state carries out in the name of the federal government as a result of the National Historic Preservation Act of 1966. Thus, the director of the Maryland Historical Trust is also the historic preservation officer for the state.

As state historic preservation officer, the director of the Maryland Trust is responsible for administering all federal programs within the state relating to preservation, most of which emanate from the Department of the Interior and its bureau, the National Park Service, as well as from the Advisory Council on Historic Preservation. These programs include the National Register of Historic Places, the Section 106 compliance review process, survey and planning activities, and grants-in-aid, all of which refer to directives to the Secretary of the Interior from Congress in the National Historic Preservation Act of 1966. (See P.L. 89-665 in Appendix A.) Also ascribed to this act are the planning activities of historic preservation reviewed annually by the National Park Service. These include the development of a comprehensive document on the preservation planning process so that the state, municipalities, federal government, and Maryland citizens know what is worthy of preservation within the state. Such a document is a guide to how the state intends to husband, conserve, and use these identified resources, as well as manage changes in the built environment, as a means of assisting the economic development of the state and its communities.

As the American preservation program continued to expand, its size made it infeasible to continue making all decisions at the federal level. Decentralization was called for. In response, the National Historic Preservation Amendments Act of 1980 was passed, establishing the Certified Local Government Program, an expanded federal/state relationship that includes local government as a partner. The Maryland Trust not only works together with local government in its survey and planning grants program, but it also works closely with the Maryland Association of Historic District Commissions. The Tax Reform Act of 1976, replaced by the Economic Recovery Tax Act of 1981 and subsequently by the Tax Reform Act of 1986, added the further responsibility of certifications for preservation projects within the state for developers wishing to take advantage of tax incentives for rehabilitation of historic properties.

All of these activities are basically federal-level responsibilities which have been redelegated to the states and in some instances by the state to local municipalities. In addition, as part of state government, the Maryland Trust has the primary responsibility of administering state historic preservation programs. In this capacity, it operates a state grant and loan program for projects, reviews and certifies projects taking advantage of the state's income tax deduction for rehabilitation, and reviews projects circulated through the state intergovernmental clearinghouse system it maintains.

As of 1985, Maryland enacted legislation similar to federal Executive Order 11593, which requires all state agencies to identify and protect historic properties in their care or those affected by projects that they undertake.

The Maryland Trust interacts closely with many other state agencies, such as the Department of Planning, the Comptroller of the Treasury, the Department of Transportation, the Department of Natural Resources, the Department of Budget and Management, the State Arts Council, and the Historic Saint Mary's Commission. Further, the Trust assists other economic and development programs within its department, such as the Maryland Main Street program, the Maryland Housing Rehabilitation program, and other neighborhood initiatives. The Trust also provides staff to the Maryland Heritage Areas Authority, the Commission on African American Heritage and Culture, and the Commission on Indian Affairs. The Maryland Environmental Trust, within the Department of Natural Resources, operates a successful easement program in land conservation which calls for cooperation with the Maryland Historical Trust, especially when man-made resources are involved, as they frequently are. (See Figure 15-1.)

In documentary research and custodianship of historical records, the Maryland Historical Trust works with the Hall of Records within the Maryland State Archives. In the absence of a state-operated museum of Maryland history, the private Maryland Historical Society in Baltimore functions as the state's premier museum and research center for history.

The partnership of public and private organizations and individuals working in preservation is not only active here through the Maryland Historical Society but through special projects with universities, colleges, and historical societies throughout the state. It is especially effective through Preservation Maryland, Inc., the private statewide organization, previously named the Society for the Preservation of Maryland Antiquities. This focal point for private preservation in the state, like the Association for the Preservation of Virginia Antiquities, is long established and has an active outreach program that works hand in glove with the community educational activities of the Maryland Trust. Like the APVA, Preservation Maryland maintains historic properties across the state as well.

Statistically, the Maryland Trust's activities are impressive. In 2002, Maryland added thirty-three individual properties sites and eight districts, representing 12,878 contributing property to the National Register. (The Maryland Inventory of Historic Properties contained approximately 80,000 entries in 2003.)

The Maryland Trust provides technical assistance to all levels of government and to the private sector, responding to requests for assistance on a variety of preservation and rehabilitation activities. Trust staff have responded to tornado and hurricane-damaged communities, made hundreds of site visits, offered advice on practices in such areas as compatibility of design, availability of experienced contractors and craftsmen, and gave general counsel on restoration and rehabilitation.

Also in 2002, in its continuing effort to protect historic properties under its venue as legal liaison to the federal government, the Maryland Trust reviewed more than 3,290 federal projects and over 1,027 state-assisted ventures within its purview.

Maryland makes active use of the preservation easement as one of the most effective tools for protection of historic property, because such

Figure 15-1
A 500-acre tract of farmland near the Chesapeake Bay in southern Maryland was donated by its owner to the state. The property contains a number of fine old buildings, such as this capacious barn, restored and adaptively used as part of the Jefferson Patterson Park and Museum.

an easement has the capability to ensure preservation without the neces-sity of public ownership. The Maryland Trust accepted its first easement as early as 1969 and now holds more than 527 such easements covering nearly 10,000 acres statewide. Some of these easements have been gifts, while some have accompanied the transfer of historic property from state to private ownership. Others have been created as owners of private property receive appropriations from the Maryland General Assembly or from Maryland Historic Trust grants and loans.

The grants and loans programs of the state of Maryland have been operative for well over a decade, and in 1987 emanated from two sources: the State Capital Grant Fund for Historic Preservation and the State Capi-tal Revolving Loan Fund for Historic Preservation.

The state makes matching and nonmatching grants for properties listed either on the National Register of Historic Places or in the Maryland Inventory of Historic Properties. The fiscal-year 2004 State Historic Preservation Grant Fund allowed the Maryland Trust to make forty-three grants totaling $1.2 million to support historic preservation and museum projects in fifteen counties and Baltimore City, as well as for projects with statewide impact. Nine non-Capital grants, totaling $208,500, will assist nonprofit organizations and local governments with research, survey planning, and educational activities involving architectural, archaeologi-cal, or culture resources. Further Capital grants totaling $6,331,500, were made to assist non-state-owned historical and cultural museums. Demand for funding far outpaced the Trust's ability to make grants: only 26.5 per-cent of applications were funded, meeting approximately one-quarter of the project funds requested.

The Historic Preservation Loan Program provides loans to nonprofit organizations, local jurisdictions, business entities, and individuals to as-sist in the protecting of historic property. Loan funds can be used to ac-quire, rehabilitate, or restore historic property listed on, or eligible for, the National Register of Historic Places. In 2002, three loans, totaling $297,500, were made.

In 1996, the Maryland legislature created a State Rehabilitation Tax Credit program similar to the federal program. All income producing and residential National Register and locally designated historic properties are eligible. Since the program's inception in 1997, it has stimulated almost $600 million in rehabilitation investments. (See Figure 15-2.)

All these programs are bolstered by a high cognizance of the value of public education and the importance of professional involvement and creativity at the staff level. The Maryland Trust works in partnership with Preservation Maryland to sponsor an annual preservation and revitaliza-tion conference each spring, as well as a popular series of educational workshops that also draw participants from neighboring states. As a fur-ther effort in public education, the MHT Press produces a range of publi-cations covering topics from countywide architectural histories to archae-ological or cultural conservation. There are currently approximately sixty titles in the MHT Press catalogue, with three new publications in 2004 on Maryland's role in aviation history in celebration of the 100th anniversary of flight, the architectural history of St. Mary's County, and Tobacco

Figure 15-2   Relocating a building or carefully dismantling it for re-erection at a new site are preservation techniques of last resort. Laurel Branch, a small workingman's house of the eighteenth century, was in an advanced state of disrepair by the time it was dismantled in the late 1950s. (The alternative was demolition to make way for new development.) The house has been moved, re-erected and restored following HABS guidelines at the National Colonial Farm in Accokeek, Maryland.

farming in Calvert County. In sum, it is obvious that the preservation program in Maryland is professional, well organized, and a pervasive presence in the continuing development of the state.

In addition to its traditional programs, MHT continues to innovate and launch new initiatives. In 1996, the state legislature established the Maryland Heritage Area Authority and authorized the creation of state heritage areas to promote historic preservation and areas of natural beauty in order to stimulate economic development through tourism. To date, the state has recognized three heritage areas and an additional nine areas have been certified, making them eligible for financial assistance through the Heritage Area Authority. The Heritage Areas Program emphasizes highly targeted economic areas with the goal of producing measurable results within a five-year period. Maryland's program differs in this respect from most "heritage areas" programs in other states, and is closer in philosophy to "enterprise zones."

The Trust has recently developed a new internet-based tool through which researchers can review Maryland's National Register listings on the Web. In addition, MHT is in the process of digitizing the entire contents of the Maryland Inventory to make the collection of information more accessible to researchers.

Figure 15-3
The successful preservation of Savannah's Isaiah Davenport House (1821) was a catalyst for the establishment of the Historic Savannah Foundation in 1955. Until the 1970s the stately brick residence served dual roles as the foundation's first headquarters and as a house museum, a use for which it is still employed.

In 2001, the Maryland Trust initiated two new programs. The Preservation Incentives for Local Governments initiative was established to provide financial incentives to counties to establish or expand their heritage preservation programs. By the program's second year, half the state's counties were participating. The Trust also implemented the State Owned Cultural Resources Assessment Program through which MHT works in partnership with other state agencies to identify and inventory historic resources under state ownership.

As of 2005, there are almost 79,000 entries on the National Register of Historic Places, of which 12,610 are listed as historic districts. It is therefore recommended that anyone in need of guidance on successful historic districts at the local level within a respective state should begin their research by contacting the office of the state historic preservation officers for advice, contacts, and other forms of assistance as may be needed.

And What of the Future?

By the first twenty-five years following the 1966 passage of the National Historic Preservation Act, everything called for in the "Conclusion to the Findings" of the report from *With Heritage So Rich* had been achieved. In addition, the State Historic Preservation Offices had fast become the working links among the federal government and public and private state and local preservation efforts in the national preservation network set up following the passage of this act. To test the success of this network in establishing preservation as a viable segment of knowledge and interest in the average American mind, try asking almost anyone what the National Register of Historic Places is. If the respondent can't identify what it is specifically, he or she has more than likely at least heard about it or read about it in the press. Part of this growing familiarity can also probably be ascribed to popular TV shows such as *This Old House* and *The Antiques Road Show*, not to mention the do-it-yourself repair/restoration movement and the vast information access of the computer world, among other sources.

Among the many changes in the preservation field that have taken place in the last several decades, several stand out for their seminal impact. Primary among these are the changes that UNESCO's training program, founded in 1959, and offered at the International Centre for the Study and Conservation of Cultural Property (ICCROM) in Rome, Italy, has had on the practice of architecture in the United States. In this program, the traditional knowledge of the architect was combined with the scientific training of the museum objects/paintings conservator who are concerned with the stabilization of such materials as wood, glass, metals, paint, and so on—the same materials the architect deals with. The prime difference between the museum objects conservator and the architectural conservator is that the latter lacks the luxury of the controlled climate of the museum gallery and must deal with the constant vagaries of weather and temperatures of the outside world on the materials he or she is working with.

One must recall that in 1959, the year ICCROM began its program in Rome, no institution of higher learning in the United States offered any preservation training courses. Design studios in American schools of architecture were exclusively twentieth-century Bauhaus-design-oriented and the older generations of architects trained in traditional design were rapidly retiring and dying. The only vehicle for training in preservation and restoration at the time was in the National Park Service Historic American Buildings Survey (HABS) program, initiated by the late Charles Peterson prior to the Second World War. A few students interested in old buildings flocked to the Rome Centre program and in a few short years, the United States could boast of approximately 100 graduates of the program. These individuals, Americans and nationals of other countries, gradually created an informal global network of specialists based on friendships made during their course of study in Italy.

Then, in the mid-1960s, Columbia University initiated a certificate program in preservation through the efforts of the late James Marston Fitch. In 1968, the Association for Preservation Technology (APT) was formed as the organizational vehicle by which these new scientific and technical players in the preservation and restoration fields could relate to each other nationally and internationally. During two well-attended programs in the 1970s, organized by the National Trust and the National Park Service, respectively, subjects including the nondestructive investigation of building fabric through the use of X-rays and the use of new twentieth-century materials, such as polymers were presented.

The impact and dissemination of these innovative approaches to preservation/restoration has been nothing short of phenomenal in the architectural world. The National Park Service and the American Institute of Architects estimate that 75 percent to 85 percent of architectural practice in this country now involves preservation, restoration, and rehabilitation to some degree, thanks primarily to changes in our tax laws in the 1970s. With preservation-related projects such a large segment of architectural practice in this country, if an architectural firm with preservation projects is not large enough to have an architectural conservator on staff, such expertise is usually hired as one of the consultants of the team working on the project at hand.

There is no denying that at this writing in 2004, a quantum change and redirection appears to be taking place in the preservation field. This is a change not necessarily based on the traditional criteria of history and architecture, but a change growing out of those values established by the historic house-museum movement and the collection of such buildings long identified as outdoor museums. Both of these preservation answers established values of time and place primarily for educational purposes.

The singling out of values of time and place applied to living neighborhoods initiated by the local citizenry and government in Charleston, South Carolina, in 1931, gave birth to the historic district concept, as we have seen, for planning purposes, not education per se. Thus, planning was established as a partner with history and architecture as a leading motivator of the preservation movement. And it is through planning as a preservation tool that the preservation movement reached out to the environmental and social values of American society in a collective effort to bring about change.

The twin issues of society and diversity and landscape and attitudes toward its use appear to be signaling a redirection of preservation interests in the last couple of decades. Evident is the realization that American culture today is more than the Eurocentric inheritance that the average American has traditionally assumed it to be. This drift to a greater inclusiveness in identifying American heritage has been brought about by the increased visibility and understanding of the cultures of the hundreds of sovereign Native American Indian nations within our country—cultures less understood in the past by the average American than more recently. Further, the cultural contributions of native Hawaiians, Micronesians and Asians as well as Latin heritage, primarily from Cuba, Mexico and Central America have broadened this inclusiveness considerably. The recognition of this wide spectrum of culture added to the existing Eurocentric and African base we called American heritage has transformed it into a rich multicultural mix unforeseen by previous generations.

Of note is that a large percentage of these cultures transmit their traditions orally rather than in writing. In oral-based societies, some sort of triangular relationship with the gods, humankind, and land usually forms the foundation of the culture. This close-knit identity with land establishes a sacredness to land and its use for the well-being of the group. It is therefore on land that oral-based populations rely, in large part, for their well-being. A case can be made that there is a basis for land to be held more sacred, therefore, by oral-based cultures than by cultures that record their history in writing. It's for reasons such as these that an oil pipeline, clear-cut logging programs, or other similar developments of a man-made nature carried forth on Native American lands can have such a negative impact on their heritage and culture.

A growing understanding and sensitivity to these issues by a broader population of the preservation constituency is an observable change in the preservation field. It has brought about an increased interest and concern for the way in which land continues to be used in our society as a developable commodity. This is especially true as it relates to leap-frogging sprawl, developing at a dizzying pace into the countryside with few if any real checks and balances in place to control it.

The highly questionable land use that sprawl creates and a nominal understanding of the concept of land's sacredness that Native American cultures demand is bringing into clearer focus for preservationists the mandates of the National Preservation Act of 1966: to create a National

Register that includes "districts, sites, buildings, structures, and objects significant in American history, architecture, archaeology and <u>culture</u> . . ." (underline added). Thus, environmental, social, and recreational values have increased in importance in the preservation field in recent decades, bringing attitudinal and ideological change in the way we visualize parameters not only for preservation and conservation but for many other allied interest groups such as folklorists and those with an interest in vernacular building. This inclusiveness, beyond the traditional Eurocentric view of preservation, should eventually demand a new preservation training initiative in schools and universities that goes beyond existing concepts currently offered in such programs.

This ongoing change has had a significant gestation period going back to the 1960s and 1970s in the public as well as the private sectors. The Endangered Species Preservation Acts of 1966 and 1973, as well as the Wild and Scenic Rivers Act of 1968, and the pivotal National Environmental Act of 1970 set the stage for private conservation organizations such as the Nature Conservancy and the Sierra Club, among others, to proclaim Earth Day in 1970, in an effort to draw attention to the ecological problems of our planet. It was during this period also that the National Trust for Historic Preservation initiated Preservation Week in a similar visibility effort regarding what we were doing to our man-made historic resources.

The concept of land trusts followed with the formation of such entities as the Chesapeake Bay Foundation, the New Jersey Conservation Foundation, and the Colorado Open Lands Organization, among others, created to protect natural and rural landscapes, including hamlets and villages, isolated buildings, bridges, canals, etc. This converged the interests of the conservationists with the preservationists and opened up their potential for recreational value as well.

Although the development of the Yorktown Battlefield in Virginia, Independence National Historical Park in Philadelphia, and Fortaleza in Puerto Rico appear to have launched the concept of partnerships by the National Park Service with state, local, and private entities; it was the Cape Cod National Seashore, dating from 1961, which was the first large-scale foray of its type—covering 40 miles of seashore in 43,500 acres. In this mix of federal, state, local, and private landowners, there are six communities and hundreds of owner-occupied buildings that the Park Service cannot demolish as long as local governments put in place zoning consistent with the purposes of the park. The end result is that this approach preserves the existing living landscape mix of fishing villages and summer cottages. An advisory commission of six local government representatives, as well as Massachusetts state representatives, and National Park Service representatives oversees and monitors the partnership agreement.

In another example, the question of how to preserve land close to Los Angeles in the Santa Monica Mountains that is subject to the pressures of sprawl stimulated a proposal to create a national park in the early 1970s. This proposal was rejected because of high land costs near an urban center where land values were expensive due to its development potential. Out of this dilemma evolved a concept very similar to the Cape Cod National Seashore and modeled essentially after the National

Parks of England and Wales. Initially called Greenline Parks (and subsequently Partnership Parks) the formula that was developed kept land acquisition to a minimum, put in place land development controls to protect the land, and utilized an inclusive planning mix of publicly and privately owned land. Oversight came from a state agency created to preserve the historical and cultural values of the area as well as its ecological, aesthetic, and recreational attributes. In essence, it refined the Cape Cod National Seashore concept, applied it to the urbanizing environment of a large city environs, preserved the state government's prime role in land use, and satisfied the federal government's priority in protecting large landscapes with significant recreational potential.

What have come to be known as National Heritage Areas evolved out of these earlier efforts of cooperative action. As opposed to the conservation of untouched nature, which drove the creation of our National Parks System, National Heritage Areas are distinct not only for their collegial cooperative community-initiated methods of administration but for their acceptance of past developments historically and physically that have laid upon the land a distinct sense of time, place, and locality (Figure E-1). They take preservation-*cum*-conservation several steps forward by addressing the preservation values of the sociological fabric of these identified areas as a major contributor to the identity of place, at the same time capitalizing on the recreational values and heritage tourism potential that areas of such distinction offer.

Figure E-1
The Schuylkill River Valley National Heritage Area extends from the mining museum at Ashland in southeastern Pennsylvania near Valley Forge to historic Fort Mifflin south of Philadelphia. The area epitomizes the story of the colonization and industrialization of America. Central to the development of this area has been the Schuylkill River which shaped the shifting currents of history in the area through which it flows.

While our great natural national parks exist because of initiating actions by our federal government, it should be emphasized that National Heritage Areas come into being by action initiated at the local level, where voicing its wishes to the federal and state levels for federal recognition and approval is needed without which it cannot exist.

The first location to be identified as a National Heritage Area in 1984 was the Illinois and Michigan Canal National Heritage Corridor, a 97-mile canal built in 1848 that connected Lake Michigan, along an Indian portage route, with the Illinois River, linking water transportation with the Great Lakes and the Mississippi watershed. This, in turn, rapidly transformed Chicago from a small settlement into the pivotal transportation center we know today. The canal and its towpath, now used for recreational purposes, are owned and managed by the state of Illinois and a nonprofit management entity which works with the government and private groups to preserve the corridor's resources.

Then, in 1985, the area now known as the John H. Chafee Blackstone River Valley National Heritage Corridor was created. It consists of 24 cities and towns on 454 square miles in the Blackstone River watershed. It ranges from Worcester, Massachusetts, to Providence, Rhode Island, and tells the story of the national impact of the American Industrial Revolution on land and society as it evolved from a farm economy to a factory economy.

Today, as of 2004, there are twenty-four National Heritage Areas (Figure E-2), the overwhelming majority of which are east of the Missis-

Figure E-2   The Blue Ridge National Heritage Area covers twenty-five counties in the Blue Ridge Mountains of western North Carolina which includes the scenic Blue Ridge Parkway. The region's distinctive qualities have arisen from a mixture of cultural influences of Eurocentric-based settlers and an intimate connection with the land largely brought about by the heritage and influences of the Cherokee Indians. The resulting rich folk-life traditions, arts, crafts and vocal/instrumental folk music that continue to play an integral role in the way of life of local communities motivates them to want to preserve and interpret these unique qualities of their lifestyle.

sippi River. Begun as a community-based effort, they have evolved into a movement, which knits the private and public sectors of our society tightly together and provides better-guided development that improves the environmental, cultural, recreational, and economic goals of these areas of our country.

The development of the National Heritage Areas concept represents perhaps the most cutting-edge development to involve preservationists' attention since Charleston, South Carolina, identified the first historic

Figure E-3   The Quinebaug and Shetucket Rivers Valley National Heritage Corridor covers 1,086 square miles and thirty-five towns in northeast Connecticut and south central Massachusetts. It is one of the last large undeveloped areas in the northeastern United States. In addition to important aboriginal archaeological sites, excellent water quality and rural landscapes, it includes architecturally significant mill structures and villages such as Beldings Mill seen in this photo. Aerial from www.glsweetnam.com.

district in 1931. Over all these years, preservationists have never been able to convince the political world that they are anything more than a window-dressing subject. Although inroads have been made over the years with this problem, the chronic underfunding of the preservation programs at the national and state levels gives clarifying testimony as to where such efforts *really* stand politically. They are seldom high on political agendas, save on a case-by-case basis within individual jurisdictions.

Preservation's primary location in a landholding agency like the National Park Service, whose primary charge is our great National Park System, remains part of this perplexing observation. When budgetary decisions need to be made, the national parks quite rightly take first priority leaving those programmatic developments (now part of the Park Service) placing America's man-made treasured resources in a secondary budgetary position. Of all the existing agencies within the federal government, however, most closely allied with preservation interests, the National Park Service is a natural choice historically. (See Figure E-3.)

With the inclusive drift of preservation in recent years, the partnership networking that now threads through the preservation movement, coupled with the concept of identity of place leading the traditional criteria of history and architecture, how such programs as National Historic Landmarks, the National Register of Historic Places, the Historic American Buildings Survey, the Historic American Engineering Record, the Historic American Landscape Survey, among others, can best serve the American public—and best be served for the public—still remains a question.

As the relatively recent developments above outlined attest, preservation is a continuum of change and not the rigid enforcement of the status quo as it is so often misconstrued. Further, the emergence of the concept of what we now call National Heritage Areas is proof of the axiom that the future of the preservation movement continues to be at the local level. The success of local preservation efforts stands in direct relationship to the ability of experts at the national and state levels to be sensitive to this and serve the movement well. Only then will the dialogue of the present about the past serve the needs of the present and the future, producing the quality of life we seek.

Selected Federal Legislation

SEVERAL LEGISLATIVE ACTIONS taken by the federal government in the twentieth century can be considered landmarks in the history of the preservation movement. They have played a major role in broadening the movement's base, expanding preservation from its beginnings as a museum/educational process to the complex planning, recreation, and economic activity it is today.

THE ANTIQUITIES ACT, 1906

An Act for the preservation of American antiquities

Be it enacted by the Senate and House of Representatives of the United States of America in Congress assembled, That any person who shall appropriate, excavate, injure, or destroy any historic or prehistoric ruin or monument, or any object of antiquity, situated on lands owned or controlled by the Government of the United States, without the permission of the Secretary of the Department of the Government having jurisdiction over the lands on which said antiquities are situated, shall upon conviction, be fined in a sum of not more than five hundred dollars or be imprisoned for a period of not more than ninety days, or shall suffer both fine and imprisonment, in the discretion of the court.

SEC. 2. That the President of the United States is hereby authorized, in his discretion, to declare by public proclamation historic landmarks, historic and prehistoric structures, and other objects of historic or scientific interest that are situated upon the lands owned or controlled by the Government of the United States to be national monuments, and may reserve as a part thereof parcels of land, the limits of which in all cases shall be confined to the smallest area compatible with the proper care and management of the objects to be protected: *Provided,* That when such objects are situated upon a tract covered by a bona fide unperfected claim or held in private ownership, the tract, or so much thereof as may be necessary for the proper care and management of the object, may be relinquished to the Government, and the Secretary of the Interior is hereby authorized to accept the relinquishment of such tracts in behalf of the Government of the United States.

SEC. 3. That permits for the examination of ruins, the excavation of archaeological sites, and the gathering of objects of antiquity upon the lands under their respective jurisdictions may be granted by the Secretaries of the Interior, Agriculture, and War to institutions which they may deem property qualified to conduct such examination, excavation, or gathering, subject to such rules and regulations as they may prescribe: *Provided,* That the examinations, excavations, and gatherings are undertaken for the benefit of reputable museums, universities, colleges, or other recognized scientific or educational institutions, with a view to increasing the knowledge of such objects, and that the gatherings shall be made for permanent preservation in public museums.

SEC. 4. That the Secretaries of the Departments aforesaid shall make and publish from time to time uniform rules and regulations for the purpose of carrying out the provisions of this Act.

Approved, June 8, 1906, [34 Stat. L. 225, Public—No. 209]

THE NATIONAL PARK SYSTEM ORGANIC ACT, 1916

An Act to establish a National Park Service, and for other purposes.

Be it enacted by the Senate and House of Representatives of the United States of America in Congress assembled, That there is hereby created in the Department of the Interior a service to be called the National Park Service, which shall be under the charge of a director, who shall be appointed by the Secretary and who shall receive a salary of $4,500 per annum. There shall also be appointed by the Secretary the following assistants and other employees at the salaries designated: One assistant director, at $2,500 per annum, one chief clerk, at $2,000 per annum, one draftsman, at $1,800 per annum; one messenger, at $600 per annum, and, in addition thereto, such other employees as the Secretary of the Interior shall deem necessary: *Provided,* That not more than $8,100 annually shall be expended for salaries of experts, assistants, and employees within the District of Columbia not herein specifically enumerated unless previously authorized by law. The service thus established shall promote and regulate the use of the Federal areas known as national parks, monuments, and reservations hereinafter specified by such means and measures as conform to the fundamental purpose of the said parks, monuments, and reservations, which purpose is to conserve the scenery and the natural and historic objects and the wild life therein and to provide for the enjoyment of the same in such manner and by such means as will leave them unimpaired for the enjoyment of future generations.

Sec. 2. That the director shall, under the direction of the Secretary of the Interior, have the supervision, management, and control of the several national parks and national monuments which are now under the jurisdiction of the Department of the Interior, and of the Hot Springs Reservation in the State of Arkansas, and of such other national parks and reservations of like character as may be hereafter created by Congress: *Provided,* That in the supervision, management, and control of national monuments contiguous to national forests the Secretary of Agriculture may cooperate with said National Park Service to such extent as may be requested by the Secretary of the Interior.

Sec. 3. That the Secretary of the Interior shall make and publish such rules and regulations as he may deem necessary or proper for the use and management of the parks, monuments, and reservations under the jurisdiction of the National Park Service, and any violations of any of the rules and regulations authorized by this Act shall be punished as provided for in section fifty of the Act entitled "An Act to codify and amend the penal laws of the United States," approved March fourth, nineteen hundred and nine, as amended by section six of the Act of June twenty-fifth, nineteen hundred and ten (Thirty-sixth United States Statutes at Large, page eight hundred and fifty-seven). He may also, upon terms and conditions to be fixed by him, sell or dispose of timber in those cases where in his judgment the cutting of such timber is required in order to control the attacks of insects or diseases or otherwise conserve the scenery or the natural or historic objects in any such park, monument, or reservation. He may also provide in his discretion for the destruction of such animals and of such plant life as may be detrimental to the use of any of said parks, monuments, or reservations. He may also grant privileges, leases, and permits for the use of land for the accommodation of visitors in the various parks, monuments, or other reservations herein provided for, but for periods not exceeding thirty years; and no natural curiosities, wonders, or objects of interest shall be leased, rented, or granted to anyone on such terms as to interfere with free access to them by the public: *Provided, however,* That the Secretary of the Interior may, under such rules and regulations and on such terms as he may prescribe, grant the privilege to graze live stock within any national park, monument, or reservation herein referred to when in his judgment such use is not detrimental to the primary purpose for which such park, monument, or reservation was created, except that this provision shall not apply to the Yellowstone National Park: *And provided further,* That the Secretary of the Interior may grant said privileges, leases, and permits and enter into contracts relating to the same with responsible persons, firms, or corporations without advertising and without securing competitive bids: *And provided further,* That no contract, lease, permit, or privilege granted shall be assigned or transferred by such grantees, permittees, or licensees, without the approval of the Secretary of the Interior first obtained in writing: *And provided further,* That the Secretary may, in his discretion, authorize such grantees, permittees, or licensees to execute mortgages and issue bonds, shares of stock, and other evidences of interest in or indebtedness upon their rights, properties, and franchises, for the purposes of installing, enlarging, or improving plant and equipment and extending facilities for the accommodation of the public within such national parks, and monuments.

Sec. 4. That nothing in this Act contained shall affect or modify the provisions of the Act approved February fifteenth, nineteen hundred and one, entitled "An Act relating to rights of way through certain parks, reservations, and other public lands."

Approved, August 25, 1916.

THE HISTORIC SITES AND BUILDINGS ACT, 1935

An Act to provide for the preservation of historic American sites, buildings, objects, and antiquities of national significance, and for other purposes.

Be it enacted by the Senate and House of Representatives of the United States of America in Congress assembled, That it is hereby declared that it is a national policy to preserve for public use historic sites, buildings and objects of national significance for the inspiration and benefit of the people of the United States.

Sec. 2. The Secretary of the Interior (hereinafter referred to as the Secretary), through the National Park Service, for the purpose of effectuating the policy expressed in section 1 hereof, shall have the following powers and perform the following duties and functions:

(a) Secure, collate, and preserve drawings, plans, photographs, and other data of historic and archaeologic sites, buildings, and objects.

(b) Make a survey of historic and archaeologic sites, buildings, and objects for the purpose of determining which possess exceptional value as commemorating or illustrating the history of the United States.

(c) Make necessary investigations and researches in the United States relating to particular sites, buildings, or objects to obtain true and accurate historical and archaeological facts and information concerning the same.

(d) For the purpose of this Act, acquire in the name of the United States by gift, purchase, or otherwise any property, personal or real, or any interest or estate therein, title to any real property to be satisfactory to the Secretary: *Provided,* That no such property which is owned by any religious or educational institution, or which is owned or administered for the benefit of the public shall be so acquired without the consent of the owner: *Provided further,* That no property shall be acquired or contract or agreement for the acquisition thereof made which will obligate the general fund of the Treasury for the payment of such property, unless or until Congress has appropriated money which is available for that purpose.

(e) Contract and make cooperative agreements with States, municipal subdivisions, corporations, associations, or individuals, with proper bond where deemed advisable, to protect, preserve, maintain, or operate any historic or archaeologic building, site, object, or property used in connection therewith for public use, regardless as to whether the title thereto is in the United States: *Provided,* That no contract or cooperative agreement shall be made or entered into which will obligate the general fund of the Treasury unless or until Congress has appropriated money for such purpose.

(f) Restore, reconstruct, rehabilitate, preserve, and maintain historic or prehistoric sites, buildings, objects, and properties of national historical or archaeological significance and where deemed desirable establish and maintain museums in connection therewith.

(g) Erect and maintain tablets to mark or commemorate historic or prehistoric places and events of national historical or archaeological significance.

(h) Operate and manage historic and archaeologic sites, buildings, and properties acquired under the provisions of this Act together with lands and subordinate buildings for the benefit of the public, such authority to include the power to charge reasonable visitation fees and grant concessions, leases, or permits for the use of land, building space, roads, or trails when necessary or desirable either to accommodate the public or to facilitate administration: *Provided,* That such concessions, leases, or permits, shall be let at competitive bidding, to the person making the highest and best bid.

(i) When the Secretary determines that it would be administratively burdensome to restore, reconstruct, operate, or maintain any particular historic or archaeologic site, building, or property donated to the United States through the National Park Service, he may cause the same to be done by organizing a corporation for that purpose under the laws of the District of Columbia or any State.

(j) Develop an educational program and service for the purpose of making available to the public facts and information pertaining to American historic and archaeologic sites, buildings, and properties of national significance. Reasonable charges may be made for the dissemination of any such facts or information.

(k) Perform any and all acts, and make such rules and regulations not inconsistent with this Act as may be necessary and proper to carry out the provisions thereof. Any person violating any of the rules and regulations authorized by this Act shall be punished by a fine of not more than $500 and be adjudged to pay all cost of the proceedings.

SEC. 3. A general advisory board to be known as the "Advisory Board on National Parks, Historic Sites, Buildings, and Monuments" is hereby established, to be composed of not to exceed eleven persons, citizens of the United States, to include representatives competent in the fields of history, archaeology, architecture, and human geography, who shall be appointed by the Secretary and serve at his pleasure. The members of such board shall receive no salary but may be paid expenses incidental to travel when engaged in discharging their duties as such members.

It shall be the duty of such board to advise on any matters relating to national parks and to the administration of this Act submitted to it for consideration by the Secretary. It may also recommend policies to the Secretary from time to time pertaining to national

parks and to the restoration, reconstruction, conservation, and general administration of historic and archaeologic sites, buildings, and properties.

SEC. 4. The Secretary, in administering this Act, is authorized to cooperate with and may seek and accept the assistance of any Federal, State, or municipal department or agency, or any educational or scientific institution, or any patriotic association, or any individual.

(b) When deemed necessary, technical advisory committees may be established to act in an advisory capacity in connection with the restoration or reconstruction of any historic or prehistoric building or structure.

(c) Such professional and technical assistance may be employed without regard to the civil-service laws, and such service may be established as may be required to accomplish the purpose of this Act and for which money may be appropriated by Congress or made available by gifts for such purpose.

SEC. 5. Nothing in this Act shall be held to deprive any State, or political subdivision thereof, of its civil and criminal jurisdiction in and over lands acquired by the United States under this Act.

SEC. 6. There is authorized to be appropriated for carrying out the purposes of this Act such sums as the Congress may from time to time determine.

SEC. 7. The provisions of this Act shall control if any of them are in conflict with any other Act or Acts relating to the same subject matter.

Approved, August 21, 1935. [S2073; Public—No. 292].

CHARTER OF THE NATIONAL TRUST FOR HISTORIC PRESERVATION, 1949

An Act to further the policy enunciated in the Historic Sites Act (49 Stat. 666) and to facilitate public participation in the preservation of sites, buildings, and objects of national significance or interest and providing a national trust for historic preservation.

Be it enacted by the Senate and House of Representatives of the United States of America in Congress assembled, That, in order to further the policy enunciated in the Act of August 21, 1935 (49 Stat. 666), entitled "An Act to provide for the preservation of historic American sites, buildings, objects, and antiquities of national significance, and for other purposes", and to facilitate public participation in the preservation of sites, buildings, and objects of national significance or interest, there is hereby created a charitable, educational, and nonprofit corporation, to be known as the National Trust for Historic Preservation in the United States, hereafter referred to as the "National Trust". The purposes of the National Trust shall be to receive donations of sites, buildings, and objects significant in American history and culture, to preserve and administer them for public benefit, to accept, hold, and administer gifts of money, securities, or other property of whatsoever character for the purpose of carrying out the preservation program, and to execute such other functions as are vested in it by this Act.

SEC. 2. The National Trust shall have its principal office in the District of Columbia and shall be deemed, for purposes of venue in civil actions, to be an inhabitant and resident thereof. The National Trust may establish offices in such other place or places as it may deem necessary or appropriate in the conduct of its business.

SEC. 3. The affairs of the National Trust shall be under the general direction of a board of trustees composed as follows: The Attorney General of the United States; the Secretary of the Interior; and the Director of the National Gallery of Art, ex officio; and not less than six general trustees who shall be citizens of the United States, to be chosen as hereinafter provided. The Attorney General, and the Secretary of the Interior, when it appears desirable in the interest of the conduct of the business of the board and to such extent as they deem it advisable, may, by written notice to the National Trust, designate any officer of their respective departments to act for them in the discharge of their duties as a member of the board of trustees. The number of general trustees shall be fixed by the Executive Board of the National Council for Historic Sites and Buildings, a corporation of the District of Columbia, and the general trustees first taking office shall be chosen by a majority vote of the members of the Executive Board from the membership of the National Council. The respective terms of office of the first general trustees so chosen shall be as prescribed by the said Executive Board but in no case shall exceed a period of five years from the date of election. A successor to a general trustee shall be chosen in the same manner as the original trustees and shall have a term expiring five years from the date of the expiration of the term for which his predecessor was chosen, except that a successor chosen to fill a vacancy occurring prior to the expiration of such term shall be chosen only for the remainder of that term. The chairman of the board of trustees shall be elected by a majority vote of the members of the board. No compensation shall be paid to the members of the board of trustees for their services as such members, but they shall be reinbursed for travel and actual expenses necessarily incurred by them in attending board meetings and performing other official duties on behalf of the National Trust at the direction of the board.

SEC. 4. To the extent necessary to enable it to carry out the functions vested in it by this Act, the National Trust shall have the following general powers:

(a) To have succession until dissolved by Act of Congress, in which event title to the properties of the National Trust, both real and personal, shall, insofar as consistent with existing contractual obligations and subject to all other legally enforceable claims or demands by or against the National Trust, pass to and become vested in the United States of America.

(b) To sue and be sued in its corporate name.

(c) To adopt, alter, and use a corporate seal which shall be judicially noticed.

(d) To adopt a constitution and to make such bylaws, rules, and regulations, not inconsistent with the laws of the United States or of any State, as it deems necessary for the administration of its functions under this Act, including among other matter, bylaws, rules, and regulations governing visitation to historic properties, administration of corporate funds, and the organization and procedure of the board of trustees.

(e) To accept, hold, and administer gifts and bequests of money, securities, or other personal property of whatsoever character, absolutely or on trust, for the purposes for which the National Trust is created. Unless otherwise restricted by the terms of the gift or bequest, the National Trust is authorized to sell, exchange, or otherwise dispose of and to invest or reinvest in such investments as it may determine from time to time the moneys, securities, or other property given or bequeathed to it. The principal of such corporate funds, together with the income therefrom and all other revenues received by it from any source whatsoever shall be placed in such depositories as the National Trust shall determine and shall be subject to expenditure by the National Trust for its corporate purposes.

(f) To acquire by gift, devise, purchase, or otherwise, absolutely or on trust, and to hold and, unless otherwise restricted by the terms of the gift or devise, to encumber, convey, or otherwise dispose of, any real property, or any estate or interest therein (except property within the exterior boundaries of national parks and national monuments), as may be necessary and proper in carrying into effect the purposes of the National Trust.

(g) To contract and make cooperative agreements with Federal, State, or municipal departments or agencies, corporations, associations, or individuals, under such terms and conditions as it deems advisable, respecting the protection, preservation, maintenance, or operation of any historic site, building, object, or property used in connection therewith for public use, regardless of whether the National Trust has acquired title to such properties, or any interest therein.

(h) To enter into contracts generally and to execute all instruments necessary or appropriate to carry out its corporate purposes, which instruments shall include such concession contracts, leases, or permits for the use of lands, buildings, or other property deemed desirable either to accommodate the public or to facilitate administration.

(i) To appoint and prescribe the duties of such officers, agents, and employees as may be necessary to carry out its functions, and to fix and pay such compensation to them for their services as the National Trust may determine.

(j) And generally to do any and all lawful acts necessary or appropriate to carry out the purposes for which the National Trust is created.

SEC. 5. In carrying out its functions under this Act, the National Trust is authorized to consult with the Advisory Board on National Parks, Historic Sites, Buildings, and Monuments, on matters relating to the selection of sites, buildings, and objects to be preserved and protected pursuant hereto.

SEC. 6. The National Trust shall, on or before the 1st day of March in each year, transmit to Congress a report of its proceedings and activities for the preceding calendar year, including the full and complete statement of its receipts and expenditures.

SEC. 7. The right to appeal, alter or amend this Act at any time is hereby expressly reserved, but no contract or individual right made or acquired shall thereby be divested or impaired.

Approved October 26, 1949. [H.R.5170; Public No. 408].

THE NATIONAL HISTORIC PRESERVATION ACT, 1966

An Act to establish a program for the preservation of additional historic properties throughout the Nation, and for other purposes.

Be it enacted by the Senate and House of Representatives of the United States of America in Congress assembled,
The Congress finds and declares—
(a) that the spirit and direction of the Nation are founded upon and reflected in its historic past;
(b) that the historical and cultural foundations of the Nation should be preserved as a living part of our community life and development in order to give a sense of orientation to the American people;
(c) that, in the face of ever-increasing extensions of urban centers, highways, and residential, commercial, and industrial developments, the present governmental and nongovernmental historic preservation programs and activities are inadequate to insure future generations a genuine opportunity to appreciate and enjoy the rich heritage of our Nation; and
(d) that, although the major burdens of historic preservation have been borne and major efforts initiated by private agencies and individuals, and both should continue to play a vital role, it is nevertheless necessary and appropriate for the Federal Government to accelerate its historic preservation programs and activities, to give maximum encouragement to agencies and individuals undertaking preservation by private means, and to assist State and local governments and the National Trust for Historic Preservation in the United States to expand and accelerate their historic preservation programs and activities.

Title I

Sec. 101. (a) The Secretary of the Interior is authorized—
(1) to expand and maintain a national register of districts, sites, buildings, structures, and objects significant in American history, architecture, archeology, and culture, hereinafter referred to as the National Register, and to grant funds to States for the purpose of preparing comprehensive statewide historic surveys and plans, in accordance with criteria established by the Secretary, for the preservation, acquisition, and development of such properties;
(2) to establish a program of matching grants-in-aid to States for projects having as their purpose the preservation for public benefit of properties that are significant in American history, architecture, archeology, and culture; and
(3) to establish a program of matching grants-in-aid to the National Trust for Historic Preservation in the United States, chartered by act of Congress approved October 26, 1949 (63 Stat. 927), as amended, for the purpose of carrying out the responsibilities of the National Trust.
(b) As used in this Act—
(1) The term "State" includes, in addition to the several States of the Union, the District of Columbia, the Commonwealth of Puerto Rico, the Virgin Islands, Guam, and American Samoa.

(2) The term "project" means programs of State and local governments and other public bodies and private organizations and individuals for the acquisition of title or interests in, and for the development of, any district, site, building, structure, or object that is significant in American history, architecture, archeology, and culture, or property used in connection therewith, and for its development in order to assure the preservation for public benefit of any such historical properties.
(3) The term "historic preservation" includes the protection, rehabilitation, restoration, and reconstruction of districts, sites, buildings, structures, and objects significant in American history, architecture, archeology, or culture.
(4) The term "Secretary" means the Secretary of the Interior.
Sec. 102. (a) No grant may be made under this Act—
(1) unless application therefor is submitted to the Secretary in accordance with regulations and procedures prescribed by him;
(2) unless the application is in accordance with the comprehensive statewide historic preservation plan which has been approved by the Secretary after considering its relationship to the comprehensive statewide outdoor recreation plan prepared pursuant to the Land and Water Conservation Fund Act of 1965 (78 Stat. 897);
(3) for more than 50 per centum of the total cost involved, as determined by the Secretary and his determination shall be final;
(4) unless the grantee has agreed to make such reports, in such form and containing such information as the Secretary may from time to time require:
(5) unless the grantee has agreed to assume, after completion of the project, the total cost of the continued maintenance, repair, and administration of the property in a manner satisfactory to the Secretary; and
(6) until the grantee has complied with such further terms and conditions as the Secretary may deem necessary or advisable.
(b) The Secretary may in his discretion waive the requirements of subsection (a), paragraphs (2) and (5) of this section for any grant under the Act to the National Trust for Historic Preservation in the United States, in which case a grant to the National Trust may include funds for the maintenance, repair, and administration of the property in a manner satisfactory to the Secretary.
(c) No State shall be permitted to utilize the value of real property obtained before the date of approval of this Act in meeting the remaining cost of a project for which a grant is made under this Act.
Sec. 103. (a) The amounts appropriated and made available for grants to the States for comprehensive statewide historic surveys and plans under this Act shall be apportioned among the States by the Secretary on the basis of needs as determined by him: *Provided, however,* That the amount granted to any one State shall not exceed 50 per centum of the total cost of the comprehensive statewide historic survey and plan for that State, as determined by the Secretary.
(b) The amounts appropriated and made available for grants to the States for projects under this Act for each fiscal year shall be apportioned among the States by

the Secretary in accordance with needs as disclosed in approved statewide historic preservation plans.

The Secretary shall notify each State of its apportionment, and the amounts thereof shall be available thereafter for payment to such State for projects in accordance with the provisions of this Act. Any amount of any apportionment that has not been paid or obligated by the Secretary during the fiscal year in which such notification is given, and for two fiscal years thereafter, shall be reapportioned by the Secretary in accordance with this subsection.

SEC. 104. (a) No grant may be made by the Secretary for or on account of any survey or project under this Act with respect to which financial assistance has been given or promised under any other Federal program or activity, and no financial assistance may be given under any other Federal program or activity for or on account of any survey or project with respect to which assistance has been given or promised under this Act.

(b) In order to assure consistency in policies and actions under this Act with other related Federal programs and activities, and to assure coordination of the planning acquisition, and development assistance to States under this Act with other related Federal programs and activities, the President may issue such regulations with respect thereto as he deems desirable, and such assistance may be provided only in accordance with such regulations.

SEC. 105. The beneficiary of assistance under this Act shall keep such records as the Secretary shall prescribe, including records which fully disclose the disposition by the beneficiary of the proceeds of such assistance, the total cost of the project or undertaking in connection with which such assistance is given or used, and the amount and nature of that portion of the cost of the project or undertaking supplied by other sources, and such other records as will facilitate an effective audit.

SEC. 106. The head of any Federal agency having direct or indirect jurisdiction over a proposed Federal or federally assisted undertaking in any State and the head of any Federal department or independent agency having authority to license any undertaking shall, prior to the approval of the expenditure of any Federal funds on the undertaking or prior to the issuance of any license, as the case may be, take into account the effect of the undertaking on any district, site, building, structure, or object that is included in the National Register. The head of any such Federal agency shall afford the Advisory Council on Historic Preservation established under title II of this Act a reasonable opportunity to comment with regard to such undertaking.

SEC. 107. Nothing in this Act shall be construed to be applicable to the White House and its grounds, the Supreme Court building and its grounds, or the United States Capitol and its related buildings and grounds.

SEC. 108. There are authorized to be appropriated not to exceed $2,000,000 to carry out the provisions of this Act for the fiscal year 1967, and not more than $10,000,000 for each of the three succeeding fiscal years. Such appropriations shall be available for the financial assistance authorized by this title and for the administrative expenses of the Secretary in connection therewith, and shall remain available until expended.

Title II

SEC. 201. (a) There is established an Advisory Council on Historic Preservation (hereinafter referred to as the "Council") which shall be composed of seventeen members as follows:

(1) The Secretary of the Interior.

(2) The Secretary of Housing and Urban Development.

(3) The Secretary of Commerce.

(4) The Administration of the General Services Administration.

(5) The Secretary of the Treasury.

(6) The Attorney General.

(7) The Chairman of the National Trust for Historic Preservation.

(8) Ten appointed by the President from outside the Federal Government. In making these appointments, the President shall give due consideration to the selection of officers of State and local governments and individuals who are significantly interested and experienced in the matters to be considered by the Council.

(b) Each member of the Council specified in paragraphs (1) through (6) of subsection (a) may designate another officer of his department or agency to serve on the Council in his stead.

(c) Each member of the Council appointed under paragraph (8) of subsection (a) shall serve for a term of five years from the expiration of his predecessor's term; except that the members first appointed under that paragraph shall serve for terms of from one to five years, as designated by the President at the time of appointment, in such manner as to insure that the terms of not less than one nor more than two of them will expire in any one year.

(d) A vacancy in the Council shall not affect its powers, but shall be filled in the same manner as the original appointment (and for the balance of the unexpired term).

(e) The Chairman of the Council shall be designated by the President.

(f) Eight members of the Council shall constitute a quorum.

SEC. 202. (a) The Council shall—

(1) advise the President and the Congress on matters relating to historic preservation; recommend measures to coordinate activities of Federal, State, and local agencies and private institutions and individuals relating to historic preservation; and advise on the dissemination of information pertaining to such activities;

(2) encourage, in cooperation with the National Trust for Historic Preservation and appropriate private agencies, public interest and participation in historic preservation;

(3) recommend the conduct of studies in such areas as the adequacy of legislative and administrative statutes and regulations pertaining to historic preservation activities of State and local governments and the effects of tax policies at all levels of government on historic preservation;

(4) advise as to guidelines for the assistance of State and local governments in drafting legislation relating to historic preservation; and

(5) encourage, in cooperation with appropriate public and private agencies and institutions, training and education in the field of historic preservation.

(b) The Council shall submit annually a comprehensive report of its activities and the results of its studies to the President and the Congress and shall from time to time submit such additional and special reports as it deems advisable. Each report shall propose such legislative enactments and other actions as, in the judgment of the Council, are necessary and appropriate to carry out its recommendations.

SEC. 203. The Council is authorized to secure directly from any department, bureau, agency, board, commission, office, independent establishment or instrumentality of the executive branch of the Federal Government information, suggestions, estimates, and statistics for the purpose of this title; and each such department, bureau, agency board, commission, office, independent establishment or instrumentality is authorized to furnish such information, suggestions, estimates, and statistics to the extent permitted by law and within available funds.

SEC. 204. The members of the Council specified in paragraphs (1) through (7) of section 201 (a) shall serve without additional compensation. The members of the Council appointed under paragraph (8) of section 201 (a) shall receive $100 per diem when engaged in the performance of the duties of the Council. All members of the Council shall receive reimbursement for necessary traveling and subsistence expenses incurred by them in the performance of the duties of the Council.

SEC. 205. (a) The Director of the National Park Service or his designee shall be the Executive Director of the Council. Financial and administrative services (including those related to budgeting, accounting, financial reporting, personnel and procurement) shall be provided the Council by the Department of the Interior, for which payments shall be made in advance, or by reimbursement, from funds of the Council in such amounts as may be agreed upon by the Chairman of the Council and the Secretary of the Interior: *Provided*, That the regulations of the Department of the Interior for the collection of indebtedness of personnel resulting from erroneous payments (5 U.S.C. 46e) shall apply to the collection of erroneous payments made to or on behalf of a Council employee, and regulations of said Secretary for the administrative control of funds (31 U.S.C. 665 (g)) shall apply to appropriations of the Council: *And provided further*, That the Council shall not be required to prescribe such regulations.

(b) The Council shall have power to appoint and fix the compensation of such additional personnel as may be necessary to carry out its duties, without regard to the provisions of the civil service laws and the Classification Act of 1949.

(c) The Council may also procure, without regard to the civil service laws and the Classification Act of 1949, temporary and intermittent services to the same extent as is authorized for the executive departments by section 15 of the Administrative Expenses Act of 1946 (5 U.S.C. 55a), but at rates not to exceed $50 per diem for individuals.

(d) The members of the Council specified in paragraphs (1) through (6) of section 201 (a) shall provided the Council, on a reimbursable basis, with such facilities and services under their jurisdiction and control as may be needed by the Council to carry out its duties, to the extent that such facilities and services are requested by the Council and are otherwise available for that purpose. To the extent of available appropriations, the Council may obtain, by purchase, rental, donation, or otherwise, such additional property, facilities, and services as may be needed to carry out its duties.

Approved October 15, 1966. [S.3035; Public No. 89-665].

EXECUTIVE ORDER #11593

For the protection and enhancement of the cultural environment, 1971

By virtue of the authority vested in me as President of the United States and in furtherance of the purposes and policies of the National Environmental Policy Act of 1969 (83 Stat. 852, 42 U.S.C. 4321 et seq.), the National Historic Preservation Act of 1966 (80 Stat. 915, 16 U.S.C. 470 et seq.), the Historic Sites Act of 1935 (49 Stat. 666, 16 U.S.C. 461 et seq.), and the Antiquities Act of 1906 (34 Stat. 225, 16 U.S.C. 431 et seq.), it is ordered as follows:

SEC. 1. **Policy.** The Federal Government shall provide leadership in preserving, restoring and maintaining the historic and cultural environment of the Nation. Agencies of the executive branch of the Government (hereinafter referred to as "Federal agencies") shall (1) administer the cultural properties under their control in a spirit of stewardship and trusteeship for future generations; (2) initiate measures necessary to direct their policies, plans and programs in such a way that federally owned sites, structures, and objects of historical, architectural or archaeological significance are preserved, restored and maintained for the inspiration and benefit of the people, and (3), in consultation with the Advisory Council on Historic Preservation (16 U.S.C. 470i); institute procedures to assure that Federal plans and programs contribute to the preservation and enhancement of non-federally owned sites, structures and objects of historical, architectural or archaeological significance.

SEC. 2. **Responsibilities of Federal agencies.** Consonant with the provisions of the acts cited in the first paragraph of this order, the heads of Federal agencies shall:

(a) no later than July 1, 1973, with the advice of the Secretary of the Interior, and in cooperation with the liaison officer for historic preservation for the State or territory involved, locate, inventory, and nominate to the Secretary of the Interior all sites, buildings, districts, and objects under their jurisdiction or control that appear to qualify for listing on the National Register of Historic Places.

(b) exercise caution during the interim period until inventories and evaluations required by subsection (a) are completed to assure that any federally owned property that might qualify for nomination is not inadvertently transferred, sold, demolished or substantially altered. The agency head shall refer any questionable actions to the Secretary of the Interior for an opinion respecting the property's eligibility for inclusion on the National Register of Historic Places. The Secretary shall consult with the liaison officer for historic preservation for the State or territory involved in arriving at his opinion. Where, after a reasonable period in which to review and evaluate the property, the Secretary determines that the property is likely to meet the criteria prescribed for listing on the National Register of Historic Places, the Federal agency head shall reconsider the proposal in light of national environmental and preservation policy. Where, after such reconsideration, the Federal agency head proposes to transfer, sell, demolish or substantially alter the property he shall not act with respect to the property until the Advisory Council on Historic Preservation shall have been provided an opportunity to comment on the proposal.

(c) initiate measures to assure that where as a result of Federal action or assistance a property listed on the National Register of Historic Places is to be substantially altered or demolished, timely steps be taken to make or have made records, including measured drawings, photographs and maps, of the property, and that copy of such records then be deposited in the Library of Congress as part of the Historic American Buildings Survey or Historic American Engineering Record for future use and reference. Agencies may call on the Department of the Interior for advice and technical assistance in the completion of the above records.

(d) initiate measures and procedures to provide for the maintenance, thorough preservation, rehabilitation, or restoration, of federally owned and registered sites at professional standards prescribed by the Secretary of the Interior.

(e) submit procedures required pursuant to subsection (d) to the Secretary of the Interior and to the Advisory Council on Historic Preservation no later than January 1, 1972, and annually thereafter, for review and comment.

(f) cooperate with purchasers and transferees of a property listed on the National Register of Historic Places in the development of viable plans to use such property in a manner compatible with preservation objectives and which does not result in an unreasonable economic burden to public or private interests.

Sec. 3. **Responsibilities of the Secretary of the Interior.** The Secretary of the Interior shall:

(a) encourage State and local historic preservation officials to evaluate and survey federally owned historic properties and, where appropriate, to nominate such properties for listing on the National Register of Historic Places.

(b) develop criteria and procedures to be applied by Federal agencies in the reviews and nominations required by section 2(a). Such criteria and procedures shall be developed in consultation with the affected agencies.

(c) expedite action upon nominations to the National Register of Historic Places concerning federally owned properties proposed for sale, transfer, demolition or substantial alteration.

(d) encourage State and Territorial liaison officers for historic preservation to furnish information upon request to Federal agencies regarding their properties which have been evaluated with respect to historic, architectural or archaeological significance and which as a result of such evaluations have not been found suitable for listing on the National Register of Historic Places.

(e) develop and make available to Federal agencies and State and local governments information concern-

ing professional methods and techniques for preserving, improving, restoring and maintaining historic properties.

(f) advise Federal agencies in the evaluation, identification, preservation, improvement, restoration and maintenance of historic properties.

(g) review and evaluate the plans of transferees of surplus Federal properties transferred for historic monument purposes to assure that the historic character of such properties is preserved in rehabilitation, restoration, improvement, maintenance and repair of such properties.

(h) review and comment upon Federal agency procedures submitted pursuant to section 2(e) of this order.

THE WHITE HOUSE,   RICHARD NIXON
May 13, 1971. [36 F.R. 8921]

EXECUTIVE ORDER 13006

Locating Federal Facilities on Historic Properties in Our Nation's Central Cities

By the authority vested in me as President by the Constitution and the laws of the United States of America, including the National Historic Preservation Act (16 U.S.C. 470 *et seq.*) and the Public Buildings Cooperative Use Act of 1976 (90 Stat. 2505), and in furtherance of and consistent with Executive Order No. 12072 of August 16, 1978, and Executive Order No. 11593 of May 13, 1971, it is hereby ordered as follows:

SEC. 1. **Statement of Policy.** Through the Administration's community empowerment initiatives, the Federal Government has undertaken various efforts to revitalize our central cities, which have historically served as the centers for growth and commerce in our metropolitan areas. Accordingly, the Administration hereby reaffirms the commitment set forth in Executive Order No. 12072 to strengthen our nation's cities by encouraging the location of Federal facilities in our central cities. The Administration also reaffirms the commitments set forth in the National Historic Preservation Act to provide leadership in the preservation of historic resources, and in the Public Buildings Cooperative Use Act of 1976 to acquire and utilize space in suitable buildings of historic, architectural, or cultural significance.

To this end, the Federal Government shall utilize and maintain, wherever operationally appropriate and economically prudent, historic properties and districts, especially those located in our central business areas. When implementing these policies, the Federal Government shall institute practices and procedures that are sensible, understandable, and compatible with current authority and that impose the least burden on, and provide the maximum benefit to, society.

SEC. 2. **Encouraging the Location of Federal Facilities on Historic Properties in Our Central Cities.** When operationally appropriate and economically prudent, and subject to the requirements of Section 601 of Title VI of the Rural Development Act of 1972, as amended (42 U.S.C. 3122), and Executive Order No. 12072, when locating Federal facilities, Federal agencies shall give first consideration to historic properties within historic districts. If no such property is

suitable, then Federal agencies shall consider other developed or undeveloped sites within historic districts.
Federal agencies shall then consider historic properties
outside of historic districts, if no suitable site within a
district exists. Any rehabilitation or construction that is
undertaken pursuant to this order must be architecturally compatible with the character of the surrounding historic district or properties.

SEC. 3. **Identifying and Removing Regulatory
Barriers.** Federal agencies with responsibilities for
leasing, acquiring, locating, maintaining, or managing
Federal facilities or with responsibilities for the planning for, or managing of, historic resources shall take
steps to reform, streamline, and otherwise minimize
regulations, policies, and procedures that impede the
Federal Government's ability to establish or maintain a
presence in historic districts or to acquire historic
properties to satisfy Federal space needs, unless such
regulations, policies, and procedures are designed to
protect human health and safety or the environment.
Federal agencies are encouraged to seek the assistance
of the Advisory Council on Historic Preservation when
taking these steps.

SEC. 4. **Improving Preservation Partnerships.** In
carrying out the authorities of the National Historic
Preservation Act, the Secretary of the Interior, the Advisory Council on Historic Preservation, and each Federal agency shall seek appropriate partnerships with
states, local governments, Indian tribes, and appropriate private organizations with the goal of enhancing
participation of these parties in the National Historic
Preservation Program. Such partnerships should embody the principles of administrative flexibility, reduced
paperwork, and increased service to the public.

SEC. 5. **Judicial Review.** This order is not intended
to create, nor does it create, any right or benefit, sub-
stantive or procedural, enforceable at law by a party
against the United States, its agencies or instrumentali-
ties, its officers or employees, or any other person.

THE WHITE HOUSE,
May 21, 1996.

The National Register's Criteria for Evaluation

THE NATIONAL REGISTER CRITERIA serve as the basis for judging, at the national, state, and local levels, all nominations for inclusion in the Register. These are the criteria against which litigation is heard in controversial situations and which determine eligibility for tax credits.

The National Register's standards for evaluating the significance of properties were developed to recognize the accomplishments of all peoples who have made a contribution to our country's history and heritage. The criteria are designed to guide state and local governments, federal agencies, and others in evaluating potential entries in the National Register.

The quality of significance in American history, architecture, archeology, engineering and culture is present in districts, sites, buildings, structures, and objects that possess integrity of location, design, setting, materials, workmanship, feeling, and association and:

(a) that are associated with events that have made a significant contribution to the broad patterns of our history; or

(b) that are associated with the lives of persons significant in our past; or

(c) that embody the distinctive characteristics of a type, period, or method of construction, or that represent the work of a master, or that possess high artistic values, or that represent a significant and distinguishable entity whose components may lack individual distinction; or

(d) that have yielded, or may be likely to yield, information important in prehistory or history.

Criteria considerations: Ordinarily cemeteries, birthplaces, or graves of historical figures, properties owned by religious institutions or used for religious purposes, structures that have been moved from their original lo-

cations, reconstructed historic buildings, properties primarily commemorative in nature, and properties that have achieved significance within the past 50 years shall not be considered eligible for the National Register. However, such properties will qualify if they are integral parts of districts that do meet the criteria or if they fall within the following categories:

(a) a religious property deriving primary significance from architectural or artistic distinction or historical importance; or

(b) a building or structure removed from its original location but which is significant primarily for architectural value, or which is the surviving structure most importantly associated with a historic person or event; or

(c) a birthplace or grave of a historical figure of outstanding importance if there is no other appropriate site or building directly associated with his productive life; or

(d) a cemetery that derives its primary significance from graves of persons of transcendent importance, from age, from distinctive design features, or from association with historic events; or

(e) a reconstructed building when accurately executed in a suitable environment and presented in a dignified manner as part of a restoration master plan, and when no other building or structure with the same association has survived; or

(f) a property primarily commemorative in intent if design, age, tradition, or symbolic value has invested it with its own historical significance; or

(g) a property achieving significance within the past 50 years if it is of exceptional importance.

Information on documentation of properties and use of the Criteria for Evaluation may be obtained by writing: National Register of Historic Places, National Park Service, U.S. Department of the Interior, Washington, D.C. 20240.

The Secretary of the Interior's Standards for Rehabilitation

and Guidelines for Rehabilitating Historic Buildings

LIKE THE NATIONAL REGISTER'S CRITERIA, the Secretary of the Interior's standards and guidelines are basic yardsticks against which restoration and rehabilitation procedures are judged. They determine whether or not certification by the National Park Service can be granted in order for the developer of a project to take advantage of tax credits provided by the tax acts of 1976, 1981, and 1986. Without certification by the National Park Service, the Internal Revenue Service will not certify eligibility for tax credits. Without both certifications, a tax claim cannot be made.

THE SECRETARY OF THE INTERIOR'S STANDARDS FOR REHABILITATION

The following Standards are to be applied to specific rehabilitation projects in a reasonable manner, taking into consideration economic and technical feasibility.

(1) A property shall be used for its historic purpose or be placed in a new use that requires minimal change to the defining characteristics of the building and its site and environment.

(2) The historic character of a property shall be retained and preserved. The removal of historic materials or alteration of features and spaces that characterize a property shall be avoided.

(3) Each property shall be recognized as a physical record of its time, place, and use. Changes that create a false sense of historical development, such as adding conjectural features or architectural elements from other buildings, shall not be undertaken.

(4) Most properties change over time; those changes that have acquired historic significance in their own right shall be retained and preserved.

(5) Distinctive features, finishes, and construction techniques or examples of craftsmanship that characterize a historic property shall be preserved.

(6) Deteriorated historic features shall be repaired rather than replaced. Where the severity of deterioration requires replacement of a distinctive feature, the new feature shall match the old in design, color, texture, and other visual qualities and, where possible, materials. Replacement of missing features shall be substantiated by documentary, physical, or pictorial evidence.

(7) Chemical or physical treatments, such as sandblasting, that cause damage to historic materials shall not be used. The surface cleaning of structures, if appropriate, shall be undertaken using the gentlest means possible.

(8) Significant archeological resources affected by a project shall be protected and preserved. If such resources must be disturbed, mitigation measures shall be undertaken.

(9) New additions, exterior alterations, or related new construction shall not destroy historic materials that characterize the property. The new work shall be differentiated from the old and shall be compatible with the massing, size, scale, and architectural features to protect the historic integrity of the property and its environment.

(10) New additions and adjacent or related new construction shall be undertaken in such a manner that if removed in the future, the essential form and integrity of the historic property and its environment would be unimpaired.

GUIDELINES FOR REHABILITATING HISTORIC BUILDINGS

BUILDING EXTERIOR

Masonry: Brick, stone, terra cotta, concrete, adobe, stucco and mortar

Recommended

Identifying, retaining, and preserving masonry features that are important in defining the overall historic character of the building such as walls, brackets, railings, cornices, window architraves, door pediments, steps, and columns; and joint and unit size, tooling and bonding patterns, coatings, and color.

Protecting and maintaining masonry by providing proper drainage so that water does not stand on flat, horizontal surfaces or accumulate in curved decorative features.

Cleaning masonry only when necessary to halt deterioration or remove heavy soiling.

Carrying out masonry surface cleaning tests after it has been determined that such cleaning is necessary. Tests should be observed over a sufficient period of time so that both the immediate effects and the long range effects are known to enable selection of the gentlest method possible.

Cleaning masonry surfaces with the gentlest method possible, such as low pressure water and detergents, using natural bristle brushes.

Inspecting painted masonry surfaces to determine whether repainting is necessary.

Removing damaged or deteriorated paint only to the next sound layer using the gentlest method possible (e.g., handscraping) prior to repainting.

Applying compatible paint coating systems following proper surface preparation.

Repainting with colors that are historically appropriate to the building and district.

Evaluating the overall condition of the masonry to determine whether more than protection and maintenance are required, that is, if repairs to the masonry features will be necessary.

Not Recommended

Removing or radically changing masonry features which are important in defining the overall historic character of the building so that, as a result, the character is diminished.

Replacing or rebuilding a major portion of exterior masonry walls that could be repaired so that, as a result, the building is no longer historic and is essentially new construction.

Applying paint or other coatings such as stucco to masonry that has been historically unpainted or uncoated to create a new appearance.

Removing paint from historically painted masonry.

Radically changing the type of paint or coating or its color.

Failing to evaluate and treat the various causes of mortar joint deterioration such as leaking roofs or gutters, differential settlement of the building, capillary action, or extreme weather exposure.

Cleaning masonry surfaces when they are not heavily soiled to create a new appearance, thus needlessly introducing chemicals or moisture into historic materials.

Cleaning masonry surfaces without testing or without sufficient time for the testing results to be of value.

Sandblasting brick or stone surfaces using dry or wet grit or other abrasives. These methods of cleaning permanently erode the surface of the material and accelerate deterioration.

Using a cleaning method that involves water or liquid chemical solutions when there is any possibility of freezing temperatures.

Cleaning with chemical products that will damage masonry, such as using acid on limestone or marble, or leaving chemicals on masonry surfaces.

Applying high pressure water cleaning methods that will damage historic masonry and the mortar joints.

Removing paint that is firmly adhering to, and thus protecting, masonry surfaces.

Using methods of removing paint which are destructive to masonry, such as sandblasting, application of caustic solutions, or high pressure waterblasting.

Failing to follow manufacturers' product and application instructions when repainting masonry.

Using new paint colors that are inappropriate to the historic building and district.

Failing to undertake adequate measures to assure the preservation of masonry features.

Recommended

Repairing masonry walls and other masonry features by repointing the mortar joints where there is evidence of deterioration such as disintegrating mortar, cracks in mortar joints, loose bricks, damp walls, or damaged plasterwork.

Removing deteriorated mortar by carefully hand-raking the joints to avoid damaging the masonry.

Duplicating old mortar in strength, composition, color, and texture.

Duplicating old mortar joints in width and in joint profile.

Repairing stucco by removing the damaged material and patching with new stucco that duplicates the old in strength, composition, color, and texture.

Using mud plaster as a surface coating over unfired, unstabilized adobe because the mud plaster will bond to the adobe.

Repairing masonry features by patching, piecing-in, or consolidating the masonry using recognized preservation methods. Repair may also include the limited replacement in kind—or with compatible substitute material—of those extensively deteriorated or missing parts of masonry features when there are surviving prototypes such as terra-cotta brackets or stone balusters.

Applying new or non-historic surface treatments such as water-repellent coatings to masonry only after repointing and only if masonry repairs have failed to arrest water penetration problems.

Replacing in kind an entire masonry feature that is too deteriorated to repair—if the overall form and detailing are still evident—using the physical evidence to guide the new work. Examples can include large sections of a wall, a cornice, balustrade, column, or stairway. If using the same kind of material is not technically or economically feasible, then a compatible substitute material may be considered.

Not Recommended

Removing nondeteriorated mortar from sound joints, then repointing the entire building to achieve a uniform appearance.

Using electric saws and hammers rather than hand tools to remove deteriorated mortar from joints prior to repointing.

Repointing with mortar of high portland cement content (unless it is the content of the historic mortar). This can often create a bond that is stronger than the historic material and can cause damage as a result of the differing coefficient of expansion and the differing porosity of the material and the mortar.

Repointing with a synthetic caulking compound.

Using a "scrub" coating technique to repoint instead of traditional repointing methods.

Changing the width or joint profile when repointing.

Removing sound stucco; or repairing with new stucco that is stronger than the historic material or does not convey the same visual appearance.

Applying cement stucco to unfired, unstabilized adobe. Because the cement stucco will not bond properly, moisture can become entrapped between materials, resulting in accelerated deterioration of the adobe.

Replacing an entire masonry feature such as a cornice or balustrade when repair of the masonry and limited replacement of deteriorated or missing parts are appropriate.

Using a substitute material for the replacement part that does not convey the visual appearance of the surviving parts of the masonry feature or that is physically or chemically incompatible.

Applying waterproof, water-repellent, or non-historic coatings such as stucco to masonry as a substitute for repointing and masonry repairs. Coatings are frequently unnecessary, expensive, and may change the appearance of historic masonry as well as accelerate its deterioration.

Removing a masonry feature that is unrepairable and not replacing it; or replacing it with a new feature that does not convey the same visual appearance.

The following work is highlighted because it represents the particularly complex technical or design aspects of rehabilitation projects and should only be considered after the preservation concerns listed above have been addressed.

Design for Missing Historic Features

Designing and installing a new masonry feature such as steps or a door pediment when the historic feature is completely missing. It may be an accurate restoration using historical, pictorial, and physical documentation; or be a new design that is compatible with the size, scale, material, and color of the historic building.

Creating a false historical appearance because the replaced masonry feature is based on insufficient historical, pictorial, and physical documentation.

Introducing a new masonry feature that is incompatible in size, scale, material and color.

Wood: Clapboard, weatherboard, shingles, and other wooden siding and decorative elements

Recommended	*Not Recommended*
Identifying, retaining, and preserving wood features that are important in defining the overall historic character of the building such as siding, cornices, brackets, window architraves, and door-way pediments; and their paints, finishes, and colors.	Removing or radically changing wood features which are important in defining the overall historic character of the building so that, as a result, the character is diminished. Removing a major portion of the historic wood from a facade instead of repairing or replacing only the deteriorated wood, then reconstructing the facade with new material in order to achieve a uniform or "improved" appearance. Radically changing the type of finish or its color or accent scheme so that the historic character of the exterior is diminished. Stripping historically painted surfaces to bare wood, then applying clear finishes or stains in order to create a "natural look." Stripping paint or varnish to bare wood rather than repairing or reapplying a special finish, i.e., a grained finish to an exterior wood feature such as a front door.
Protecting and maintaining wood features by providing proper drainage so that water is not allowed to stand on flat, horizontal surfaces or accumulate in decorative features.	Failing to identify, evaluate, and treat the causes of wood deterioration, including faulty flashing, leaking gutters, cracks and holes in siding, deteriorated caulking in joints and seams, plant material growing too close to wood surfaces, or insect or fungus infestation.
Applying chemical preservatives to wood features such as beam ends or outriggers that are exposed to decay hazards and are traditionally unpainted.	Using chemical preservatives such as creosote which can change the appearance of wood features unless they were used historically.
Retaining coatings such as paint that help protect the wood from moisture and ultraviolet light. Paint removal should be considered only where there is paint surface deterioration and as part of an overall maintenance program which involves repainting or applying other appropriate protective coatings.	Stripping paint or other coatings to reveal bare wood, thus exposing historically coated surfaces to the effects of accelerated weathering.
Inspecting painted wood surfaces to determine whether repainting is necessary or if cleaning is all that is required.	Removing paint that is firmly adhering to, and thus, protecting wood surfaces.
Removing damaged or deteriorated paint to the next sound layer using the gentlest method possible (handscraping and handsanding), then repainting.	Using destructive paint removal methods such as a propane or butane torches, sandblasting or waterblasting. These methods can irreversibly damage historic woodwork.
Using with care electric hot-air guns on decorative wood features and electric heat plates on flat wood surfaces when paint is so deteriorated that total removal is necessary prior to repainting.	Using thermal devices improperly so that the historic woodwork is scorched.
Using chemical strippers primarily to supplement other methods such as handscraping, handsanding and the above-recommended thermal devices. Detachable wooden elements such as shutters, doors, and columns may—with the proper safeguards—be chemically dip-stripped.	Failing to neutralize the wood thoroughly after using chemicals so that new paint does not adhere. Allowing detachable wood features to soak too long in a caustic solution so that the wood grain is raised and the surface roughened.
Applying compatible paint coating systems following proper surface preparation.	Failing to follow manufacturers' product and application instructions when repainting exterior woodwork.
Repainting with colors that are appropriate to the historic building and district.	Using new colors that are inappropriate to the historic building or district.

Recommended

Not Recommended

Evaluating the overall condition of the wood to determine whether more than protection and maintenance are required, that is, if repairs to wood features will be necessary.

Failing to undertake adequate measures to assure the preservation of wood features.

Repairing wood features by patching, piecing-in, consolidating, or otherwise reinforcing the wood using recognized preservation methods. Repair may also include the limited replacement in kind—or with compatible substitute material—of those extensively deteriorated or missing parts of features where there are surviving prototypes such as brackets, moldings, or sections of siding.

Replacing an entire wood feature such as a cornice or wall when repair of the wood and limited replacement of deteriorated or missing parts are appropriate.

Using substitute materials for the replacement part that does not convey the visual appearance of the surviving parts of the wood feature or that is physically or chemically incompatible.

Replacing in kind an entire wood feature that is too deteriorated to repair—if the overall form and detailing are still evident—using the physical evidence to guide the new work. Examples of wood features include a cornice, entablature or balustrade. If using the same kind of material is not technically or economically feasible, then a compatible substitute material may be considered.

Removing an entire wood feature that is unrepairable and not replacing it; or replacing it with a new feature that does not convey the same visual appearance.

The following work is highlighted to indicate that it represents the particularly complex technical or design aspects of rehabilitation projects and should only be considered after the preservation concerns listed above have been addressed.

Design for Missing Historic Features

Designing and installing a new wood feature such as a cornice or a doorway when the historic feature is completely missing. It may be an accurate restoration using historical, pictorial, and physical documentation; or be a new design that is compatible with the size, scale, material, and color of the historic building.

Creating a false historic appearance because the replaced wood feature is based on insufficient historical, pictorial, and physical documentation.

Introducing a new wood feature that is incompatible in size, scale, material, and color.

Architectural Metals: Cast iron, steel, pressed tin, copper, aluminum, and zinc

Recommended

Not Recommended

Identifying, retaining, and preserving architectural metal features such as columns, capitals, window hoods, or stairways that are important in defining the overall historic character of the building; and their finishes and colors.

Removing or radically changing architectural metal features which are important in defining the overall historic character of the building so that, as a result, the character is diminished.

Removing a major portion of the historic architectural metal from a facade instead of repairing or replacing only the deteriorated metal, then reconstructing the facade with new material in order to create a uniform, or "improved" appearance.

Radically changing the type of finish or its historical color or accent scheme.

Protecting and maintaining architectural metals from corrosion by providing proper drainage so that water does not stand on flat, horizontal surfaces or accumulate in curved, decorative features.

Failing to identify, evaluate, and treat the causes of corrosion, such as moisture from leaking roofs or gutters.

Placing incompatible metals together without providing a reliable separation material. Such incompatibility can result in galvanic corrosion of the less noble metal, e.g., copper will corrode cast iron, steel, tin, and aluminum.

Exposing metals which were intended to be protected from the environment.

Cleaning architectural metals, when necessary, to remove corrosion prior to repainting or applying other appropriate protective coatings.

Applying paint or other coatings to metals such as copper, bronze, or stainless steel that were meant to be exposed.

Recommended	Not Recommended

Recommended

Identifying the particular type of metal prior to any cleaning procedure and then testing to assure that the gentlest cleaning method possible is selected or determining that cleaning is inappropriate for the particular metal.

Cleaning soft metals such as lead, tin, copper, terneplate, and zinc with appropriate chemical methods because their finishes can be easily abraded by blasting methods.

Using the gentlest cleaning methods for cast iron, wrought iron, and steel—hard metals—in order to remove paint buildup and corrosion. If handscraping and wire brushing have proven ineffective, low pressure dry grit blasting may be used as long as it does not abrade or damage the surface.

Applying appropriate paint or other coating systems after cleaning in order to decrease the corrosion rate of metals or alloys.

Repainting with colors that are appropriate to the historic building or district.

Applying an appropriate protective coating such as lacquer to an architectural metal feature such as a bronze door which is subject to heavy pedestrian use.

Evaluating the overall condition of the architectural metals to determine whether more than protection and maintenance are required, that is, if repairs to features will be necessary.

Repairing architectural metal features by patching, splicing, or otherwise reinforcing the metal following recognized preservation methods. Repairs may also include the limited replacement in kind—or with a compatible substitute material—of those extensively deteriorated or missing parts of features when there are surviving prototypes such as porch balusters, column capitals or bases; or porch cresting.

Replacing in kind an entire architectural metal feature that is too deteriorated to repair—if the overall form and detailing are still evident—using the physical evidence to guide the new work. Examples could include cast iron porch steps or steel sash windows. If using the same kind of material is not technically or economically feasible, then a compatible substitute material may be considered.

Not Recommended

Using cleaning methods which alter or damage the historic color, texture, and finish of the metal; or cleaning when it is inappropriate for the metal.

Removing the patina of historic metal. The patina may be a protective coating on some metals, such as bronze or copper, as well as a significant historic finish.

Cleaning soft metals such as lead, tin, copper, terneplate, and zinc with grit blasting which will abrade the surface of the metal.

Failing to employ gentler methods prior to abrasively cleaning cast iron, wrought iron or steel; or using high pressure grit blasting.

Failing to re-apply protective coating systems to metals or alloys that require them after cleaning so that accelerated corrosion occurs.

Using new colors that are inappropriate to the historic building or district.

Failing to assess pedestrian use or new access patterns so that architectural metal features are subject to damage by use or inappropriate maintenance such as salting adjacent sidewalks.

Failing to undertake adequate measures to assure the preservation of architectural metal features.

Replacing an entire architectural metal feature such as a column or a balustrade when repair of the metal and limited replacement of deteriorated or missing parts are appropriate.

Using a substitute material for the replacement part that does not convey the visual appearance of the surviving parts of the architectural metal features or that is physically or chemically incompatible.

Removing an architectural metal feature that is unrepairable and not replacing it; or replacing it with a new architectural metal feature that does not convey the same visual appearance.

The following work is highlighted to indicate that it represents the particularly complex technical or design aspects of rehabilitation projects and should only be considered after the preservation concerns listed above have been addressed.

Design for Missing Historic Features

Designing and installing a new architectural metal feature such as a sheet metal cornice or cast iron capital when the historic feature is completely missing. It may be an accurate restoration using historical, pictorial and physical documentation; or be a new design that is compatible with the size, scale, material, and color of the historic building.

Creating a false historic appearance because the replaced architectural metal feature is based on insufficient historical, pictorial, and physical documentation.

Introducing a new architectural metal feature that is incompatible in size, scale, material, and color.

Roofs

Recommended	*Not Recommended*

Identifying, retaining, and preserving roofs—and their functional and decorative features—that are important in defining the overall historic character of the building. This includes the roof's shape, such as hipped, gambrel, and mansard; decorative features such as cupolas, cresting, chimneys, and weathervanes; and roofing material such as slate, wood, clay tile, and metal, as well as its size, color, and patterning.

Radically changing, damaging, or destroying roofs which are important in defining the overall historic character of the building so that, as a result, the character is diminished.

Removing a major portion of the roof or roofing material that is repairable, then reconstructing it with new material in order to create a uniform, or "improved" appearance.

Changing the configuration of a roof by adding new features such as dormer windows, vents, or skylights so that the historic character is diminished.

Stripping the roof of sound historic material such as slate, clay tile, wood, and architectural metal.

Applying paint or other coatings to roofing material which has been historically uncoated.

Protecting and maintaining a roof by cleaning the gutters and downspouts and replacing deteriorated flashing. Roof sheathing should also be checked for proper venting to prevent moisture condensation and water penetration; and to insure that materials are free from insect infestation.

Failing to clean and maintain gutters and downspouts properly so that water and debris collect and cause damage to roof fasteners, sheathing, and the underlying structure.

Providing adequate anchorage for roofing material to guard against wind damage and moisture penetration.

Allowing roof fasteners, such as nails and clips to corrode so that roofing material is subject to accelerated deterioration.

Protecting a leaking roof with plywood and building paper until it can be properly repaired.

Permitting a leaking roof to remain unprotected so that accelerated deterioration of historic building materials—masonry, wood, plaster, paint and structural members—occurs.

Repairing a roof by reinforcing the historic materials which comprise roof features. Repairs will also generally include the limited replacement in kind—or with compatible substitute material—of those extensively deteriorated or missing parts of features when there are surviving prototypes such as cupola louvers, dentils, dormer roofing; or slates, tiles, or wood shingles on a main roof.

Replacing an entire roof feature such as a cupola or dormer when repair of the historic materials and limited replacement of deteriorated or missing parts are appropriate.

Using a substitute material for the replacement part that does not convey the visual appearance of the surviving parts of the roof or that is physically or chemically incompatible.

Replacing in kind an entire feature of the roof that is too deteriorated to repair—if the overall form and detailing are still evidence—using the physical evidence to guide the new work. Examples can include a large section of roofing, or a dormer or chimney. If using the same kind of material is not technically or economically feasible, then a compatible substitute material may be considered.

Removing a feature of the roof that is unrepairable, such as a chimney or dormer, and not replacing it; or replacing it with a new feature that does not convey the same visual appearance.

The following work is highlighted to indicate that it represents the particularly complex technical or design aspects of rehabilitation projects and should only be considered after the preservation concerns listed above have been addressed.

Design for Missing Historic Features

Designing and constructing a new feature when the historic feature is completely missing, such as a chimney or cupola. It may be an accurate restoration using historical, pictorial and physical documentation; or be a new design that is compatible with the size, scale, material, and color of the historic building.

Creating a false historical appearance because the replaced feature is based on insufficient historical, pictorial, and physical documentation.

Introducing a new roof feature that is incompatible in size, scale, material, and color.

Alterations/Additions for the New Use

Recommended

Installing mechanical and service equipment on the roof such as air conditioning, transformers, or solar collectors when required for the new use so that they are inconspicuous from the public right-of-way and do not damage or obscure character-defining features.

Designing additions to roofs such as residential, office or storage spaces; elevator housing; decks and terraces; or dormers or skylights when required by the new use so that they are inconspicuous from the public right-of-way and do not damage or obscure character-defining features.

Not Recommended

Installing mechanical or service equipment so that it damages or obscures character-defining features; or is conspicuous from the public right-of-way.

Radically changing a character-defining roof shape or damaging or destroying character-defining roofing material as a result of incompatible design or improper installation techniques.

Windows

Recommended

Identifying, retaining, and preserving windows—and their functional and decorative features—that are important in defining the overall historic character of the building. Such features can include frames, sash, muntins, glazing, sills, heads, hoodmolds, panelled or decorated jambs and moldings, and interior and exterior shutters and blinds.

Not Recommended

Removing or radically changing windows which are important in defining the overall historic character of the building so that, as a result, the character is diminished.

Changing the number, location, size or glazing pattern of windows, through cutting new openings, blocking-in windows, and installing replacement sash which does not fit the historic window opening.

Changing the historic appearance of windows through the use of inappropriate designs, materials, finishes, or colors which radically change the sash, depth of reveal, and muntin configuration; the reflectivity and color of the glazing; or the appearance of the frame.

Obscuring historic window trim with metal or other material.

Stripping windows of historic material such as wood, iron, cast iron, and bronze.

Protecting and maintaining the wood and architectural metal which comprise the window frame, sash, muntins, and surrounds through appropriate surface treatments such as cleaning, rust removal, limited paint removal, and re-application of protective coating systems.

Making windows weathertight by recaulking and replacing or installing weatherstripping. These actions also improve thermal efficiency.

Evaluating the overall condition of materials to determine whether more than protection and maintenance are required, i.e. if repairs to windows and window features will be required.

Failing to provide adequate protection of materials on a cyclical basis so that deterioration of the windows results.

Retrofitting or replacing windows rather than maintaining the sash, frame, and glazing.

Failing to undertake adequate measures to assure the preservation of historic windows.

Repairing window frames and sash by patching, splicing, consolidating or otherwise reinforcing. Such repair may also include replacement in kind of those parts that are either extensively deteriorated or are missing when there are surviving prototypes such as architraves, hoodmolds, sash, sills, and interior or exterior shutters and blinds.

Replacing an entire window when repair of materials and limited replacement of deteriorated or missing parts are appropriate.

Failing to reuse serviceable window hardware such as brass lifts and sash locks.

Using a substitute material for the replacement part that does not convey the visual appearance of the surviving parts of the window or that is physically or chemically incompatible.

Recommended

Replacing in kind an entire window that is too deteriorated to repair—if the overall form and detailing are still evident—using the physical evidence to guide the new work. If using the same kind of material is not technically or economically feasible, then a compatible substitute material may be considered.

Not Recommended

Removing a character-defining window that is unrepairable and blocking it in; or replacing it with a new window that does not convey the same visual appearance.

The following work is highlighted to indicate that it represents the particularly complex technical or design aspects of rehabilitation projects and should only be considered after the preservation concerns listed above have been addressed.

Design for Missing Historic Features

Designing and installing new windows when the historic windows (frame, sash and glazing) are completely missing. The replacement windows may be an accurate restoration using historical, pictorial and physical documentation; or be a new design that is compatible with the window openings and the historic character of the building.

Creating a false historical appearance because the placed window is based on insufficient historical, pictorial, and physical documentation.

Introducing a new design that is incompatible with the historic character of the building.

Alterations/Additions for the New Use

Designing and installing additional windows on rear or other non-character-defining elevations if required by the new use. New window openings may also be cut into exposed party walls. Such design should be compatible with the overall design of the building, but not duplicate the fenestration pattern and detailing of a character-defining elevation.

Installing new windows, including frames, sash, and muntin configuration that are incompatible with the building's historic appearance or obscure, damage, or destroy character-defining features.

Providing a setback in the design of dropped ceilings when they are required for the new use to allow for the full height of the window openings.

Inserting new floors or furred-down ceilings which cut across the glazed areas of windows so that the exterior form and appearance of the windows are changed.

Entrances and Porches

Recommended

Identifying, retaining, and preserving entrances—and their functional and decorative features—that are important in defining the overall historic character of the building such as doors, fanlights, sidelights, pilasters, entablatures, columns, balustrades, and stairs.

Not Recommended

Removing or radically changing entrances and porches which are important in defining the overall historic character of the building so that, as a result, the character is diminished.

Stripping entrances and porches of historic material such as wood, iron, cast iron, terra cotta, tile and brick.

Removing an entrance or porch because the building has been re-oriented to accommodate a new use.

Cutting new entrances on a primary elevation.

Altering utilitarian or service entrances so they appear to be formal entrances by adding panelled doors, fanlights, and sidelights.

Protecting and maintaining the masonry, wood, and architectural metal that comprise entrances and porches through appropriate surface treatments such as cleaning, rust removal, limited paint removal, and re-application of protective coating systems.

Failing to provide adequate protection to materials on a cyclical basis so that deterioration of entrances and porches results.

Evaluating the overall condition of materials to determine whether more than protection and maintenance are required, that is, if repairs to entrance and porch features will be necessary.

Failing to undertake adequate measures to assure the preservation of historic entrances and porches.

Recommended

Repairing entrances and porches by reinforcing the historic materials. Repair will also generally include the limited replacement in kind—or with compatible substitute material—of those extensively deteriorated or missing parts of repeated features where there are surviving prototypes such as balustrades, cornices, entablatures, columns, sidelights, and stairs.

Replacing in kind an entire entrance or porch that is too deteriorated to repair—if the form and detailing are still evident—using the physical evidence to guide the new work. If using the same kind of material is not technically or economically feasible, then a compatible substitute material may be considered.

Not Recommended

Replacing an entire entrance or porch when the repair of materials and limited replacement of parts are appropriate.

Using a substitute material for the replacement parts that does not convey the visual appearance of the surviving parts of the entrance and porch or that is physically or chemically incompatible.

Removing an entrance or porch that is unrepairable and not replacing it; or replacing it with a new entrance or porch that does not convey the same visual appearance.

The following work is highlighted to indicate that it represents the particularly complex technical or design aspects of rehabilitation projects and should only be considered after the preservation concerns listed above have been addressed.

Design for Missing Historic Features

Designing and constructing a new entrance or porch if the historic entrance or porch is completely missing. It may be a restoration based on historical, pictorial, and physical documentation; or be a new design that is compatible with the historic character of the building.

Creating a false historical appearance because the replaced entrance or porch is based on insufficient historical, pictorial, and physical documentation.

Introducing a new entrance or porch that is incompatible in size, scale, material, and color.

Alterations/Additions for the New Use

Designing enclosures for historic porches when required by the new use in a manner that preserves the historic character of the building. This can include using large sheets of glass and recessing the enclosure wall behind existing scrollwork, posts, and balustrades.

Enclosing porches in a manner that results in a diminution or loss of historic character such as using solid materials such as wood, stucco, or masonry.

Recommended

Designing and installing additional entrances or porches when required for the new use in a manner that preserves the historic character of the building, i.e., limiting such alteration to non-character-defining elevations.

Not Recommended

Installing secondary service entrances and porches that are incompatible in size and scale with the historic building or obscure, damage, or destroy character-defining features.

Storefronts

Recommended

Identifying, retaining, and preserving storefronts—and their functional and decorative features—that are important in defining the overall historic character of the building such as display windows, signs, doors, transom, kick plates, corner posts, and entablatures.

Not Recommended

Removing or radically changing storefronts—and their features—which are important in defining the overall historic character of the building so that, as a result, the character is diminished.

Changing the storefront so that it appears residential rather than commercial in character.

Removing historic material from the storefront to create a recessed arcade.

Introducing coach lanterns, mansard overhangings, wood shakes, nonoperable shutters, and small-paned windows if they cannot be documented historically.

Changing the location of a storefront's main entrance.

Recommended

Protecting and maintaining masonry, wood, and architectural metals which comprise storefronts through appropriate treatments such as cleaning, rust removal, limited paint removal, and reapplication of protective coating systems.

Protecting storefronts against arson and vandalism before work begins by boarding up windows and installing alarm systems that are keyed into local protection agencies.

Evaluating the overall condition of storefront materials to determine whether more than protection and maintenance are required, that is, if repairs to features will be necessary.

Repairing storefronts by reinforcing the historic materials. Repairs will also generally include the limited replacement in kind—or with compatible substitute material—of those extensively deteriorated or missing parts of storefronts where there are surviving prototypes such as transoms, kick plates, pilasters, or signs.

Replacing in kind an entire storefront that is too deteriorated to repair—if the overall form and detailing are still evident—using the physical evidence to guide the new work. If using the same material is not technically or economically feasible, then compatible substitute materials may be considered.

Not Recommended

Failing to provide adequate protection to materials on a cyclical basis so that deterioration of storefront features results.

Permitting entry into the building through unsecured or broken windows and doors so that interior features and finishes are damaged through exposure to weather or through vandalism.

Stripping storefronts of historic material such as wood, cast iron, terra cotta, carrara glass, and brick.

Failing to undertake adequate measures to assure the preservation of the historic storefront.

Replacing an entire storefront when repair of materials and limited replacement of its parts are appropriate.

Using substitute material for the replacement parts that does not convey the same visual appearance as the surviving parts of the storefront or that is physically or chemically incompatible.

Removing a storefront that is unrepairable and not replacing it; or replacing it with a new storefront that does not convey the same visual appearance.

The following work is highlighted to indicate that it represents the particularly complex technical or design aspects of rehabilitation projects and should only be considered after the preservation concerns listed above have been addressed.

Design for Missing Historic Features

Recommended

Designing and constructing a new storefront when the historic storefront is completely missing. it may be an accurate restoration using historical, pictorial, and physical documentation; or be a new design that is compatible with the size, scale, material, and color of the historic building. Such new design should generally be flush with the façade; and the treatment of secondary design elements, such as awnings or signs, kept as simple as possible. For example, new signs should fit flush with the existing features of the façade, such as the fascia board or cornice.

Not Recommended

Creating a false historical appearance because the replaced storefront is based on insufficient historical, pictorial, and physical documentation.

Introducing a new design that is incompatible in size, scale, material, and color.

Using new illuminated signs; inappropriately scaled signs and logos; signs that project over the sidewalk unless they were a characteristic feature of the historic building; or other types of signs that obscure, damage, or destroy remaining character-defining features of the historic building.

BUILDING INTERIOR

Structural System

Recommended

Identifying, retaining, and preserving structural systems—and individual features of systems—that are important in defining the overall historic character of the building, such as post and beam systems, trusses, summer beams, vigas, cast iron columns, above-grade stone foundation walls, or loadbearing brick or stone walls.

Not Recommended

Removing, covering, or radically changing features of structural systems which are important in defining the overall historic character of the building so that, as a result, the character is diminished.

Putting a new use into the building which could overload the existing structural system; or installing equipment or mechanical systems which could damage the structure.

Recommended	*Not Recommended*
	Demolishing a loadbearing masonry wall that could be augmented and retained and replacing it with a new wall (i.e., brick or stone), using the historic masonry only as an exterior veneer.
	Leaving known structural problems untreated such as deflection of beams, cracking and bowing of walls, or racking of structural members.
	Utilizing treatments or products that accelerate the deterioration of structural material such as introducing urea-formaldehyde foam insulation into frame walls.
Protecting and maintaining the structural system by cleaning the roof gutters and downspouts; replacing roof flashing; keeping masonry, wood, and architectural metals in a sound condition; and assuring that structural members are free from insect infestation.	Failing to provide proper building maintenance on a cyclical basis so that deterioration of the structural system results.
Examining and evaluating the physical condition of the structural system and its individual features using nondestructive techniques such as X-ray photography.	Utilizing destructive probing techniques that will damage or destroy structural material.
Repairing the structural system by augmenting or upgrading individual parts or features. For example, weakened structural members such as floor framing can be spliced, braced, or otherwise supplemented and reinforced.	Upgrading the building structurally in a manner that diminishes the historic character of the exterior, such as installing strapping channels or removing a decorative cornice; or damages interior features or spaces.
	Replacing a structural member or other feature of the structural system when it could be augmented and retained.
Replacing in kind—or with substitute material—those portions or features of the structural system that are either extensively deteriorated or are missing when there are surviving prototypes such as cast iron columns, roof rafters or trusses, or sections of loadbearing walls. Substitute material should convey the same form, design, and overall visual appearance as the historic feature; and, at a minimum, be equal to its loadbearing capabilities.	Installing a replacement feature that does not convey the same visual appearance, e.g., replacing an exposed wood summer beam with a steel beam.
	Using substitute material that does not equal the loadbearing capabilities of the historic material and design or is otherwise physically or chemically incompatible.

The following work is highlighted to indicate that it represents the particularly complex technical or design aspects of rehabilitation projects and should only be considered after the preservation concerns listed above have been addressed.

Alterations/Additions for the New Use

Recommended	*Not Recommended*
Limiting any new excavations adjacent to historic foundations to avoid undermining the structural stability of the building or adjacent historic buildings.	Carrying out excavations or regrading adjacent to or within a historic building which could cause the historic foundation to settle, shift, or fail; or could have a similar effect on adjacent historic buildings.
Correcting structural deficiencies in preparation for the new use in a manner that preserves the structural system and individual character-defining features.	Radically changing interior spaces or damaging or destroying features or finishes that are character-defining while trying to correct structural deficiencies in preparation for the new use.
Designing and installing new mechanical or electrical systems when required for the new use which minimize the number of cutouts or holes in structural members.	Installing new mechanical and electrical systems or equipment in a manner which results in numerous cuts, splices, or alterations to the structural members.
Adding a new floor when required for the new use if such an alteration does not damage or destroy the structural system or obscure, damage, or destroy character-defining spaces, features, or finishes.	Inserting a new floor when such a radical change damages a structural system or obscures or destroys interior spaces, features, or finishes.
	Inserting new floors or furred-down ceilings which cut across the glazed areas of windows so that the exterior form and appearance of the windows are radically changed.

Recommended

Creating an atrium or a light well to provide natural light when required for the new use in a manner that assures the preservation of the structural system as well as character-defining interior spaces, features, and finishes.

Not Recommended

Damaging the structural system or individual features; or radically changing, damaging, or destroying character-defining interior spaces, features, or finishes in order to create an atrium or a light well.

Interior: Spaces, Features, and Finishes

Recommended

Interior Spaces

Identifying, retaining, and preserving a floor plan or interior spaces that are important in defining the overall historic character of the building. This includes the size, configuration, proportion, and relationship of features to spaces; and the spaces themselves such as lobbies, reception halls, entrance halls, double parlors, theaters, auditoriums, and important industrial or commercial use spaces.

Not Recommended

Radically changing a floor plan or interior spaces—including individual rooms—which are important in defining the overall historic character of the building so that, as a result, the character is diminished.

Altering the floor plan by demolishing principal walls and partitions to create a new appearance.

Altering or destroying interior spaces by inserting floors, cutting through floors, lowering ceilings, or adding or removing walls.

Relocating an interior feature such as a staircase so that the historic relationship between features and spaces is altered.

Interior Features and Finishes

Identifying, retaining, and preserving interior features and finishes that are important in defining the overall historic character of the building, including columns, cornices, baseboards, fireplaces and mantles, paneling, light fixtures, hardware, and flooring; and wallpaper, plaster, paint, and finishes such as stenciling, marbling, and graining; and other decorative materials that accent interior features and provide color, texture, and patterning to walls, floors, and ceilings.

Removing or radically changing features and finishes which are important in defining the overall historic character of the building so that, as a result, the character is diminished.

Installing new decorative material that obscures or damages character-defining interior features or finishes.

Removing paint, plaster, or other finishes from historically finished surfaces to create a new appearance (e.g., removing plaster to expose masonry surfaces such as brick walls or a chimney piece).

Applying paint, plaster, or other finishes to surfaces that have been historically unfinished to create a new appearance.

Stripping historically painted wood surfaces to bare wood, then applying clear finishes or stains to create a "natural look."

Stripping paint to bare wood rather than repairing or reapplying grained or marbled finishes to features such as doors and paneling.

Radically changing the type of finish or its color, such as painting a previously varnished wood feature.

Protecting and maintaining masonry, wood, and architectural metals which comprise interior features through appropriate surface treatments such as cleaning, rust removal, limited paint removal, and reapplication of protective coatings systems.

Failing to provide adequate protection to materials on a cyclical basis so that deterioration of interior features results.

Protecting interior features and finishes against arson and vandalism before project work begins, erecting protective fencing, boarding-up windows, and installing fire alarm systems that are keyed to local protection agencies.

Permitting entry into historic buildings through unsecured or broken windows and doors so that interior features and finishes are damaged by exposure to weather or through vandalism.

Stripping interiors of features such as woodwork, doors, windows, light fixtures, copper piping, radiators; or of decorative materials.

Recommended

Protecting interior features such as a staircase, mantel, or decorative finishes and wall coverings against damage during project work by covering them with heavy canvas or plastic sheets.

Installing protective coverings in areas of heavy pedestrian traffic to protect historic features such as wall coverings, parquet flooring and panelling.

Removing damaged or deteriorated paints and finishes to the next sound layer using the gentlest method possible, then repainting or refinishing using compatible paint or other coating systems.

Repainting with colors that are appropriate to the historic building.

Limiting abrasive cleaning methods to certain industrial or warehouse buildings where the interior masonry or plaster features do not have distinguishing design, detailing, tooling, or finishes; and where wood features are not finished, molded, beaded, or worked by hand. Abrasive cleaning should *only* be considered after other, gentler methods have been proven ineffective.

Evaluating the overall condition of materials to determine whether more than protection and maintenance are required, that is, if repairs to interior features and finishes will be necessary.

Repairing interior features and finishes by reinforcing the historic materials. Repair will also generally include the limited replacement in kind—or with compatible substitute material—of those extensively deteriorated or missing parts of repeated features when there are surviving prototypes such as stairs, balustrades, wood panelling, columns; or decorative wall coverings or ornamental tin or plaster ceilings.

Replacing in kind an entire interior feature or finish that is too deteriorated to repair—if the overall form and detailing are still evident—using the physical evidence to guide the new work. Examples could include wainscoting, a tin ceiling, or interior stairs. If using the same kind of material is not technically or economically feasible, then a compatible substitute material may be considered.

Not Recommended

Failing to provide proper protection of interior features and finishes during work so that they are gouged, scratched, dented, or otherwise damaged.

Failing to take new use patterns into consideration so that interior features and finishes are damaged.

Using destructive methods such as propane or butane torches or sandblasting to remove paint or other coatings. These methods can irreversibly damage the historic materials that comprise interior features.

Using new paint colors that are inappropriate to the historic building.

Changing the texture and patina of character-defining features through sandblasting or use of other abrasive methods to remove paint, discoloration or plaster. This includes both exposed wood (including structural members) and masonry.

Failing to undertake adequate measures to assure the preservation of interior features and finishes.

Replacing an entire interior feature such as a staircase, panelled wall, parquet floor, or cornice; or finish such as a decorative wall covering or ceiling when repair of materials and limited replacement of such parts are appropriate.

Using a substitute material for the replacement part that does not convey the visual appearance of the surviving parts or portions of the interior feature or finish or that is physically or chemically incompatible.

Removing a character-defining feature or finish that is unrepairable and not replacing it; or replacing it with a new feature or finish that does not convey the same visual appearance.

The following work is highlighted to indicate that it represents the particularly complex technical or design aspects of rehabilitation projects and should only be considered after the preservation concerns listed above have been addressed.

Design for Missing Historic Features

Designing and installing a new interior feature or finish if the historic feature or finish is completely missing. This could include missing partitions, stairs, elevators, lighting fixtures, and wall coverings; or even entire rooms if all historic spaces, features and finishes are missing or have been destroyed by inappropriate "renovations." The design may be a restoration based on historical, pictorial, and physical documentation; or be a new design that is compatible with the historic character of the building, district, or neighborhood.

Creating a false historical appearance because the replaced feature is based on insufficient physical, historical, and pictorial documentation or on information derived from another building.

Introducing a new interior feature or finish that is incompatible with the scale, design, materials, color, and texture of the surviving interior features and finishes.

Alterations/Additions for the New Use

Recommended

Accommodating service functions such as bathrooms, mechanical equipment, and office machines required by the building's new use in secondary spaces such as first floor service areas or on upper floors.

Reusing decorative material or features that have had to be removed during the rehabilitation work including wall and baseboard trim, door moulding, paneled doors, and simple wainscoting; and relocating such material or features in areas appropriate to their historic placement.

Installing permanent partitions in secondary spaces; removable partitions that do not destroy the sense of space should be installed when the new use requires the subdivision of character-defining interior spaces.

Enclosing an interior stairway where required by code so that its character is retained. In many cases, glazed fire-rated walls may be used.

Placing new code-required stairways or elevators in secondary and service areas of the historic building.

Creating an atrium or a light well to provide natural light when required for the new use in a manner that preserves character-defining interior spaces, features, and finishes as well as the structural system.

Adding a new floor if required for the new use in a manner that preserves character-defining structural features, and interior spaces, features, and finishes.

Not Recommended

Dividing rooms, lowering ceilings, and damaging or obscuring character-defining features such as fireplaces, niches, stairways or alcoves, so that a new use can be accommodated in the building.

Discarding historic material when it can be reused within the rehabilitation project or relocating it in historically inappropriate areas.

Installing permanent partitions that damage or obscure character-defining spaces, features, or finishes.

Enclosing an interior stairway with fire-rated construction so that the stairwell space or any character-defining features are destroyed.

Radically changing, damaging, or destroying character-defining spaces, features, or finishes when adding new code-required stairways and elevators.

Destroying character-defining interior spaces, features, or finishes; or damaging the structural system in order to create an atrium or light well.

Inserting a new floor within a building that alters or destroys the fenestration; radically changes a character-defining interior space; or obscures, damages, or destroys decorative detailing.

Mechanical Systems: Heating, Air Conditioning, Electrical, and Plumbing

Recommended

Identifying, retaining, and preserving visible features of early mechanical systems that are important in defining the overall historic character of the building, such as radiators, vents, fans, grilles, plumbing fixtures, switchplates, and lights.

Protecting and maintaining mechanical, plumbing, and electrical systems and their features through cyclical cleaning and other appropriate measures.

Preventing accelerated deterioration of mechanical systems by providing adequate ventilation of attics, crawlspaces, and cellars so that moisture problems are avoided.

Repairing mechanical systems by augmenting or upgrading system parts, such as installing new pipes and ducts; rewiring; or adding new compressors or boilers.

Replacing in kind—or with compatible substitute material—those visible features of mechanical systems that are either extensively deteriorated or are missing when there are surviving prototypes such as ceiling fans, switchplates, radiators, grilles, or plumbing fixtures.

Not Recommended

Removing or radically changing features of mechanical systems that are important in defining the overall historic character of the building so that, as a result, the character is diminished.

Failing to provide adequate protection of materials on a cyclical basis so that deterioration of mechanical systems and their visible features results.

Enclosing mechanical systems in areas that are not adequately ventilated so that deterioration of the systems results.

Replacing a mechanical system or its functional parts when it could be upgraded and retained.

Installing a replacement feature that does not convey the same visual appearance.

The following work is highlighted to indicate that it represents the particularly complex technical or design aspects of rehabilitation projects and should only be considered after the preservation concerns listed above have been addressed.

Alterations/Additions for the New Use

Recommended

Installing a completely new mechanical system if required for the new use so that it causes the least alteration possible to the building's floor plan, the exterior elevations, and the least damage to historic building material.

Installing the vertical runs of ducts, pipes, and cables in closets, service rooms, and wall cavities.

Installing air conditioning units if required by the new use in such a manner that the historic materials and features are not damaged or obscured.

Installing heating/air conditioning units in the window frames in such a manner that the sash and frames are protected. Window installations should be considered only when all other viable heating/cooling systems would result in significant damage to historic materials.

Not Recommended

Installing a new mechanical system so that character-defining structural or interior features are radically changed, damaged, or destroyed.

Installing vertical runs of ducts, pipes, and cables in places where they will obscure character-defining features.

Concealing mechanical equipment in walls or ceilings in a manner that requires the removal of historic building material.

Installing "dropped" acoustical ceilings to hide mechanical equipment when this destroys the proportions of character-defining interior spaces.

Cutting through features such as masonry walls in order to install air conditioning units.

Radically changing the appearance of the historic building or damaging or destroying windows by installing heating/air conditioning units in historic window frames.

BUILDING SITE

Recommended

Identifying, retaining, and preserving buildings and their features as well as features of the site that are important in defining its overall historic character. Site features can include driveways, walkways, lighting, fencing, signs, benches, fountains, wells, terraces, canal systems, plants and trees, berms, and drainage or irrigation ditches; and archeological features that are important in defining the history of the site.

Retaining the historic relationship between buildings, landscape features, and open space.

Protecting and maintaining buildings and the site by providing proper drainage to assure that water does not erode foundation walls; drain toward the building; nor erode the historic landscape.

Minimizing disturbance of terrain around buildings or elsewhere on the site, thus reducing the possibility of destroying unknown archeological materials.

Not Recommended

Removing or radically changing buildings and their features or site features which are important in defining the overall historic character of the building site so that, as a result, the character is diminished.

Removing or relocating historic buildings or landscape features, thus destroying the historic relationship between buildings, landscape features, and open space.

Removing or relocating historic buildings on a site or in a complex of related historic structures—such as a mill complex or farm—thus diminishing the historic character of the site or complex.

Moving buildings onto the site, thus creating a false historical appearance.

Lowering the grade level adjacent to a building to permit development of a formerly below-grade area such as a basement in a manner that would drastically change the historic relationship of the building to its site.

Failing to maintain site drainage so that buildings and site features are damaged or destroyed; or, alternatively, changing the site grading so that water no longer drains properly.

Introducing heavy machinery or equipment into areas where their presence may disturb archeological materials.

Recommended	Not Recommended
Surveying areas where major terrain alteration is likely to impact important archeological sites.	Failing to survey the building site prior to the beginning of rehabilitation project work so that, as a result, important archeological material is destroyed.
Protecting, e.g. preserving in place known archeological material whenever possible.	Leaving known archeological material unprotected and subject to vandalism, looting, and destruction by natural elements such as erosion.
Planning and carrying out any necessary investigation using professional archeologists and modern archeological methods when preservation in place is not feasible.	Permitting unqualified project personnel to perform data recovery so that improper methodology results in the loss of important archeological material.
Protecting the building and other features of the site against arson and vandalism before rehabilitation work begins, i.e., erecting protective fencing and installing alarm systems that are keyed into local protection agencies.	Permitting buildings and site features to remain unprotected so that plant materials, fencing, walkways, archeological features, etc. are damaged or destroyed.
	Stripping features from buildings and the site such as wood siding, iron fencing, masonry balustrades; or removing or destroying landscape features, including plant material.
Providing continued protection of masonry, wood, and architectural metals which comprise building and site features through appropriate surface treatments such as cleaning, rust removal, limited paint removal, and re-application of protective coating systems; and continued protection and maintenance of landscape features, including plant material.	Failing to provide adequate protection of materials on a cyclical basis so that deterioration of building and site features results.
Evaluating the overall condition of materials to determine whether more than protection and maintenance are required, that is, if repairs to building and site features will be necessary.	Failing to undertake adequate measures to assure the preservation of building and site features.
Repairing features of buildings and the site by reinforcing the historic materials. Repair will also generally include replacement in kind—with a compatible substitute material—of those extensively deteriorated or missing parts of features where there are surviving prototypes such as fencing and paving.	Replacing an entire feature of the building or site such as a fence, walkway, or driveway when repair of materials and limited replacement of deteriorated or missing parts are appropriate.
	Using a substitute material for the replacement part that does not convey the visual appearance of the surviving parts of the building or site feature or that is physically or chemically incompatible.
Replacing in kind an entire feature of the building or site that is too deteriorated to repair—if the overall form and detailing are still evident—using the physical evidence to guide the new work. This could include an entrance or porch, walkway, or fountain. If using the same kind of material is not technically or economically feasible, then a compatible substitute material may be considered.	Removing a feature of the building or site that is unrepairable and not replacing it; or replacing it with a new feature that does not convey the same visual appearance.

The following work is highlighted to indicate that it represents the particularly complex technical or design aspects of rehabilitation projects and should only be considered after the preservation concerns listed above have been addressed.

Design for Missing Historic Features

Recommended	Not Recommended
Designing and constructing a new feature of a building or site when the historic feature is completely missing, such as an outbuilding, terrace, or driveway. It may be based on historical, pictorial, or physical documentation; or be a new design that is compatible with the historic character of the building and site.	Creating a false historical appearance because the replaced feature is based on insufficient historical, pictorial, and physical documentation.
	Introducing a new building or site feature that is out of scale or otherwise inappropriate.
	Introducing a new landscape feature or plant material that is visually incompatible with the site or that destroys site patterns or vistas.

Alterations/Additions for the New Use

Recommended

Designing new onsite parking, loading docks, or ramps when required by the new use so that they are as unobtrusive as possible and assure the preservation of character-defining features of the site.

Designing new exterior additions to historic buildings or adjacent new construction which is compatible with the historic character of the site and which preserve the historic relationship between a building or buildings, landscape features, and open space.

Removing nonsignificant buildings, additions, or site features which detract from the historic character of the site.

Not Recommended

Placing parking facilities directly adjacent to historic buildings where automobiles may cause damage to the buildings or landscape features or be intrusive to the building site.

Introducing new construction onto the building site which is visually incompatible in terms of size, scale, design, materials, color and texture or which destroys historic relationships on the site.

Removing a historic building in a complex, a building feature, or a site feature which is important in defining the historic character of the site.

DISTRICT/NEIGHBORHOOD

Recommended

Identifying, retaining, and preserving buildings, and streetscape, and landscape features which are important in defining the overall historic character of the district or neighborhood. Such features can include streets, alleys, paving, walkways, street lights, signs, benches, parks and gardens, and trees.

Retaining the historic relationship between buildings, and streetscape and landscape features such as a town square comprised of row houses and stores surrounding a communal park or open space.

Protecting and maintaining the historic masonry, wood, and architectural metals which comprise building and streetscape features, through appropriate surface treatments such as cleaning, rust removal, limited paint removal, and reapplication of protective coating systems; and protecting and maintaining landscape features, including plant material.

Protecting buildings, paving, iron fencing, etc. against arson and vandalism before rehabilitation work begins by erecting protective fencing and installing alarm systems that are keyed into local protection agencies.

Evaluating the overall condition of building, streetscape and landscape materials to determine whether more than protection and maintenance are required, that is, if repairs to features will be necessary.

Repairing features of the building, streetscape, or landscape by reinforcing the historic materials. Repair will also generally include the replacement in kind—or with a compatible substitute material—of those extensively deteriorated or missing parts of features when there are surviving prototypes such as porch balustrades, paving materials, or streetlight standards.

Not Recommended

Removing or radically changing those features of the district or neighborhood which are important in defining the overall historic character so that, as a result, the character is diminished.

Destroying streetscape and landscape features by widening existing streets, changing paving material, or introducing inappropriately located new streets or parking lots.

Removing or relocating historic buildings, or features of the streetscape and landscape, thus destroying the historic relationship between buildings, features and open space.

Failing to provide adequate protection of materials on a cyclical basis so that deterioration of building, streetscape, and landscape features results.

Permitting buildings to remain unprotected so that windows are broken; and interior features are damaged.

Stripping features from buildings or the streetscape such as wood siding, iron fencing, or terra cotta balusters; or removing or destroying landscape features, including plant material.

Failing to undertake adequate measures to assure the preservation of building, streetscape, and landscape features.

Replacing an entire feature of the building, streetscape, or landscape such as a porch, walkway, or streetlight, when repair of materials and limited replacement of deteriorated or missing parts are appropriate.

Using a substitute material for the replacement part that does not convey the visual appearance of the surviving parts of the building, streetscape, or landscape feature or that is physically or chemically incompatible.

Recommended

Replacing in kind an entire feature of the building, streetscape, or landscape that is too deteriorated to repair—when the overall form and detailing are still evident—using the physical evidence to guide the new work. This could include a storefront, a walkway, or a garden. If using the same kind of material is not technically or economically feasible, then a compatible substitute material may be considered.

Not Recommended

Removing a feature of the building, streetscape, or landscape that is unrepairable and not replacing it; or replacing it with a new feature that does not convey the same visual appearances.

The following work is highlighted because it represents the particularly complex technical or design aspects of rehabilitation projects and should only be considered after the preservation concerns listed above have been addressed.

Recommended

Design for Missing Historic Features

Designing and constructing a new feature of the building, streetscape, or landscape when the historic feature is completely missing, such as row house steps, a porch, streetlight, or terrace. It may be a restoration based on historical, pictorial, and physical documentation; or be a new design that is compatible with the historic character of the district or neighborhood.

Alterations/Additions for the New Use

Designing required new parking so that it is as unobtrusive as possible, i.e., on side streets or at the rear of buildings. "Shared" parking should also be planned so that several businesses can utilize one parking lot as opposed to introducing random, multiple lots.

Designing and constructing new additions to historic buildings when required by the new use. New work should be compatible with the historic character of the district or neighborhood in terms of size, scale, design, material, color, and texture.

Removing nonsignificant buildings, additions, or streetscape and landscape features which detract from the historic character of the district or the neighborhood.

Not Recommended

Creating a false historical appearance because the replaced feature is based on insufficient historical, pictorial and physical documentation.

Introducing a new building, streetscape or landscape feature that is out of scale or otherwise inappropriate to the setting's historic character, e.g., replacing picket fencing with chain link fencing.

Placing parking facilities directly adjacent to historic buildings which cause the removal of historic plantings, relocation of paths and walkways, or blocking of alleys.

Introducing new construction into historic districts that is visually incompatible or that destroys historic relationships within the district or neighborhood.

Removing a historic building, building feature, or landscape or streetscape feature that is important in defining the overall historic character of the district or the neighborhood.

ENERGY EFFICIENCY

Recommended

District/Neighborhood

Maintaining those existing landscape features which moderate the effects of the climate on the setting such as deciduous trees, evergreen wind-blocks, and lakes or ponds.

Building Site

Retaining plant materials, streets, and landscape features, especially those which perform passive solar energy functions such as sun shading and wind breaks.

Installing freestanding solar collectors in a manner that preserves the historic property's character-defining features.

Designing attached solar collectors, including solar greenhouses, so that the character-defining features of the property are preserved.

Not Recommended

Stripping the setting of landscape features and landforms so that the effects of the wind, rain, and the sun result in accelerated deterioration of historic materials.

Removing plant materials, trees, and landscape features, so that they no longer perform passive solar energy functions.

Installing freestanding solar collectors that obscure, damage, or destroy historic landscape or archeological features.

Locating solar collectors where they radically change the property's appearance; or damage or destroy character-defining features.

Recommended	*Not Recommended*

Masonry/Wood/Architectural Metals

Installing thermal insulation in attics and in unheated cellars and crawlspaces to increase the efficiency of the existing mechanical systems.

Applying urea of formaldehyde foam or any other thermal insulation with a water content into wall cavities in an attempt to reduce energy consumption.

Installing insulating material on the inside of masonry walls to increase energy efficiency where there is no character-defining interior moulding around the window or other interior architectural detailing.

Resurfacing historic building materials with more energy efficient but incompatible materials, such as covering historic masonry with exterior insulation.

Installing passive solar devices such as a glazed "trombe" wall on a rear or inconspicuous side of all the historic building.

Installing passive solar devices such as an attached glazed "trombe" wall on primary or other highly visible elevations; or where historic material must be removed or obscured.

Roofs

Placing solar collectors on noncharacter-defining roofs or roofs of nonhistoric adjacent buildings.

Placing solar collectors on roofs when such collectors change the historic roofline or obscure the relationship of the roof to character-defining roof features such as dormers, skylights, and chimneys.

Windows

Utilizing the inherent energy conserving features of a building by maintaining windows and louvered blinds in good operable condition for natural ventilation.

Removing historic shading devices rather than keeping them in an operable condition.

Improving thermal efficiency with weatherstripping, storm windows, caulking, interior shades, and, if historically appropriate, blinds and awnings.

Replacing historic multi-paned sash with new thermal sash utilizing false muntins.

Installing interior storm windows with airtight gaskets, ventilating holes, and/or removable clips to insure proper maintenance and to avoid condensation damage to historic windows.

Installing interior storm windows that allow moisture to accumulate and damage the window.

Installing exterior storm windows which do not damage or obscure the windows and frames.

Installing new exterior storm windows which are inappropriate in size or color, which are inoperable.

Replacing windows or transoms with fixed thermal glazing or permitting windows and transoms to remain inoperable rather than utilizing them for their energy conserving potential.

Considering the use of lightly tinted glazing on non-character-defining elevations if other energy retro-fitting alternatives are not possible.

Using tinted or reflective glazing on character-defining or other conspicuous elevations.

Entrances and Porches

Utilizing the inherent energy conserving features of a building by maintaining porches, and double vestibule entrances in good condition so that they can retain heat or block the sun and provide natural ventilation.

Enclosing porches located on character defining elevations to create passive solar collectors or airlock vestibules. Such enclosures can destroy the historic appearance of the building.

Interior Features

Retaining historic interior shutters and transoms for their inherent energy conserving features.

Removing historic interior features which play a secondary energy conserving role.

New Additions to Historic Buildings

Placing new additions that have an energy conserving function such as a solar greenhouse on non-character-defining elevations.

Installing new additions such as multistory solar greenhouse additions which obscure, damage, destroy character-defining features.

Mechanical Systems

Installing thermal insulation in attics and in unheated cells and crawlspaces to conserve energy.

Apply urea formaldehyde foam or any other thermal insulation with a water content or that may collect moisture into wall cavities.

NEW ADDITIONS TO HISTORIC BUILDINGS

Recommended

Placing functions and services required for the new use in non-character-defining interior spaces rather than installing a new addition.

Constructing a new addition so that there is the least possible loss of historic materials and so that character-defining features are not obscured, damaged, or destroyed.

Locating the attached exterior addition at the rear or on an inconspicuous side of a historic building; and limiting its size and scale in relationship to the historic building.

Designing new additions in a manner that makes clear what is historic and what is new.

Considering the attached exterior addition both in terms of the new use and the appearance of other buildings in the historic district or neighborhood. Design for the new work may be contemporary or may reference design motifs from the historic building. In either case, it should always be clearly differentiated from the historic building and be compatible in terms of mass, materials, relationship of solids to voids, and color.

Placing new additions such as balconies and greenhouses on non-character-defining elevations and limiting the size and scale in relationship to the historic building.

Designing additional stories, when required for the new use, that are set back from the wall plane and are as inconspicuous as possible when viewed from the street.

Not Recommended

Expanding the size of the historic building by constructing a new addition when the new use could be met by altering non-character-defining interior spaces.

Attaching a new addition so that the character-defining features of the historic building are obscured, damaged, or destroyed.

Designing a new addition so that its size and scale in relation to the historic building are out of proportion, thus diminishing the historic character.

Duplicating the exact form, material, style, and detailing of the historic building in the new addition so that the new work appears to be part of the historic building.

Imitating a historic style or period of architecture in new additions, especially for contemporary uses such as drive-in banks or garages.

Designing and constructing new additions that result in the diminution or loss of the historic character of the resource, including its design, materials, workmanship, location, or setting.

Using the same wall plane, roof line, cornice height, materials, siding lap or window type to make additions appear to be a part of the historic building.

Designing new additions such as multistory greenhouse additions that obscure, damage, or destroy character-defining features of the historic building.

Constructing additional stories so that the historic appearance of the building is radically changed.

ACCESSIBILITY CONSIDERATIONS

Recommended

Not Recommended

HEALTH AND SAFETY CONSIDERATIONS

Recommended

Identifying the historic building's character-defining spaces, features, and finishes so that code-required work will not result in their damage or loss.

Complying with health and safety code, including seismic codes and barrier-free access requirements, in such a manner that character-defining spaces, features, and finishes are preserved.

Working with local code officials to investigate alternative life safety measures or variances available under some codes so that alterations and additions to historic buildings can be avoided.

Providing barrier-free access through removable or portable, rather than permanent, ramps.

Not Recommended

Undertaking code-required alterations to a building or site before identifying those spaces, features, or finishes which are character-defining and must therefore be preserved.

Altering, damaging, or destroying character-defining spaces, features, and finishes while making modifications to a building or site to comply with safety codes.

Making changes to historic buildings without first seeking alternatives to code requirements.

Installing permanent ramps that damage or diminish character-defining features.

Recommended

Providing seismic reinforcement to a historic building in a manner that avoids damaging the structural system and character-defining features.

Upgrading historic stairways and elevators to meet health and safety codes in a manner that assures their preservation, i.e., so that they are not damaged or obscured.

Installing sensitively designed fire suppression systems, such as a sprinkler system for wood frame mill buildings, instead of applying fire-resistant sheathing to character-defining features.

Applying fire-retardant coatings, such as intumescent paints, which expand during fire to add thermal protection to steel.

Adding a new stairway or elevator to meet health and safety codes in a manner that preserves adjacent character-defining features and spaces.

Placing a code-required stairway or elevator that cannot be accommodated within the historic building in a new exterior addition. Such an addition should be located at the rear of the building or on an inconspicuous side; and its size and scale limited in relationship to the historic building.

Not Recommended

Reinforcing a historic building using measures that damage or destroy character-defining structural and other features.

Damaging or obscuring historic stairways and elevators or altering adjacent spaces in the process of doing work to meet code requirements.

Covering character-defining wood features with fire-resistant sheathing which results in altering their visual appearance.

Using fire-retardant coatings if they damage or obscure character-defining features.

Radically changing, damaging, or destroying character-defining spaces, features, or finishes when adding a new code-required stairway or elevator.

Constructing a new addition to accommodate code-required stairs and elevators on character-defining elevations highly visible from the street; or where it obscures, damages or destroys character-defining features.

Preservation Resources

Following are some notable organizations that address historic preservation. Several offer their own publications and can be used for further research.

NATIONAL ORGANIZATIONS

Advisory Council on Historic Preservation
(USICCROM Member)
http://www.achp.gov/iccrom.html
1100 Pennsylvania Avenue NW, Suite 809
Old Post Office Building
Washington, D.C. 20004
Tel. 202-606-8503

American Association of Museums
http://www.aam-us.org/
1575 Eye Street NW, Suite 400
Washington, D.C. 20005
Tel. 202-289-1818
Fax 202-289-6578

American Association for State and Local History
http://www.aaslh.org/
1717 Church Street
Nashville, TN 37203-2991
Tel. 615-320-3203
Fax 615-327-9013

The American Institute of Architects Historic Resources Committee
http://www.aia.org/hrc_default
1735 New York Avenue NW
Washington, D.C. 20006-5292
Tel. 202-626-7300
Fax 202-626-7547

The Getty Conservation Institute (GCI)
http://www.getty.edu/conservation/
1200 Getty Center Drive, Suite 700
Los Angeles, CA 90049-1684
Tel. 310-440-7325
Fax 310-440-7702

The Getty Grant Program
http://www.getty.edu/grants/conservation/
1200 Getty Center Drive
Los Angeles, CA 90049-1679
Tel. 310-440-7300

National Trust for Historic Preservation
http://www.nationaltrust.org/
1785 Massachusetts Avenue NW
Washington, D.C. 20036-2117
Tel. 202-588-6000

National Park Service
http://www.nps.gov
1849 C Street NW
Washington, D.C. 20240
Tel. 202-208-6843
National Park Service cultural resources publications service-wide may be found online at
http://www.cr.nps.gov/linkpubs.htm

National Conference of State Historic Preservation Officers
http://www.ncshpo.org/
Suite 342 Hall of the States
444 North Capitol Street NW
Washington, D.C. 20001-7572
Tel. 202-624-5465
Fax 202-624-5419

United States Committee, International Council on Monuments and Sites (USICOMOS)
http://www.icomos.org/usicomos/
401 F Street, NW Suite 331
Washington, D.C. 20001-2728
Tel. 202-842-1866
Fax 202-842-1861

World Monuments Fund (WMF)
http://wmf.org/
95 Madison Avenue, 9th Floor
New York, NY 10016
Tel. 646-424-9594
Fax 646-424-9593

INTERNATIONAL ORGANIZATIONS

Aga Khan Trust for Culture
http://www.akdn.org/agency/aktc.html
1-3 Avenue de la Paix
1202 Geneva, Switzerland
Tel. (41.22) 909 72 00
Fax (41.22) 909 72 92

Documentation and Conservation of the Modern Movement (DOCOMOMO)
http://www.docomomo.com
Institut Français d'Architecture
Palais de la Porte Dorée
293 av. Daumesnil
75012 Paris, France
Tel. +33 (0)1 58 51 52 65
Fax +33 (0)1 58 51 52 20

International Centre for the Study of the Preservation and Restoration of Cultural Property (ICCROM)
http://www.iccrom.org/
Via di San Michele 13
I-00153 Rome, Italy
Tel. +39 06 585531

International Council on Monuments and Sites (ICOMOS)
http://www.icomos.org/
49-51 rue de la Fédération 75015 Paris, France
Tel. +33 (0)1 45 67 67 70
Fax +33 (0)1 45 66 06 22

International Council of Museums (ICOM)
http://icom.museum
ICOM, Maison de l'UNESCO
1 rue Miollis
75732 Paris cedex 15, France.
Tel. (33 1) 4734 0500
Fax (33 1) 4306 7862

Organization of World Heritage Cities
http://www.ovpm.org
15, rue Saint-Nicolas
Québec (Québec), Canada, G1K 1M8
Tel. 418-692-0000
Fax 418-692-5558

United Nations Educational, Scientific, and Cultural Organization (UNESCO)
http://www.unesco.org/culture
7, Place de Fontenoy
75352 Paris 07 SP, France
Tel. +33 (0)1 45 68 10 00
Fax +33 (0)1 45 67 16 90

The World Bank Group
http://www.worldbank.org
1818 H Street NW
Washington, D.C. 20433
Tel. 202-473-1000
Fax 202-477-6391

World Heritage Centre (WHC)
http://whc.unesco.org/
7 Place de Fontenoy 75007 Paris, France
+33 (0)1 45 68 1571
+33 (0)1 45 68 5570

Glossary

OVER the years, and especially since 1966, a specialized vocabulary of words and phrases has developed which is basic to an understanding of preservation. The definitions that follow constitute a majority of terms in current usage, but not all. Please note that some terms, such as *renovation, handicapped access*, and others may have slightly different meanings here than they do in common parlance. Since many of them represent the relatively new language of recent forms of preservation, a percentage may not be found in conventional dictionaries. The publications of the National Park Service and the National Trust for Historic Preservation have been the primary sources from which the definitions have been taken verbatim or adapted by the author. The reader is advised to consult the publications of both of these organizations for further information.

Abandonment. Giving up ownership or control of property.

Above-ground archaeology. The close scrutiny of a building or an above-ground artifact visible to the eye.

Adaptive use. The process of converting a building to a use other than that for which it was designed, e.g., changing a factory into housing. Such a conversion is accomplished with varying alterations to the building.

Ambiance. A French term signifying environment and the atmosphere of the sense of place.

Amenity. A structure or environmental feature that by common consent is seen to make a positive aesthetic contribution of more than a utilitarian nature to the environment.

Amicus curiae. A Latin term used in law meaning a "friend of the court," in which an organization or individual, usually with special expertise, is allowed to testify in a court of law on the issue in question before that court.

Antineglect ordinance. A municipal statute that prevents the local preservation effort from being undermined by individual property owners in the designated preservation area who willfully allow their property to deteriorate.

Archaeology. The study of past human lifeways through evidence found in the ground.

Architectural scientific conservation. The act of applying museum scientific object methodologies and materials to existing historic buildings in an effort to stabilize and retain original building fabric in the restoration process rather than replacing it with new parts.

Artifact. A man-made object that is a form of archaeological data.

Background buildings. In the built environment, buildings that are essential in maintaining a sense of place and locality and which identify the environment of landmarks, but which are not themselves of landmark quality. (*See* Sense of place.)

Balance. The harmonious integration of the sum of the parts of a building which gives it visual appeal and character.

Blockbusting. The process by which speculators attempt to depress a given area's property values for purchase and ultimate resale at inflated prices.

Boutique syndrome. The replacement of service-oriented businesses by specialty shops catering to tourism.

Built environment. That portion of the environment that has been created by human efforts. In an urban setting the built portion approaches totality of environment. Preservation is based on the idea that the built environment should be respected and conserved as carefully as the natural environment. The term is preferred over *man-made environment*.

Certificate of appropriateness. A permit to proceed with new construction or alterations to a property within a historic district after the proposed changes have been reviewed against applicable criteria by a local body (usually called an *architectural review board, preservation commission*, or some similar title).

Certified historic structure. Any building that is listed individually in the National Register of Historic Places, or a building that is located in a registered historic district and certified by the secretary of the interior as being of historic significance to the district.

Certified rehabilitation. Any rehabilitation of a certified historic structure that the secretary of the interior has determined is consistent with the historic character of the property and/or the district where it may be located.

Cityscape. *See* Urban Landscape, Townscape, Streetscape.

Codes. Regulations of building practices, the enforcement of which helps to ensure neighborhood upkeep and stability.

Commercial archaeology. The study of structures and artifacts of commercial activity, such as diners, motels, gasoline stations, and signs.

Conservation archaeology. The practice of minimal excavation to preserve the archaeological site for future investigation and/or interpretation by visitors.

Cultural landscape. A geographic area, including both cultural and natural resources and the wildlife or domestic animals therein, associated with an historic event, activity or person, or exhibiting other cultural or aesthetic values.

Cultural resource. A building, structure, district, site, or object that is significant in American history, architecture, archaeology, or culture.

Curator. A professionally trained person responsible for the care, custodianship, study and interpretation of artifacts in a museum or at an archaeological or similar site.

Demolition. The premeditated process of completely destroying a building by tearing it down or imploding it. (*See* Implosion.)

Demolition by neglect. The gradual destruction of a building because of lack of maintenance.

Demolition delay. A temporary halt to the destruction of a building, usually by court injunction, which allows preservationists time to negotiate.

Design guidelines. Criteria, locally developed, that identify local design concerns, drawn up in an effort to assist property owners to respect and maintain the character of the designated district or buildings in the process of rehabilitation and new construction.

Design review. The local process of determining whether new construction or proposed changes to buildings in an historic district meet the standards of appropriateness established by the local review board.

Destruction. The process of destroying a site, building, object, district, or structure, in part or completely, usually by an accident such as fire or earthquake.

Deterioration. The process of making a structure's condition worse, by lack of maintenance, normal wear and tear, and/or exposure to weather.

Disinvestment. *See* Reinvestment.

Dismantle. To take a structure apart systematically, usually with the intention of re-erecting it somewhere else.

Displacement. The removal of individuals, commercial businesses, and industry from a given area because of increased property values created by escalating real estate activities.

Docent. A guide in a museum, responsible for educating visitors about the collections and/or buildings.

Double decking. The practice of inserting a mezzanine or new floor in a high-ceilinged room to double the usable square footage.

Easement. A partial interest in real property, through donation or purchase, recorded in the deed, protecting the identifying elements of the interior/exterior or space around the property deemed important to be preserved.

Eminent domain. The right of government to acquire private property for the public benefit, with just compensation to the owner.

Enabling legislation. The legal authorization of federal or state governing bodies to delegate powers or enact specific measures such as historic district ordinances, taxation, or zoning.

Fabric. The physical material or component parts of a building or city plan, interwoven as in the warp and woof of cloth.

Façadism. The retention of only the façade of a historic building during the conversion

process, in which the remainder of the structure is severely altered or totally destroyed.

Feasibility study. An evaluative analysis of anticipated conversion costs, physical condition, appropriate use, anticipated revenues, time schedule, and other factors of a proposed project.

Gentrification. The replacement of lower socioeconomic individuals by more affluent groups in a neighborhood rehabilitation/preservation process.

Handicapped access. Accessibility to a building by the handicapped by means that minimally intrude on the architectural integrity of a historic building.

Heritage tourism. Traveling to experience the places and activities that authentically represent the stories and people of the past and present.

Historic district. A geographically definable area—urban or rural, large or small—possessing a significant concentration, linkage, or continuity of sites, buildings, structures, and/or objects united by past events or aesthetically by plan or physical development.

Historic district ordinance. A local law that designates and attempts to protect a neighborhood or area of preservable potential.

Historic house museum. A public or private educational institution, usually nonprofit, whose structure is itself of historical or architectural importance and whose interpretation relates primarily to the building's architecture, furnishings, and history. (*See* Interpretation.)

Historic landscape. An area that has had associated with it an event or series of events of historical note. A historic landscape may also be the visual perception of a particular period of civilization, a way of life, or pattern of living.

Historical archaeology. The study of cultural remains of literate societies with recorded histories.

Homesteading. A local program by which abandoned buildings are given or sold for token fees to individuals agreeing to rehabilitate them and live in them for a specified period of time.

Implosion. The destruction of a building by blowing it up so that it collapses inward.

Industrial archaeology. The study of the history and development of the physical evidence of engineering and industry.

Infill. Descriptive of buildings that have been designed and built to replace missing structures or otherwise fill gaps in the streetscape. Infilling can mean replacing a rowhouse destroyed by fire, for example. Preservationists are concerned that the design of infill architecture be compatible in such elements as height, proportion, and materials.

Interpretation. The educational methods by which the history and meaning of historic sites, buildings, objects, districts, and structures are explained by use of docents, leaflets, tape recordings, signs, film, and other means.

Landmarks register. A listing of sites, buildings, objects, districts, and structures of potential preservation interest which may carry some sort of legal protection when listed.

Landscape. A view or vista of land in which natural and built environments are sometimes combined.

Landscape archaeology. The study of the land contours and vegetative evidence as indicators of original use and sites of potential archaeological interest and value.

Leverage. Maximizing the use of a small amount of funding by attracting additional funds to provide sufficient capital for a project.

Living history. A relatively recent interpretive approach at a historic site in which historical events and techniques are acted out, emphasizing the participation of visitors.

Living history farm. A working farm which is operated by using the everyday objects and tools of the past for educational purposes. (*See* Material culture.)

Mass. The physical volume or bulk of a building, its arrangement and organization.

Material culture. The concern for an interest in objects of everyday past life which are modified over time.

Mixed use. A term used to signify an authorized variety of uses in a given area, as opposed to the single use called for in most zoned areas.

Mixed-use development. A large real estate development, which may incorporate historic buildings, characterized by a comprehensive plan of variable revenue-producing uses, such as retail, office, residential, and hotel.

Museum village. *See* Outdoor museum.

National Heritage Area. A place where natural, cultural, historic, and scenic resources combine to form a cohesive, nationally distinctive landscape arising from patterns of human activity shaped by geography.

Nonconforming intrusion. Any building or structure in a neighborhood or historic district that has a high degree of incongruity with other buildings and structures in the area, producing a negative visual effect detrimental to the cohesiveness of the sense of place and locality.

Outdoor museum. A restored, re-created or replicated village site in which several or many structures have been restored, rebuilt, or moved and whose purpose is to interpret a historical or cultural setting, period, or activity.

Period room. A collection of artifacts, furnishings, and ceiling, wall, and floor treatments arranged in a gallery or museum space to approximate the way they would have been arranged during the period of time that they represent.

Police power. The right of government to restrict the use of property (through zoning, for example) and individual conduct (denial of demolition, for example) in the interest of the public safety, health, and welfare.

Prehistoric archaeology. The study of extant cultural remains of societies that existed prior to recorded history.

Preservation. The act or process of applying measures to sustain the existing form, integrity, and material of a building or structure and the existing form and vegetative cover of a site. It may include initial stabilization work, where necessary, as well as ongoing maintenance of the historic building materials and vegetation.

Preservation commission. A generic term usually applied to a municipal agency with the basic responsibility of designating and regulating historic landmarks and districts, sometimes referred to as an *architectural board of review* or by some similar title.

Preservation technology. The understanding of the original construction of historic structures and their settings, the analysis and diagnosis of the current conditions, and the application of this knowledge and new technology to the maintenance and conservation of historic properties.

Proportion. As an expression of artistic endeavor, the relation between parts in relevance to the whole (height to width, for example), which helps create visual order in architecture.

Public archaeology. Government-funded archaeological programs and projects.

Raze. To totally demolish a building by any process.

Reconstruction. The act or process of reproducing by new construction the exact form and detail of a vanished building, structure, or object or a part thereof, as it appeared at a specific period of time.

Redlining. The arbitrary refusal of financial and insurance institutions to invest in areas considered to be high risk.

Redundant building. *See* Surplus property.

Registered historic district. Any district that is listed in the National Register of Historic Places or a district that is designated under a state or local statute certified by the secretary of the interior as containing criteria sufficient to achieve preservation of the buildings in the district. Such a designation certifies that the area substantially meets all the requirements for listing in the National Register.

Rehabilitation. The act or process of returning a property to a state of utility through repair or alteration that makes possible an efficient contemporary use, while preserving those portions or features of the property that are significant to its historical, architectural, and cultural values.

Rehabilitation guide. Standards developed to assist property owners in preserving or restoring the historic architectural qualities of their buildings.

Reinvestment. The organized channeling of public and private monies into a depressed neighborhood to combat the withdrawal of investment (known as *disinvestment*).

Relocation. The process of moving households or businesses to a new location, usually because of urban renewal or similar governmental actions. (*See* Displacement.)

Renovation. Questionable modernization of a historic building in which inappropriate alterations are made and important features and details eliminated.

Rescue archaeology. *See* Salvage archaeology.

Restoration. The act or process of accurately recovering the form and details of a property and its setting as it appeared at a particular period of time by means of the removal of later work or by the replacement of missing earlier work.

Rhythm. The sense of movement created by the regular recurrence of elements, as in the spacing of doors and windows, across the façade of a building.

Rural preservation. The protection of the countryside, including the preservation of buildings and villages of cultural significance, the protection of their surroundings, and the enhancement of the local economy and social institutions.

Salvage archaeology. The retrieval of archaeological materials and data threatened by destruction, sometimes referred to as *rescue archaeology*.

Scale. Those qualities in architecture and landscape that relate to human size, enhancing the importance of the human individual rather than diminishing the individual.

Seascape. A view or vista of water, sometimes combined with elements of the natural shoreline, which may also sustain a minimum of built intrusions. Also called *Waterscape*.

Sense of place. The sum total of those parts that give a particular site, area, or neighborhood a distinctive character unique to its locality.

Shrine. An early term of reference to historic sites and buildings that reflects the intense patriotic associations such sites as Mount Vernon held for pioneers in the American preservation movement.

Sprawl. The straggling expansion of an urban area into the adjoining countryside often in a leap-frogging manner.

Stabilization. The act or process of applying measures designed to reestablish a weather-resistant enclosure and structural stability while maintaining the essential form as it exists at present.

Street furniture. A planner's term for elements of the streetscape other than buildings, such as light fixtures, fire hydrants, benches, and signs.

Streetscape. A view or vista of a specific street, the distinguishing characteristics of which are created by the width of the street and sidewalks, their paving materials and color, the design of street furniture, the potential use of plant materials such as trees and shrubs, and the setback, mass, proportion, and scale of those buildings that enclose the street.

Style. The manner in which ornament and structure are combined to create the distinctive character of artistic architectural endeavor expressive of an era or period in time.

Surplus property. Any building or site no longer needed for the use for which it was originally erected. In Great Britain, such a building or site is termed *redundant*.

Sustainable development. Development that meets the needs and aspirations of the current generation without compromising the ability to meet those of future generations.

Sustainable tourism. An attempt to make a low impact on the environment and local culture while helping to generate income, employment, and the conservation of local ecosystems. Responsible tourism that is both ecologically and culturally sensitive.

Sweat equity. The investment of labor as a form of payment in the restoration/rehabilitation process.

Taking. The power of government to expropriate private property.

Tout ensemble. A French term, meaning "all together," used (primarily in Louisiana) to connote the cohesive sense of an entire area or neighborhood.

Townscape. A view or vista of land comprised of a distinctive relationship of buildings, spaces, materials, and textures, which create an atmosphere, scale, and image. (*See also* Urban landscape.)

Traditional cultural property. Property that has an association with cultural practices or beliefs of a living community, which are rooted in that community's history and are important in maintaining the continuing cultural identity of the community.

Underwater archaeology. The study of submerged or inundated sites.

Urban landscape. A view or vista of land comprised of elements of the built environment, usually of a high density, sometimes referred to as a *cityscape*. (*See also* Townscape.)

Visual pollution. A term applied to intrusions in the man-made or natural environment, which are generally considered offensive to the sight.

Waterscape. *See* Seascape.

Bibliography

THE NATIONAL TRUST LIBRARY at the University of Maryland includes well over 10,000 volumes, making it a most comprehensive collection of literature on the subject of historic preservation. Of these thousands of titles, the following are considered among those basic to a general understudying of the subject. (The Government Printing Office in Washington, D.C., which has issued a number of these publications, is abbreviated as GPO.)

Abramson, Paul, ed. *Surplus Schools: Adaptive Reuse.* New York: Educational Facilities Laboratory, 1985.

Adler, Leopold, II, Walter C. Kidney, and Arthur P. Zeigler, Jr. *Revolving Funds for Historic Preservation: A Manual of Practice.* Pittsburgh: Ober Park Associates, 1975.

Advisory Council on Historic Preservation. *Annual Reports to the President and the Congress of the United States.* Washington, D.C.: GPO, 1968–1968.

———. *Assessing the Energy Conservation Benefits of Historic Preservation.* Washington, D.C.: GPO, 1979.

———. *The Contribution of Historic Preservation to Urban Revitalization.* Washington, D.C.: GPO, 1979.

———. *Historic Preservation Case Law: A Special Report.* Washington, D.C.: Advisory Council on Historic Preservation, 1985.

———. *The National Historic Preservation Act of 1966: An Assessment of Its Implementation over Twenty Years.* Washington, D.C.: Advisory Council on Historic Preservation, September 1986.

———. *Where to Look: A Guide to Preservation Information.* Washington, D.C.: GPO, 1982.

Albright, Horace Marden. *The Birth of the National Park Service: The Founding Years, 1913–33.* Salt Lake City: Howe Brothers, 1985.

———. *Origins of National Park Service Administration of Historic Sites.* Philadelphia: Eastern National Park and Monument Association, 1971.

Albright, Horace Marden, Russell E. Dickerson, William Penn Mott, Jr., and Mary Lu Moore. *National Park Service: The Story Behind the Scenery.* Las Vegas, Nev. KC Publications, 1987.

Alderson, William T., and Shirley Payne Low. *Interpretation of Historic Sites.* Nashville, Tenn.: American Association for State and Local History, 1979.

Alexander, Edward P. *Museums in Motion: An Introduction to the History and Function of Museums.* Nashville, Tenn.: American Association for State and Local History, 1979.

———. *Museum Masters: Their Museums and Their Influence.* Nashville, Tenn.: American Association for State and Local History, 1983.

American Association for State and Local History. *Historic Landscapes and Gardens: Procedures for Restoration.* Nashville, Tenn.: AASLH, 1974.

————. *Technical Leaflet Series.* Nashville, Tenn.: AASLH, 1965.

American Association of Museums. *The Official Museum Directory.* Skokie, Ill.: National Register Publishing Co., 1983.

American Institute of Timber Construction. *Timber Construction Manual.* 3rd ed. New York: John Wiley & Sons, 1986.

Anderson, Jay. *Time Machines: The World of Living History.* Nashville, Tenn.: American Association for State and Local History, 1984.

Andrews, Gregory E. *Tax Incentives for Historic Preservation.* Rev ed. Washington, D.C.: Preservation Press, 1981.

"Annotated Bibliography of Law-Related Journal Citations on Historic Preservation." *Northern Kentucky Law Review,* vol. 9, 1982.

Association for Living Historical Farms and Agricultural Museums. *Selected Living Historical Farms, Villages and Agricultural Museums in the United States and Canada.* Washington, D.C.: ALHFAG, 1975.

Association for Preservation Technology. *The Journal of the Association for Preservation Technology.* Ottawa, Ontario: APT. Published quarterly.

Auer, Michael, John A. Burns, and H. Ward Jandl. *Yesterday's Houses of Tomorrow: Innovative American Homes, 1850–1950.* Washington, D.C.: Preservation Press, 1991.

Avrami, E., R. Mason, and M. de la Torre, eds. "Values and Heritage Conservation." Los Angeles: The Getty Conservation Institute, 2000.

Bachmann, Konstanze, ed. *Conservation Concerns: A Guide for Collectors and Curators.* Washington, D.C.: Smithsonian Institution Press, 1992.

Baker, D. *Living with the Past: The Historic Environment.* Bletsoe, Bedford, Great Britain: D. Baker, 1983.

Balthazar, Korab. *Archabet: An Architectural Alphabet.* Washington, D.C.: National Trust for Historic Preservation, 1985.

Banks, Elizabeth. *Creating Period Gardens.* Washington, D.C.: Preservation Press, 1991.

Barnett, Jonathan. *Urban Design as Public Policy.* New York: Architectural Record Books, 1974.

Becker, Norman. *The Complete Book of Home Inspection for the Buyer or Owner.* New York: McGraw-Hill, 1980.

Bendix, Regina. *In Search of Authenticity: The Formation of Folklore Studies.* Madison: University of Wisconsin Press, 1999.

Bernhard, Sandy, and Thomas Ela. *The House Journal.* Washington, D.C.: Preservation Press, 1993.

Binford, Sally R., and Lewis R. Binford, eds. *New Perspectives in Archeology.* Chicago: Aldine Publishing 1968.

Birnbaum, Charles A., Jane Brown Gillette, Nancy Slade, eds. *Preserving Modern Landscape Architecture: Proceedings from the Wave Hill Conference.* Washington, D.C.: Spacemaker Press, 1999.

Birnbaum, Charles A., Jane Brown Gillette, and Nancy Slade, eds. *Preserving Modern Landscape Architecture II: Making Postwar Landscapes Visible.* Washington, D.C.: Spacemaker Press, 2004.

Birnhaum, Charles A., and Robin Karson. *Pioneers of American Landscape Design.* New York: McGraw-Hill, 2000.

Blake, Peter. *God's Own Junkyard: The Planned Deterioration of America's Landscape.* Rev. ed. New York: Holt, Rinehart and Winston, 1979.

Blumenson, John J. G. *Identifying American Architecture: A Pictorial Guide to Styles and Terms, 1600–1945.* Foreword by Nikolaus Pevsner. Rev. ed. Nashville, Tenn.: American Association for State and Local History, 1981.

Blumenthal, Sara K., ed. *Federal Historic Preservation Laws.* Washington, D.C.: National Parks Service, 1990.

Bonderman, J. David, Stephan N. Dennis, and Christopher Duerksen, eds. *Handbook on Historic Preservation Law.* Washington, D.C.: Conservation Foundation and National Center of Preservation Law, 1983.

Borchers, Perry E. *Photogrammetric Recording of Cultural Resources.* U.S. Dept. of the Interior, Technical Preservation Services. Washington, D.C.: GPO, 1977.

Bowsher, Alice Meriwether. *Design Review in Historic Districts: A Handbook for Virginia Review Boards.* 1978. Reprint. Washington, D.C.: Preservation Press, 1980.

Boyer, M. Christine. *The City of Collective Memory: Its Historical Imagery and Architectural Entertainments.* Cambridge: The MIT Press, 1996.

Brand, Stewart. *How Buildings Learn: What Happens After They're Built.* New York: Viking Press, 2004.

Brandt, Susan, and Sherban Cantacuzino. *Saving Old Buildings.* London: Architectural Press, 1980.

Brenneman, Russell L., and Sarah Bates. *Land Saving Action.* Covelo, Calif.: Island Press, 1984.

Brickerhoff, Parsons, and Louis G. Silano, eds. *Bridge Inspection and Rehabilitation: A Practical Guide.* New York: John Wiley & Sons, 1993.

Brown, Michael F. *Who Owns Native Culture?* Cambridge and London: Harvard University Press, 2003.

Bucher, Ward, ed. *Dictionary of Building Preservation.* New York: John Wiley & Sons, Inc., 1996.

Bullock, Orin M. *The Restoration Manual: An Illustrated Guide to the Preservation and Restoration of Old Buildings.* 1966. Reprint. New York: Van Nostrant Reinhold, 1983.

Burns, John, ed. *Recording Historic Structures,* 2nd ed. Hoboken: John Wiley & Sons, Inc., 2003.

Burrows, Tracy. *A Survey of Zoning Definitions.* Chicago: American Planning Association, 1989.

Campagna, Barbara A., Marcie F. Feuerstein, and Lynda H. Schneekloth, eds. *Changing Places: Remaking Institutional Buildings.* Fredonia, N.Y.: White Pine Press, 1992.

Carlson, Daniel. *Reusing America's Schools: A Guide for Local Officials, Developers, Neighborhood Residents, Planners, and Preservationists.* Washington, D.C.: Preservation Press, 1991.

Cassidy, Robert. *Livable Cities: A Grass-Roots Guide to Rebuilding Urban America.* New York: Holt, Rinehart and Winston, 1980.

Cawley, Frederick C. *Property Owner's Guide to Paint Restoration and Preservation.* Technical Series no. 1. Albany, N.Y.: Preservation League of New York State, 1976.

Chambers, J. Henry. *Cyclical Maintenance for Historic Buildings.* Technical Preservation Services, U.S. Department of the Interior. Washington, D.C.: GPO, 1976.

Chambers, S. Allen Jr., and the National Park Foundation Staff. *National Landmarks, America's Treasures: The National Park Foundation's Complete Guide to National Historic Landmarks.* New York: John Wiley & Sons, Inc., 2000.

Chang, Kwang-chih, ed. *Settlement Archeology.* Palo Alto, Calif.: National Press, 1968.

Chittenden, Betsy. *A Profile of the National Register of Historic Places.* Preservation Policy Research Series. Washington, D.C.: National Trust for Historic Preservation, 1984.

Chittenden, Betsy, and Jacques Gordon. *Older and Historic Buildings and the Preservation Industry.* Washington, D.C.: National Trust for Historic Preservation, 1984.

Choay, Françoise. *The Invention of the Historic Monument.* Translated by L.M. O'Connell. Cambridge: Cambridge University Press, 2001.

Clark, John, et al. *Small Seaports: Revitalization Through Conserving Heritage Resources.* Washington, D.C.: Conservation Foundation, 1979.

Clay, Grady. *Close-Up: How to Read an American City.* 1973. Reprint. Chicago: University of Chicago Press, 1980.

Closs, Christopher W. *Saving Large Estates.* Information Series, National Trust for Historic Preservation. Washington, D.C.: Preservation Press, 1982.

Cole, Katherine H., and H. Ward Jandl. *Houses by Mail: A Field Guide to Mail-Order Houses from Sears, Roebuck and Company.* Washington, D.C.: Preservation Press, 1986.

Coleman, Lawrence Vail. *Historic House Museums.* Reprint. Detroit: Gale Research Company, 1973.

———. *The Museum in America: A Critical Study.* Washington, D.C.: American Association of Museums, 1939.

Colin, Pearson, ed. *Conservation of Marine Archaeological Objects.* London: Butterworths, 1987.

Collins, Richard C., Anthony Bruce Dotson, and Elizabeth B. Waters. *America's Down-*

towns: Growth, Politics, and Preservation. Washington, D.C.: Preservation Press, 1991.

The Conservation Foundation. *National Parks for a New Generation: Visions, Realities, Prospects.* Washington, D.C.: The Conservation Foundation, 1985.

———. National Trust for Historic Preservation, and American Bar Association. *Reusing Old Buildings: Preservation Law and the Development Process.* Washington, D.C.: National Trust for Historic Preservation, 1984.

Costonis, John J. *Icons and Aliens: Law, Aesthetics and Environmental Change.* Urbana: University of Illinois Press, 1989.

———. *Space Adrift: Landmark Preservation and the Marketplace.* Urbana: National Trust for Historic Preservation by the University of Illinois Press, 1974.

———. *Space Adrift: Saving Urban Landmarks Through the Chicago Plan.* Champaign, Ill.: University of Illinois Press, 1974.

Coughlin, Thomas, III. *Easements and Other Legal Techniques to Protect Historic Houses in Private Ownership.* Washington, D.C.: Historic House Program, 1981.

Craig, Tracey Linton, ed. *Directory of Historical Societies and Agencies in the United States and Canada.* 12th ed. Nashville, Tenn.: American Association for State and Local History, 1982.

Cranz, Galen. *The Politics of Park Design: A History of Urban Parks in America.* Cambridge, Mass.: MIT Press, 1982.

Cullen, Gordon. *The Concise Townscape.* New York: Van Nostrand Reinhold, 1961.

Cullinance, John J. *Understanding Architectural Drawings: A Guide for Non-architects.* Washington, D.C.: Preservation Press, 1993.

Curtis, John O. *Moving Historic Buildings.* U.S. Department of the Interior, Technical Preservation Services Branch. Washington, D.C.: GPO, 1979.

Dale, Antony, et al. *Historic Preservation in Foreign Countries.* Edited by Robert E. Stipe. 2 vols. Washington, D.C.: International Council on Monuments and Sites, 1983.

Dawson, Alexandra D. *Land Use Planning and the Law.* New York: Garland, 1982.

Dean, Jeff. *Architectural Photography: Techniques for Architects, Preservationists, Historians, Photographers and Urban Planners.* Nashville, Tenn.: American Association for State and Local History. 1982.

Deetz, James. *Invitation to Archaeology.* Garden City, N.Y.: Natural History Press, 1967.

———. *In Small Things Forgotten: The Archeology of Early American Life.* Garden City, N.Y.: Anchor Press, 1977.

De la Torre, Marta, ed. *Assessing the Values of Cultural Heritage.* Los Angeles: The Getty Conservation Institute, 2002.

Dennis, Stephen, ed. *Directory of Preservation Lawyers.* Washington, D.C.: National Trust for Historic Preservation, 1984.

———. *Preservation Law Update.* Washington, D.C.: National Center for Preservation Law, 1986.

Derry, Anne, et al. *Guidelines for Local Surveys: A Basis for Preservation Planning.* National Register of Historic Places, Department of the Interior. Washington, D.C.: GPO, 1977.

Diehl, Janet, and Thomas Barrett. *The Conservation Easement Handbook: Managing Land Conservation and Historic Preservation Easement Programs.* San Francisco: Trust for Public Land, 1988.

Dietz, Albert G.H. *Dwelling House Construction.* 5th ed. Cambridge: The MIT Press, 1991.

Dornsife, Samuel, ed. *Exterior Decoration: A Treatise on the Artistic Use of Colors in the Ornamentation of Buildings.* Philadelphia: The Athenaeum of Philadelphia, 1976.

Duerksen, Christopher, ed. *Handbook on Preservation Law.* Washington, D.C.: Conservation Foundation, 1983.

Dwight, Pamela, ed. *Landmark Yellow Pages; Where to Find All the Names, Addresses, Facts, and Figures You Need.* 2nd ed. Washington, D.C.: Preservation Press, 1993.

Easton, Bob, and Peter Nabokov. *Native American Architecture.* New York: Oxford University Press, 1986.

Edlin, Herbert L. *What Wood Is That?: A Manual of Wood Identification.* New York: Viking Press, 1969.

Educational Facilities Laboratories. *Movie Palaces: Renaissance and Reuse.* New York: Academy for Educational Development, 1982.

Ellsworth, Linda. *The History of a House: How to Trace It.* Nashville, Tenn.: American Association for State and Local History, 1976.

Faherty, Keith F., and Thomas G. Williamson, eds. *Wood Engineering and Construction Handbook.* New York: McGraw-Hill, 1989.

Fallon, Stacie A. *Getting the Lead Out: State Policy on Lead Paint.* Lombard, Ill.: Midwestern Legislative Conference, Council of State Governments, 1993.

Favretti, Rudy J., and Joy Putman Favretti. *Landscapes and Gardens for Historic Buildings: A Handbook for Reproducing and Creating Authentic Landscape Settings.* Nashville, Tenn.: American Association for State and Local History. 1978.

"Federal Historic Preservation Laws." Washington, D.C.: U.S. Department of the Interior, National Park Service, National Center for Cultural Resources, 2002.

Feilden, Bernard M. *Conservation of Historic Buildings.* Woburn, Mass.: Butterworths, 1982.

———. *Conservation of Historic Buildings.* 3rd ed. London: Butterworths, 2003.

Finley, David E. *History of the National Trust for Historic Preservation 1947–1963.* Washington, D.C.: National Trust for Historic Preservation, 1965.

Fisher, Charles, et al. *Interiors Handbook for Historic Buildings.* Washington, D.C.: Historic Preservation Education Foundation, 1988.

Fitch, James Marston. *Historic Preservation: Curatorial Management of the Built World.* New York, McGraw-Hill, 1982.

Fleming, John, Hugh Honour, and Nikolaus Pevsner. *The Penguin Dictionary of Architecture.* 4th ed. London: Penguin Books, 1991.

Fleming, Ronald Lee. *Facade Stories: Changing Faces of Main Street Storefronts and How to Care for Them.* New York: Hastings House, 1982.

Folsom, Franklin and Mary. *America's Ancient Treasures: A Guide to Archeological Sites and Museums in the United States and Canada.* 4th ed. Albuquerque: University of New Mexico Press, 1993.

Forbes, Peter, Ann Armbrecht Forbes, and Helen Whybrow, eds. *Our Land, Ourselves: Readings on People and Place.* 2nd ed. San Francisco: The Trust for Public Land, 1999.

Foulks, William G., ed. *Historic Building Façades.* New York: John Wiley & Sons, Inc., 1997.

Fox, Stephen. *John Muir and His Legacy: The American Conservation Movement.* Boston: Little, Brown, 1981.

French, Thomas R. "Annotated Bibliography of Law-Related Journal Citations on Historic Preservation." *Northern Kentucky Law Review,* vol. 9, 1982.

Friedman, Donald, and Nathaniel Oppenheimer. *The Design of Renovations.* New York: Norton, 1997.

Gardner, James B., and George Rollie Adams, eds. *Ordinary People and Everyday Life: Perspectives on the New Social History.* Nashville, Tenn.: American Association for State and Local History, 1983.

Garnham, Harry L. *Maintaining the Spirit of the Place.* Mesa, Ariz.: PDA Publishers Corporation, 1985.

Garvery, Robert R., and Terry B. Morton. *The United States Government in Historic Preservation: A Brief History of the 1966 National Historic Preservation Act and Others.* Rev. ed. Washington, D.C.: National Trust for Historic Preservation, 1973.

Gaughenbaugh, Michael, and Herbert Camburn. *Old House, New House: A Child's Exploration of American Architectural Styles.* Washington, D.C.: Preservation Press, 1993.

Gayle, Margot, David W. Look, and John G. Waite. *Metals in America's Historic Buildings: Uses and Preservation Treatments.* U.S. Department of the Interior, Technical Preservation Services. Washington, D.C.: GPO, 1980.

Getzels, Judith, and Charles Thurow, eds. *Rural and Small Town Planning.* Old West Regional Commission. Chicago, Ill.: American Planning Association, 1980.

Giljahn, Jack W., and Thomas R. Matheny. *A Guide for the Adaptive Use of Surplus*

Schools. Columbus, Ohio: Columbus Landmarks Foundation, 1981.

Gladstone, Bernard. *The Simon and Schuster Complete Guide to Home Repair and Maintenance.* New York: Simon and Schuster, 1984.

Glenn, Patricia Brown, and Joe Stites. *Under Every Roof: A Kid's Style and Field Guide to the Architecture of American Houses.* Washington, D.C.: Preservation Press, 1993.

Gobert, Ernest G., and Thomas A. Oxley. *Dampness in Buildings: Diagnosis, Treatment, Instruments.* London: Butterworths, 1983.

Goodall, Harrison, and Renee Friedman. *Log Structures: Preservation and Problem-Solving.* Nashville, Tenn.: American Association for State and Local History, 1980.

Gordon, J.E. *Structures: Or Why Things Don't Fall Down.* Cambridge: Da Capo Press, 2003.

Gottfried, Herbert, and Jan Jennings. *American Vernacular Design, 1870–1940.* Ames: Iowa State University Press, 1993.

———. *American Vernacular Interior Architecture, 1870–1940.* New York: Van Nostrand Reinhold, 1988.

Goulty, Sheena MacKellar. *Heritage Gardens: Care, Conservation and Management.* London: Routledge, 1993.

Gowans, Alan. *Images of American Living: Four Centuries of Architecture and Furniture as Cultural Expression.* 1964. Reprint. New York: Harper & Row, 1976.

Gowans, Alan. *The Comfortable House: North American Suburban Architecture, 1890–1939.* Cambridge, Mass.: MIT Press, 1986.

Gratz, Roberta Brandes. *The Living City: Thinking Big in a Small Way.* New York: Simon and Schuster, 1989.

Greenberg, Ronald M., and Sarah A. Marusin, eds. *National Register of Historic Places.* Vols I, II. National Park Service, U.S. Department of the Interior. Washington, D.C.: GPO, 1976, 1979.

Greenbil, Barrie B. *Spaces: Dimensions of the Human Landscape.* New Haven, Conn.: Yale University Press, 1981.

Greer, Nora Richter. *Architecture Transformed: New Life for Old Buildings.* Gloucester: Rockport Publishes, 1998.

Greiff, Constance M., ed. *Lost America: From the Atlantic to the Mississippi.* Foreword by James Biddle. Princeton, N.J.: Pyne Press, 1971.

———. *Lost America: From the Mississippi to the Pacific.* Princeton, N.J.: Pyne Press, 1972.

Groth, Paul, and Todd Bressi, eds. *Understanding Ordinary Landscapes.* New Haven: Yale University Press, 1997.

Grow, Lawrence. *The Sixth Old House Catalogue.* Pittstown, N.J.: The Main Street Press, 1988.

Guthe, Carl E. *The Management of Small History Museums.* 2nd ed. Nashville, Tenn.: American Association for State and Local History, 1964.

Hansel, David A., Stephen L. Kass, and Judith M. LaBelle. *Rehabilitating Older and Historic Buildings: Law, Taxation, Strategies.* New York: John Wiley & Sons, 1985.

Harris, Cyril M., ed. *Historic Architecture Sourcebook.* New York: Dover, 1983.

Harris, Neil. *Building Lives: Constructing Rites and Passages.* New Haven: Yale University Press, 1999.

Harris, Samuel Y. *Building Pathology.* New York: John Wiley & Sons, Inc., 2001.

Herbers, Jill. *Great Adaptations: New Residential Uses for Older Buildings.* New York: Whitney Library of Design, 1990.

Hitchcock, Henry-Russell. *American Architectural Books: A List of Books, Portfolios, and Pamphlets on Architecture and Related Subjects Published in America Before 1895.* 1946. Reprint. New York: Da Capo, 1975.

———. *Architecture: Nineteenth and Twentieth Centuries.* 2nd ed. 1963. Reprint. Baltimore: Penguin Books, 1971.

Hitchcock, Henry-Russell, and William Seale. *Temples of Democracy.* New York: Harcourt, Brace, Jovanovich, 1976.

Hole, Frank, and Robert T. Heizer. *Prehistoric Archaeology: A Brief Introduction.* 2nd ed. New York: Holt, Rinehart and Winston, 1982.

Holland, F. Ross, Jr. *America's Lighthouses: Their Illustrated History Since 1716.* Rev. ed. Brattleboro, Vt.: Stephen Greene Press, 1981.

Hosmer, Charles B., Jr. *Presence of the Past: A History of the Preservation Movement in the United States before Williamsburg*. Foreword by Walter Muir Whitehill. New York: Putnam, 1965.

————. *Preservation Comes of age: From Williamsburg to the National Trust, 1926–1949*. Charlottesville: University Press of Virginia, 1981.

Howard, Hugh. *How Old Is This House: A Skeleton Key to Dating and Identifying Three Centuries of American Houses*. New York: Noonday Press, 1989.

Howe, Barbara J. *Houses and Homes: Exploring Their History*. Nashville, Tenn.: American Association for State and Local History, 1987.

Howe, Barbara, et al. *House Histories*. Nashville, Tenn.: American Association for State and Local History, 1986.

Hutt, Sherry, Elwood W. Jones, and Martin Edward McAllister. *Archeological Resource Protection*. Washington, D.C.: Preservation Press, 1992.

Huxtable, Ada Louise. *Goodbye History, Hello Hamburger*. Washington, D.C.: Preservation Press, 1986.

————. *The Unreal America: Architecture and Illusion*. New York: The New Press, 1997.

————. *Will They Ever Finish Bruckner Boulevard?* New York: Macmillan, 1970.

Jackson, Donald C. *Saving Historic Bridges*. Information Series, National Trust for Historic Preservation. Washington, D.C.: Preservation Press, 1984.

Jackson, John B. *Discovering the Vernacular Landscape*. New Haven: Yale University Press, 1984.

————. *A Sense of Place, A Sense of Time*. New Haven: Yale University Press, 1994.

Jacobs, Jane. *The Death and Life of Great American Cities*. New York: Random House, 1961.

Jennings, Jan. *Roadside America: The Automobile in Design and Culture*. Ames: Iowa State University Press, 1990.

Jokilheto, Jukka. *A History of Architectural Conservation*. Oxford: Butterworth-Heinemann, 1999.

Jones, Bernie. *Neighborhood Planning: A Guide for Citizens and Planners*. Chicago: Planners Press, 1990.

Jordy, William H., and William Harvey Pierson. *American Buildings and Their Architects*. 4 vols. Garden City, N.Y.: Doubleday, 1970.

Kammen, Michael. *Mystic Chords of Memory: The Transformation of Tradition in American Culture*. New York: Alfred A. Knopf, 1991.

Keller, Genevieve P., et al. *Saving America's Countryside: A Guide to Rural Conservation*. Baltimore, Md.: Johns Hopkins University Press, 1989.

Kemp, Emory L., and Theodore Anton Sande, eds. *Historic Preservation of Engineering Works*. New York: American Society of Civil Engineers, 1981.

Keune, Russell V., ed. *The Historic Preservation Yearbook*. Bethesda, Md.: Adler and Adler, 1984.

Kidney, Walter. *Working Places: The Adaptive Use of Industrial Buildings*. Pittsburgh: Ober Park Associates, 1976.

King, Thomas F. *The Archeological Survey: Methods and Uses*. U.S. Department of the Interior. National Park Service. Washington, D.C.: GPO, 1978.

King, Thomas F., Patricia Parker Hickman, and Gary Berg. *Anthropology in Historic Preservation: Caring for Culture's Clutter*. New York: Academic Press, 1977.

Kitchen, Judith L. *Characteristics of Effective Local Historic Preservation Legislation*. Columbus: Ohio State Historic Preservation Office, 1989.

————. *Caring for Your Old House: A Guide for Owners and Residents*. Washington, D.C.: Preservation Press, 1991.

————. *Old-Building Owner's Manual*. Columbus: Ohio Historic Preservation Office, 1983.

Klein, Marilyn W., David P. Fogle, and Wolcott B. Etienne. *Clues to American Architecture*. Washington, D.C.: Starrhill Press, 1985.

Klimoski, Gretchen, and Judy Williams. *Manual of Practice for South Carolina Local Preservation Commissions*. Columbus, Ohio: Neighborhood Works, 1994.

Koch, James H. *Profits from Country Property: How to Select, Buy, Maintain, and Improve Country Property.* New York: McGraw-Hill, 1981.

Kornwolfe, James, and Georgiana A.W. *Architecture and Town Planning in Colonial North America.* Baltimore: The Johns Hopkins University Press, 2002.

Kyvig, David E., and Myron A. Marty. *Nearby History: Exploring the Past Around You.* Nashville, Tenn.: American Association for State and Local History, 1982.

Lebovich, William L. *America's City Halls.* U.S. Department of the Interior, National Park Service, Historic American Buildings Survey. Washington, D.C.: Preservation Press, 1984.

Leighton, Ann. *American Gardens of the Nineteenth Century: "For Comfort and Affluence."* Amherst: University of Massachusetts Press, 1987.

Liebs, Chester. *Main Street to Miracle Mile: American Roadside Architecture.* Boston: New York Graphic Society, 1985.

Limerick, Jeffrey, et al. *America's Grand Resort Hotels.* New York: Pantheon, 1979.

Lingeman, Richard. *Small Town America: A Narrative History, 1620–the Present.* New York: Putnam, 1980.

London, Mark. *Masonry: How to Care for Old and Historic Brick and Stone.* Washington, D.C.: Preservation Press, 1988.

Longstreth, Richard. *The Buildings of Main Street.* Washington, D.C.: Preservation Press, 1987.

Lottman, Herbert R. *How Cities Are Saved.* New York: Universe Books, 1976.

Lowenthal, David. *The Past Is a Foreign Country.* Cambridge: Cambridge University Press, 1985.

Lowenthal, David, and Marcus Binney, eds. *Our Past Before Us: Why Do We Save It?* London: Temple Smith, 1981.

Lynch, Kevin. *Managing the Sense of a Region.* Cambridge, Mass.: MIT Press, 1976.

———. *What Time Is This Place?* Cambridge, Mass.: MIT Press, 1972.

Lynch, Michael F. *How to Care for Religious Properties.* Albany, N.Y.: Preservation League of New York State, 1982.

Mackintosh, Barry. *The History Sites Survey and the National Historic Landmarks Program: A History.* Washington, D.C.: National Park Service, 1985.

———. *The National Historic Preservation Act and the National Park Service: A History.* Washington, D.C.: The National Park Service, 1986.

———. *The National Parks: Shaping the System.* Washington, D.C.: U.S. Department of the Interior, 1985.

MacLeish, A. Bruce. *The Care of Antiques and Historical Collections.* Rev. ed. Nashville, Tenn.: American Association for State and Local History, 1985.

Maddex, Diane, ed. *All About Old Buildings: The Whole Preservation Catalog.* Washington, D.C.: The Preservation Press, 1985.

———. *Built in the USA: American Buildings from Airports to Zoos.* Washington, D.C.: Preservation Press, 1985.

———. *Master Builders: A Guide to Famous American Architects.* Washington, D.C.: Preservation Press, 1985.

Maddex, Diane, and Ellen R. Marsh, eds. *The Brown Book: A Directory of Preservation Information.* Washington, D.C.: Preservation Press, 1983.

Markowitz, Arnold L., ed. *Historic Preservation: A Guide to Information Sources.* Detroit: Gale Research Company, 1980.

Maryland Historical Trust. *Preservation Easements: A Publication.* Rev. Ed. Annapolis: Maryland Historical Trust, Department of Economic and Community Development, 1977.

Matero, Frank G., and Martin E. Weaver. *Conserving Buildings: A Guide to Techniques and Materials.* New York: John Wiley & Sons, 1993.

McAlester, Virginia and Lee McAlester. *A Field Guide to American Houses.* New York: Alfred A. Knopf, 1984.

McGimsey, Charles R., III. *Public Archeology.* New York: Seminar Press, 1972.

McGimsey, Charles R., III, and Hester A. Davis, eds. *The Management of Archaeological Resources: The Airlie House Report.* Washington, D.C.: Society for American Archeology, 1977.

McGrath, Norman. *Photographing Buildings Inside and Out.* 2nd ed. New York: Whitney Library of Design, 1993.

McHargue, Georgess, and Michael Roberts. *A Field Guide to Conservation Archaeology in North America.* Philadelphia: Lippincott, 1977.

McKee, Harley J. *Introduction to Early American Masonry: Stone, Brick, Mortar and Plaster.* Washington, D.C.: Preservation Press, 1973.

———. *Recording Historic Buildings.* Historic American Buildings Survey, U.S. Department of the Interior. Washington, D.C.: GPO, 1976.

McNulty, Robert H., and Stephen A. Kliment, eds. *Neighborhood Conservation: A Handbook of Methods and Techniques.* 1976. Reprint. New York: Whitney Library of Design, 1979.

Meinig, D.W., ed. *The Interpretation of Ordinary Landscapes: Geographical Essays.* New York: Oxford University Press, 1979.

Melnick, Robert Z., Daniel Sponn, and Emma Jane Saxe. *Cultural Landscapes: Rural Historic Districts in the National Park System.* Washington, D.C.: Park Historic Architecture Division, U.S. Dept. of the Interior, 1984.

Merritt, Carole. *Historic Black Resources: A Handbook for the Identification, Documentation, and Evaluation of Historic African-American Properties in Georgia.* Atlanta: Historic Preservation Section, Georgia Department of Natural Resources, 1984.

Metcalf, Fay D., and Matthew T. Downey. *Using Local History in the Classroom.* Nashville, Tenn.: American Association for State and Local History, 1982.

Moore, Charles W., Kathryn Smith, and Peter Becker, eds. *Home Sweet Home: American Domestic Vernacular Architecture.* New York: Rizzoli, 1983.

Morton, Terry B., ed. *Monumentum,* Vol. XIII. Washington, D.C.: International Council on Monuments and Sites, 1976.

Morton, W. Brown III, and Gary L. Hume. *The Secretary of the Interior's Standards for Historic Preservation Projects, with Guidelines for Applying the Standards.* Technical

Preservation Services, U.S. Department of the Interior. Washington, D.C.: GPO, 1979.

Moss, Robert. *Century of Color: Exterior Decoration for American Buildings, 1820–1920.* Watkins Glen, N.Y.: American Life Foundation, 1981.

———. *Lighting for Historic Buildings: A Guide to Selecting Reproductions.* Washington, D.C.: Preservation Press, 1988.

Mulloy, Elizabeth D. *The History of the National Trust for Historic Preservation. 1963–1973.* Washington, D.C.: Preservation Press, 1976.

Munro, Roxie, and Diane Maddex. *Architects Make Zigzags: Looking at Architecture from A to Z.* Washington, D.C.: Preservation Press, 1986.

Munsell, Kenneth, and Anne Smith Denman. **Historic Preservation Resource Book for Small Communities.** Ellensburg, Wash.: Small Towns Institute, 1983.

Murtagh, William J. "Aesthetic and Social Dimensions of Historic Districts," in *Historic Districts: Identification, Social Aspects and Preservation.* Washington, D.C.: Preservation Press, 1975.

Myers, Denys Peter. *Gaslighting in America: A Guide for Historical Preservation.* Technical Preservation Services, U.S. Department of the Interior. Washington, D.C.: GPO, 1978.

Myers, Phyllis, and Gordon Binder. *Neighborhood Conservation: Lessons from Three Cities.* Washington, D.C.: The Conservation Foundation, 1977.

Naeve, Milo M. *Identifying American Furniture: A Pictorial Guide to Styles and Terms.* Nashville, Tenn.: American Association for State and Local History, 1982.

National Association of Counties Research Foundation. *Disappearing Farmlands: A Citizen's Guide to Agricultural Land Preservation.* 2nd ed. Washington, D.C.: NACRF, 1980.

National Heritage Preservation Institute Staff, et al. *Caring for Your Historic House.* New York: Harry N. Abrams, 1998.

National Main Street Center. *National Main Street Center Training Manual.* Washington, D.C.: National Main Street Center, 1981.

National Park Service. *Preservation of Historic Adobe Buildings*. Preservation Brief #5. National Park Service, U.S. Department of the Interior. Washington, D.C.: GPO 1978.

———. *Respectful Rehabilitation: Answers to Your Questions About Old Buildings*. Technical Preservation Services, U.S. Department of the Interior. Washington, D.C.: Preservation Press, 1982.

———. *Technical Preservation Briefs*. Series. Technical Preservation Services, U.S. Department of the Interior. Washington, D.C.: GPO. Published periodically.

"The National Park Service and Historic Preservation." *The Public Historian: A Journal of Public History* 9 (Spring 1987).

National Trust for Historic Preservation and Colonial Williamsburg Foundation. *Historic Preservation Today: Essays Presented to the Seminar on Preservation and Restoration, Williamsburg, Virginia, 1963*. Charlottesville: University Press of Virginia, 1966.

———. *Historic Preservation Tomorrow*. Charlottesville: University Press of Virginia, 1967.

National Trust for Historic Preservation and Land Trust Exchange. *Appraising Easements. Guidelines for Valuation of Historic Preservation and Land Conservation Easements*. Washington, D.C.: National Trust for Historic Preservation, 1984.

National Trust for Historic Preservation. *Attic to Basement: Maintaining Your Old House*. Austin, Tex.: Preservation Productions, 1993. Videocassette.

———. *Basic Preservation Procedures*. Washington, D.C.: Preservation Press, 1983.

———. *Conserve Neighborhoods Notebook*. Rev. ed. Neighborhood Conservation Office. Washington, D.C.: National Trust for Historic Preservation, 1981.

———. *Conserving the Historic and Cultural Landscape: Selected Papers*. Washington, D.C.: Preservation Press, 1976.

———. *Directory of Private, Nonprofit Preservation Organizations: State and Local Levels*. Washington, D.C.: Preservation Press, 1980.

———. *Federal Tax Incentives for Rehabilitation of Historic Buildings*. Information Series. Washington, D.C.: Preservation Press, 1984.

———. *The First National Maritime Preservation Conference: Proceedings*. Washington, D.C.: Preservation Press, 1977.

———. *Information: A Preservation Sourcebook*. Washington, D.C.: Preservation Press, 1979–85.

———. *New Energy from Old Buildings*. Washington, D.C.: Preservation Press, 1981.

———. *Old & New Architecture: Design Relationship*. Washington, D.C.: Preservation Press, 1980.

———. *Preservation Law Reporter*. Washington, D.C.: National Trust for Historic Preservation. Published quarterly.

———. *Preservation: Toward an Ethic in the 1980s*. Washington, D.C.: Preservation Press, 1980.

———. *Preservation and Conservation: Principles and Practices*. International Centre for the Study of the Preservation and Restoration of Cultural Property. Washington, D.C.: Preservation Press, 1976.

Naylor, David. *American Picture Palaces: The Architecture of Fantasy*. New York: Van Nostrand Reinhold, 1981.

"Neighborhood Organizing Guide: Ideas for Bringing the Neighborhood Together." *Conserve Neighborhoods*. (September–October 1981). Washington, D.C.: National Trust for Historic Preservation.

Nelson, Carl. *Protecting the Past from Natural Disasters*. Washington, D.C.: Preservation Press, 1993.

Newton, Norman T. *Design on the Land: The Development of Landscape Architecture*. Cambridge, Mass.: The Belknap Press of Harvard University, 1971.

New York Landmarks Conservancy. *Repairing Old and Historic Windows*. Washington, D.C.: Preservation Press, 1992.

Nielson, Sally E., ed. *Insulating the Old House: A Handbook for the Owner*. Portland, Me.: Greater Portland Landmarks, 1979.

Noble, Allen G. *Wood, Brick and Stone: The North American Settlement Landscape*. 2 vols. Amherst: University of Massachusetts Press, 1984.

Noel-Hume, Ivor. *Historical Archaeology: A Comprehensive Guide for Both Amateurs* and Professionals to the Techniques and Methods of Excavating Historical Sites. New York: Alfred A. Knopf, 1969.

Nylander, Jane C. Fabrics for Historic Buildings. 3rd ed. Washington, D.C.: Preservation Press, 1983.

Nylander, Richard. Wallpapers for Historic Buildings. Washington, D.C.: Preservation Press, 1983.

Old House Journal Editors. The Old House Journal 1988 Catalog: A Buyers Guide for the Pre-1939 House. Brooklyn, N.Y.: Old House Journal, 1987.

Page, Max and Randall Mason, eds. Giving Preservation a History. New York and London: Routledge, 2004.

Paseltiner, Ellen Kettler, and Deborah Tyler. Zoning and Historic Preservation: A Survey of Current Zoning Techniques in U.S. Cities to Encourage Historic Preservation. Rev. ed. Chicago: Landmarks Preservation Council of Illinois, 1984.

Percy, David O. Living Historical Farms: The Working Museums. Accokeek, Md.: National Colonial Farm, 1981.

Peterson, Charles E., ed. Building Early America. Philadelphia: Chilton Book Company, 1976.

Phillips, Charles, and Patricia Hogan. A Culture at Risk: Who Cares for America's Heritage? Nashville, Tenn.: American Association for State and Local History, 1985.

Phillips, Steven J. Old House Dictionary: An Illustrated Guide to American Domestic Architecture. Washington, D.C.: Preservation Press, 1992.

Placzek, Adolf K., ed. The Macmillan Encyclopedia of Architects. New York: Macmillan, 1982.

Poore, Patricia. The Old House Journal Guide to Restoration. New York: Dutton, 1992.

Poppeliers, John, S. Allen Chambers, and Nancy B. Schwartz. What Style Is It? A Guide to American Architecture. Rev. ed. Washington, D.C.: Preservation Press, 1984.

Practicing Law Institute Handbooks. Historic Preservation Law. New York: Practicing Law Institute, 1981, 1982.

———. Rehabilitating Historic Properties. New York: Practicing Law Institute, 1984.

Preservation Action. Blueprint for Lobbying: A Citizens Guide to the Politics of Preservation. Washington, D.C.: Preservation Action, 1984.

Prycer, Donald G. Preserving a Fragile Art: A Manual for Surveying Significant Interiors. New York: American Society of Interior Designers, 1982.

Quick, Polly McW., ed. Proceedings: Conference on Reburial Issues. Washington, D.C.: Society for American Archaeology and Society of Professional Archaeologists, 1985.

Rains, Albert, and Laurance G. Henderson. With Heritage So Rich. United States Conference of Mayors. Rev. ed. Washington, D.C.: Preservation Press, 1983.

Ramati, Raquel. How to Save Your Own Street. Urban Design Group, New York Department of City Planning. New York: Doubleday, 1981.

Ramsey, Charles George, and Harold Reeve Sleeper. Ramsey/Sleeper Architectural Graphics Standards. 9th ed. New York: John Wiley & Sons, 1994.

Reiner, Laurence E. How to Recycle Buildings. New York: McGraw-Hill, 1979.

Reps, John W. The Making of Urban America: A History of City Planning in the United States. Princeton: Princeton University Press, 1965.

"Revolving Funds—Recycling Resources for Neighborhoods." Conserve Neighborhoods 18 (May/June 1981).

Richardson, Ralph W. Historic Districts of America: The South. Bowie, Md.: Heritage Books, 1987.

Robin, Peggy. Saving the Neighborhood: You Can Fight Developers and Win. Kensington, Md.: Woodbine House, 1990.

Robinson, Nicholas A. Environmental Regulations of Real Property. New York: Law Journal Seminars Press, 1982.

Roddewig, Richard J. Preparing a Historic Preservation Ordinance. Chicago: American Planning Association, 1983.

Roddewig, Richard J., and Bradford J. White. Preservation Law for the 1990s. Chicago: Authors, 1990.

Roddewig, Richard J., and Christopher J. Duerksen. Responding to the Takings Challenge: A Guide for Officials and Planners. Washington, D.C.: National Trust for Historic Preservation, 1989.

Rosenberg, Sam, ed. *Travel Historic Rural America: A Guide to Agricultural Museums and Events in the U.S. and Canada*. St. Joseph, Mich.: American Society of Agricultural Engineers, 1982.

Roth, Leland M. *America Builds: Source Documents in American Architecture and Planning*. New York: Harper & Row, 1983.

Runte, Alfred. *National Parks: The American Experience*. 2nd ed. Lincoln: University of Nebraska Press, 1987.

Rypkema, Donavan D. *The Economics of Historic Preservation: A Community Leader's Guide*. Washington, D.C.: National Trust for Historic Preservation, 1994.

Savage, Beth L., ed. *African-American Historic Places: National Register of Historic Places*. Washington, D.C.: Preservation Press, 1994.

Saylor, Henry H. *Dictionary of Architecture*. 1952. Reprint. New York: John Wiley, 1963.

Schiffer, Michael B., and George J. Gumerman. *Conservation Archeology: A Guide for Cultural Resource Management Studies*. New York: Academic Press, 1977.

Schlereth, Thomas J. *Artifacts and the American Past*. Nashville, Tenn.: American Association for State and Local History, 1981.

———. ed. *Material Culture Studies in America*. Nashville, Tenn.: American Association for State and Local History, 1982.

Schmertz, Mildred F., and Editors of Architectural Record. *New Life for Old Buildings*. New York: McGraw-Hill, 1982.

Scott, John S. *Dictionary of Civil Engineering*. 3rd ed. London: Collins, 1985.

Seale, William. *Of Houses and Time: Personal Histories of America's National Trust Properties*. New York: H.N. Abrams, 1992.

———. *The President's House: A History*. Washington, D.C.: White House Historical Association with the cooperation of the National Geographic Society, 1986.

———. *Recreating the Historic House Interior*. Nashville, Tenn.: American Association for State and Local History, 1979.

———. *The Tasteful Interlude: American Interiors Through the Camera's Eye, 1860–1917*. 1975. Rev. ed. Nashville, Tenn.: American Association for State and Local History, 1980.

The Secretary of the Interior's 20th Anniversary Report on the National Historic Preservation Act. Washington, D.C.: U.S. Department of the Interior, 1986.

Shivers, Natalie W. *Walls and Molding: How to Care for Old and Historic Wood and Plaster*. Washington, D.C.: Preservation Press, 1990.

Shopsin, William C., and Grania Bolton Marcus. *Saving Large Estates: Conservation, Historic Preservation, and Adaptive Reuse*. Setauket, N.Y.: Society for the Preservation of Long Island Antiquities, 1977.

Siesler, Jeffrey M., and Henry Londner. *Conserving Energy in Older Houses: A Do-It-Yourself Manual*. Alexandria, Va.: Analytech, 1983.

Smith, Herbert H. *The Citizen's Guide to Zoning*. Chicago: Planners Press, 1983.

South, Stanley. *Method and Theory in Historical Archeology*. New York: Academic Press, 1977.

Southern, Kathleen Pepi. *Historic Preservation in Rural North Carolina: Problems and Potentials*. Raleigh: Historic Preservation Society of North Carolina, 1982.

Steele, Fritz. *The Sense of Place*. Boston: CBI Publishing Co., 1981.

Stephen, George. *New Life for Old Houses*. Washington, D.C.: Preservation Press, 1989.

Stevenson, Katherine Cole, and H. Ward Jandl. *Houses by Mail: A Guide to Houses from Sears, Roebuck and Company*. Washington, D.C.: Preservation Press, 1986.

Stilgoe, John R. *Common Landscape of America, 1580 to 1845*. New Haven: Yale University Press, 1982.

Stipe, Robert E., ed. *A Richer Heritage*. Chapel Hill: The University of North Carolina Press, 2003.

Stipe, Robert E., for the Heritage Conservation and Recreation Service, U.S. Department of the Interior. *New Directions in Rural Preservation*. Washington, D.C.: GPO, 1980.

Stipe, Robert E., and Antoinette J. Lee, eds. *American Mosaic: Preserving a Nation's Heritage*. Washington, D.C.: International Council on Monuments and Sites, 1987.

Stipe, Robert E., et al. "The Impact of Law on Preservation Activities in the United States." Edited by Terry B. Morton. *Momentum*, vol. XIII. Washington, D.C.: International Council on Monuments and Sites, 1976.

Stokes, Samuel N., et al. *Saving America's Countryside*. Baltimore: Johns Hopkins University Press, 1989.

Strangstad, Lynette. *A Graveyard Preservation Primer*. Nashville, Tenn.: American Association for State and Local History, 1988.

Sullivan, George, ed. *Discover Archaeology: An Introduction to the Tools and Techniques of Archaeological Fieldwork*. New York: Penguin, 1981.

Sutro, Suzanne. *Reinventing the Village: Planning, Zoning, and Design Strategies*. Chicago: American Planning Association, 1990.

Thomas Vonier Associates. *Energy Conservation and Solar Energy for Historic Buildings: Guidelines for Appropriate Designs*. Technical Preservation Services, U.S. Department of the Interior. Washington, D.C.: National Center for Architecture & Urbanism, 1981.

Thompson, John M.A., ed. *The Manual of Curatorship: A Guide to Museum Practice*. Reprint. London: Butterworths, 1986.

Thurber, Pamela, ed. *Controversies in Preservation: Understanding the Movement Today*. Preservation Policy Research Series. Washington, D.C.: National Trust for Historic Preservation, 1985.

Tilden, Freeman. *Interpreting Our Heritage*. Rev. ed. Chapel Hill: University of North Carolina Press, 1977.

Traub, Gerald P. *3 R's for Schools: Rescue, Renovation, Reuse*. Raleigh, N.C.: Historic Preservation Foundation of North Carolina, 1994.

Tschudi-Madsen, Stephan. *Restoration and Anti-Restoration: A Study in English Restoration Philosophy*. 2nd ed. Oslo/Bergen/Tromso: Universitetsforlaget, 1976.

Tubesing, Richard. *Architectural Preservation and Urban Renovation: An Annotated Bibliography of U.S. Congressional Documents*. New York: Garland Publishing, 1982.

Tung, Anthony M. *Preserving the World's Great Cities: The Destruction and Renewal of the Historic Metropolis*. New York: Crown Publishing Group, 2001.

UNESCO. *"Appropriate Techniques" in the Conservation of Cultural Properties*. Paris: UNESCO Press, 1981.

U.S. Department of Commerce, Office of Coastal Zone Management. *Improving Your Waterfront: A Practical Guide*. Washington, D.C.: GPO, 1980.

U.S. Department of the Interior. National Park Service. Interagency Resources Division. *National Register Bulletin (No. 12): Definition of National Register Boundaries for Archeological Properties*. Washington, D.C.: National Park Service, 1985.

———. *National Register Bulletin (No. 13): How to Apply National Register Criteria to Post Offices*. Washington, D.C.: National Park Service.

———. *National Register Bulletin (No. 15): How to Apply the National Register Criteria for Evaluation*. Washington, D.C.: National Park Service, 1991.

———. *National Register Bulletin (No. 16A): How to Complete the National Register Registration Form*. Washington, D.C.: National Park Service, 1991.

———. *National Register Bulletin (No. 16B): How to Complete the National Register Multiple Property Documentation Form*. Washington, D.C.: National Park Service, 1991.

———. *National Register Bulletin (No. 17): Certification of State and Local Statutes and Historic Districts*. Washington, D.C.: National Park Service, 1987.

———. *National Register Bulletin (No. 18): How to Evaluate and Nominate Designed Historic Landscapes*, by Timothy Keller and Genevieve P. Keller. Washington, D.C.: National Park Service, 1987.

———. *National Register Bulletin (No. 19): Policies and Procedures for Processing National Register Nominations*. Washington, D.C.: National Park Service, 1986.

———. *National Register Bulletin (No. 20): Nominating Historic Vessels and Shipwrecks* to the National Register of Historic Places, by James P. Delgado. Washington, D.C.: National Park Service, 1987.

———. *National Register Bulletin (No. 21): How to Establish Boundaries for National Register Properties.* Washington, D.C.: National Park Service, 1987.

———. *National Register Bulletin (No. 22): Guidelines for Evaluating and Nominating Properties That Have Achieved Significance within the Last Fifty Years.* Washington, D.C.: National Park Service, 1989.

———. *National Register Bulletin (No. 24): Guidelines for Local Surveys: A Basis for Preservation Planning,* by Patricia L. Parker. Washington, D.C.: National Park Service, 1992.

———. *National Register Bulletin (No. 28): Using the UTM Grid System to Record Historic Sites,* by Wilfred P. Cole. Washington, D.C.: National Park Service, 1992.

———. *National Register Bulletin (No. 29): Guidelines for Restricting Information About Historic and Prehistoric Resources,* by John Knoerl, Diane Miller, and Rebecca H. Shrimpton. Washington, D.C.: National Park Service, n.d.

———. *National Register Bulletin (No. 30): Guidelines for Evaluating and Documenting Rural Historic Landscapes,* by Linda Flint McClelland, J. Timothy Keller, Genevieve P. Keller, and Robert Z. Melnick. Washington, D.C.: National Park Service, 1990.

———. *National Register Bulletin (No. 32): Guidelines for Evaluating and Documenting Properties Associated with Significant Persons,* by Beth Grosvenor Boland. Washington, D.C.: National Park Service, 1989.

———. *National Register Bulletin (No. 34): Guidelines for Evaluating and Documenting Historic Aids to Navigation,* by James P. Delgado and Kevin J. Foster. Washington, D.C.: National Park Service, 1990.

———. *National Register Bulletin (No. 35): National Register Casebook: Examples of Documentation.* Washington, D.C.: National Park Service, 1988.

———. *National Register Bulletin (No. 36): Guidelines for Evaluating and Registering Historical Archeological Sites and Districts,* by John Knoerl, John H. Sprinkle, Jr., and Jan Townsend. Washington, D.C.: National Park Service, 1993.

———. *National Register Bulletin (No. 38): Guidelines for Evaluating and Documenting Traditional Cultural Properties,* by Patricia L. Parker and Thomas F. King. Washington, D.C.: National Park Service, 1992.

———. *National Register Bulletin (No. 39): Researching a Historic Property,* by Eleanor O'Donnell. Washington, D.C.: National Park Service, 1991.

———. *National Register Bulletin (No. 40): Guidelines for Identifying, Evaluating, and Registering America's Historic Battlefields,* by Patrick W. Andrus. Washington, D.C.: National Park Service, 1992.

———. *National Register Bulletin (No. 41): Guidelines for Evaluating and Registering Cemeteries and Burial Places,* by Elisabeth Walton Potter and Beth M. Boland. Washington, D.C.: National Park Service, 1992.

———. *National Register Bulletin (No. 42): Guidelines for Identifying, Evaluating, and Registering Historic Mining Properties,* by Bruce J. Noble, Jr., and Robert Spude. Washington, D.C.: National Park Service, 1992.

U.S. Department of the Interior. *Urban Waterfront Revitalization: The Role of Recreation and Heritage.* Washington, D.C.: GPO, 1980.

U.S. Department of the Interior. Heritage Conservation and Recreation Service. *Epoxies for Wood Repairs in Historic Buildings,* by Morgan W. Phillips and Judith E. Selwyn. Washington, D.C.: Heritage Conservation and Recreation Service, 1978.

———. *The Repair of Historic Wooden Windows,* by John H. Myers. Preservation Brief No. 9. Washington, D.C.: Heritage Conservation and Recreation Service, 1980.

———. *Repointing Mortar Joints in Historic Brick Buildings,* by James Askins, Robert C. Mack, and De Teel Patterson Tiller. Preservation Brief No. 2. Washington, D.C.: Heritage Conservation and Recreation Service, 1980.

———. *X-Ray Examination of Historic Structures,* by David M. Hart. Washington, D.C.: Heritage Conservation and Recreation Service, 1975.

U.S. Department of the Interior. National Park Service. *Affordable Housing Through Historic Preservation: A Case Study Guide to Combining the Tax Credits,* by William F. Delvac. Washington, D.C.: National Park Service, 1994.

———. *Aluminum and Vinyl Sidings on Historic Buildings: The Appropriateness of Substitute Materials for Resurfacing Historic Wood Frame Buildings,* by John H. Myers. Preservation Brief No. 8. Washington, D.C.: National Park Service, 1984.

———. *Applied Decoration for Historic Interiors Preserving Composition Ornament,* by William Adair and Jonathan Thornton. Preservation Brief No. 34. Washington, D.C.: National Park Service, 1994.

———. *Architectural Character: Identifying the Visual Aspects of Historic Buildings as an Aid to Preserving Their Character,* by Lee H. Nelson. Preservation Brief No. 17. Washington, D.C.: National Park Service, 1988.

———. *The Cleaning and Waterproof Coating of Masonry Buildings,* by Robert C. Mack. Preservation Brief No. 1. Washington, D.C.: National Park Service, 1975.

———. *Choosing an Archeological Consultant.* Washington, D.C.: National Park Service, 1987.

———. *Conserving Energy in Historic Buildings,* by Baird M. Smith. Preservation Brief No. 3. Washington, D.C.: National Park Service, 1984.

———. *Dangers of Abrasive Cleaning to Historic Buildings,* by Anne E. Grimmer. Preservation Brief No. 6. Washington, D.C.: National Park Service, 1984.

———. *Exterior Paint Problems on Historic Woodwork,* by David W. Look and Kay D. Weeks. Preservation Brief No. 10. Washington, D.C.: National Park Service, 1984.

———. *"Historic Preservation" and "Historic Properties"?* Washington, D.C.: National Park Service, 1988.

———. *Is There Archeology in Your Community?* by Patricia Parker. Washington, D.C.: National Park Service, 1987.

———. *Keeping It Clean: Removing Dirt, Paint, Stains, and Graffiti from Historic Masonry Buildings,* by Anne E. Grimmer. Washington, D.C.: National Park Service, 1988.

———. *Local Preservation: A Selected Bibliography.* Washington, D.C.: National Park Service, 1988.

———. *Making Historic Properties Accessible,* by Thomas C. Jester and Sharon C. Park. Preservation Brief No. 32. Washington, D.C.: National Park Service, 1993.

———. *Moisture Problems in Historic Masonry Walls: Diagnosis and Treatment,* by Baird M. Smith. Washington, D.C.: National Park Service, 1984.

———. *Mothballing Historic Buildings,* by Sharon C. Park. Preservation Brief No. 31. Washington, D.C.: National Park Service, 1993.

———. *New Exterior Additions to Historic Buildings: Preservation Concerns,* by Kay D. Weeks. Preservation Brief No. 14. Washington, D.C.: National Park Service, 1986.

———. *Painting Historic Interiors,* by Susan B. Chase. Preservation Brief No. 28. Washington, D.C.: National Park Service, 1992.

———. *Pioneers of American Landscape Design: An Annotated Bibliography,* edited by Charles A. Birnbaum, Sally Boazberg, and Lisa E. Crowder. Washington, D.C.: National Park Service, 1993.

———. *The Preservation and Repair of Historic Clay Tile Roofs,* by Anne E. Grimmer and Paul Kelsey Williams. Preservation Brief No. 30. Washington, D.C.: National Park Service, 1993.

———. *The Preservation and Repair of Historic Stucco,* by Anne E. Grimmer. Preservation Brief No. 22. Washington, D.C.: National Park Service, 1990.

———. *Preservation of Historic Adobe Buildings.* Preservation Brief No. 5. Washington, D.C.: National Park Service, 1984.

———. *The Preservation of Historic Barns,* by Michael Auer. Preservation Brief No. 20. Washington, D.C.: National Park Service, 1989.

———. *Preservation of Historic Concrete: Problems and General Approaches,* by William B. Coney. Preservation Brief No. 15. Denver, Col.: National Park Service Rocky Mountain Regional Office, 1991.

————. *The Preservation of Historic Glazed Architectural Terra-Cotta*, by De Teel Patterson Tiller. Preservation Brief No. 7. Washington, D.C.: National Park Service, 1984.

————. *The Preservation of Historic Pigmented Structural Glass (Vitrolite and Carrara Glass)*. Preservation Brief No. 12. Washington, D.C.: National Park Service, 1984.

————. *Preserving Historic Ornamental Plaster*, by David Flaharty. Preservation Brief No. 23. Washington, D.C.: National Park Service, 1991.

————. *Protecting Cultural Landscapes: Planning, Treatment and Management of Historic Landscapes*, by Charles A. Birnbaum. Preservation Brief No. 36. Washington, D.C.: National Park Service, 1994.

————. *Questions and Answers About Historic Properties Survey*, by Patricia Parker. Washington, D.C.: National Park Service, 1987.

————. *Questions and Answers About Your "SHPO"*, by Patricia Parker. Washington, D.C.: National Park Service, 1987.

————. *Rehabilitating Historic Storefronts*, by H. Ward Jandl. Preservation Brief No. 11. Washington, D.C.: National Park Service, 1982.

————. *Rehabilitating Interiors in Historic Buildings: Identifying and Preserving Character-Defining Elements*, by H. Ward Jandl. Preservation Brief No. 18. Washington, D.C.: National Park Service, 1988.

————. *The Repair and Replacement of Historic Wooden Shingle Roofs*, by Sharon C. Park. Preservation Brief No. 19. Washington, D.C.: National Park Service, 1989.

————. *The Repair and Thermal Upgrading of Historic Steel Windows*, by Sharon C. Park. Preservation Brief No. 13. Washington, D.C.: National Park Service, 1984.

————. *The Repair, Replacement, and Maintenance of Historic Slate Roofs*, by Jeffrey S. Levine. Preservation Brief No. 29. Washington, D.C.: National Park Service, 1993.

————. *Repairing Historic Flat Plaster: Walls and Ceilings*, by Mary Lee MacDonald. Preservation Brief No. 21. Washington, D.C.: National Park Service, 1989.

————. *The Secretary of the Interior's Standards for Rehabilitation and Guidelines for Rehabilitating Historic Buildings*. Washington, D.C.: National Park Service, 1991.

————. *Understanding Old Buildings: The Process of Architectural Investigation*, by Travis C. McDonald. Preservation Brief No. 35. Washington, D.C.: National Park Service, 1995.

————. *The Use of Substitute Materials on Historic Building Exteriors*, by Sharon C. Park. Preservation Brief No. 16. Washington, D.C.: National Park Service, 1988.

————. *What Are the Historic Preservation Tax Incentives?* Washington, D.C.: National Park Service, 1988.

————. *What Are the National Register Criteria?* by Patricia Parker. Washington, D.C.: National Park Service, 1987.

————. *What Is "Section 106 Review"?* by Thomas F. King. Washington, D.C.: National Park Service, 1987.

————. *What Is the National Historic Preservation Act?* by Patricia Parker. Washington, D.C.: National Park Service, 1987.

————. *When Preservation Commissions Go to Court: A Summary of Favorable Treatment of Challenges to Ordinances and Commission Decisions*, by Stephen N. Dennis. Washington, D.C.: National Park Service, 1988.

————. *The Window Handbook: Successful Strategies for Rehabilitating Windows in Historic Buildings*. Washington, D.C.: National Park Service, 1986.

————. *Zoning and Historic Preservation*, by Stephen A. Morris. Washington, D.C.: National Park Service, 1989.

U.S. Department of Transportation. *Recycling Historic Railroad Stations: A Citizens Manual*. In association with Anderson, Notter, Finegold. Washington, D.C.: GPO, 1978.

United States Environmental Protection Agency and National Institute of Occupational Safety and Health. *Building Air Quality: A Guide for Building Owners and Facility Managers*. Washington, D.C.: GPO, 1991.

Upton, Dell, ed. *America's Architectural Roots: Ethnic Groups That Built America*. Washington, D.C.: Preservation Press, 1986.

Upton, Dell, and John Michael Vlach, eds. *Common Places: Readings in American Ver-*

nacular Architecture. Athens: University of Georgia Press, 1985.

Valerio, Joseph M., and Daniel Friedman. *Movie Palaces: Renaissance and Reuse.* New York: Educational Facilities Laboratories, 1982.

Vieyra, Daniel. *"Fill 'Er Up": An Architectural History of American Gas Stations.* New York: Collier Books, 1979.

Von Rosenstiel, Helene, and Gail C. Winkler. *Floor Coverings for Historic Buildings: A Guide to Selecting Reproductions.* Washington, D.C.: Preservation Press, 1988.

Von Tscharner, Renata, and Ronald Lee Fleming. *New Providence: A Changing Cityscape.* San Diego: Harcourt Brace Jovanovich, 1987.

Warner, Raynor M., Sibyl M. Groff, and Ranne P. Warner, *New Profits from Old Buildings: Private Enterprise Approaches to Making Preservation Pay.* 1978. Reprint. New York: McGraw-Hill, 1979.

Watson, A. Elizabeth. *Establishing an Easement Program to Protect Historic, Scenic and Natural Resources.* Rev. ed. Information Series. Washington, D.C.: National Trust for Historic Preservation, 1982.

Watson, A. Elizabeth, et al. *Rural Conservation.* Rev. ed. Information Series, National Trust for Historic Preservation. Washington, D.C.: Preservation Press, 1984.

Weaver, Martin E. *Conserving Buildings.* New York: John Wiley & Sons, Inc., 1992.

Weinberg, Nathan G. *Preservation in American Towns and Cities.* Boulder, Colo.: Westview Press, 1979.

Whiffen, Marcus. *American Architecture Since 1780: A Guide to the Styles.* Cambridge, Mass.: MIT Press, 1992.

Whiffen, Marcus, and Frederick Koeper. *American Architecture, 1607–1976.* Cambridge, Mass.: MIT Press, 1981.

Will, Margaret Thomas. *Architectural Conservation in Europe: A Selected Bibliography of Publications in English.* Monticello, Ill.: Vance Bibliographies, 1980.

Willey, Gordon R., and Jeremy A. Sabloff. *A History of American Archeology.* London: Thames and Hudson, 1974.

Williams, Norman, Jr., Edmund H. Kellog, and Frank B. Gilbert. *Readings in Historic Preservation.* New Brunswick, N.J.: Center for Urban Policy Research, 1983.

Wilson, Chris, and Paul Groth, eds. *Everyday America: Cultural Landscape Studies After J.B. Jackson.* University of California Press, 2003.

Wilson, Forrest. *Bridges Go from Here to There.* Washington, D.C.: Preservation Press, 1993.

———. *What It Feels Like to Be a Building.* Washington, D.C.: Preservation Press, 1988.

Wilson, Rex L., and Gloria Loyola, eds. *Rescue Archaeology: Papers from the First New World Conference on Rescue Archaeology.* Government of Ecuador, Organization of American States, and National Trust for Historic Preservation. Washington, D.C.: Preservation Press, 1982.

Winkler, Gail C., and Roger W. Moss. *Victorian Interior Decoration: American Interiors, 1830–1900.* New York: H. Holt, 1986.

With Heritage So Rich, A Report of a Special Committee on Historic Preservation Under the Auspices of the United States Conference of Mayors with a Grant from the Ford Foundation. New York: Random House, 1965.

"With Heritage Still So Rich, Special National Park Service Supplement." Preservation News (October 1986).

Worskett, Roy. *The Character of Towns: An Approach to Conservation.* London: Architectural Press, 1969.

Wrenn, Tony P., and Elizabeth D. Mulloy. *America's Forgotten Architecture.* National Trust for Historic Preservation. New York: Pantheon, 1976.

Wright, Russell. *A Guide to Delineating Edges of Historic Districts.* Washington, D.C.: Preservation Press, 1976.

Wyeneth, Robert R. *Historic Preservation for a Living City: Historic Charleston Foundation 1947–1997.* University of South Carolina Press, 2000.

Zick, Steven J. *Preservation Easements: The Legislative Framework.* Preservation Policy Research Series. Washington, D.C.: National Trust for Historic Preservation, 1984.

Zick, William, et al. *Methods of Modifying Historic Bridges for Contemporary Use*. Charlottesville: Virginia Highway and Transportation Research Council, 1980.

Ziegler, Arthur P., Jr., and Walter C. Kidney. *Historic Preservation in Small Towns: A Manual of Practice*. Nashville, Tenn.: American Association for State and Local History, 1980.

Ziegler, Arthur P., Jr., Leopold Adler II, and Walter C. Kidney. *Revolving Funds for Historic Preservation: A Manual of Practice*. Pittsburgh: Ober Park Associates, 1975.

Zurier, Rebecca. *The American Firehouse: An Architectural and Social History*. New York: Abbeville Press, 1982.

Information series from the National Trust for Historic Preservation. Bulletins include:

Historic Districts

41 "Design and Development: Infill Housing Compatible with Historic Neighborhoods"

43 "Factory-Built Housing: Finding a Home in Historic Neighborhoods"

58 "Maintaining Community Character: How to Establish a Local Historic District"

62 "Reviewing New Construction in Historic Areas"

85 "Design Review in Historic Districts"

Organizational Development

14 "Legal Considerations in Establishing a Historic Preservation Organization"

26 "Using Professional Consultants in Preservation"

37 "Investing in Volunteers: A Guide to Effective Volunteer Management"

39 "Building on Experience: Improving Organizational Capacity to Handle Development Projects"

40 "Business Ventures for Nonprofits"

45 "A Self-Assessment Guide for Community Preservation Organizations"

49 "Membership Development: A Guide for Nonprofit Preservation Organizations"

54 "Steering Nonprofits: Advice for Boards and Staff"

63 "Building Support Through Public Relations: A Guide for Nonprofit Preservation Organizations"

66 "Strategic Planning for Nonprofit Organizations"

75 "A Quest for Funds Revisited: A Fund-Raising Starter Kit"

79 "Personnel Issues for Preservation Nonprofit Organizations"

80 "Sharing Your Success: Fund-Raising Ideas"

90 "Risk Management and Liability Insurance for Nonprofit Preservation Organizations"

Preservation Issues

10 "Commercial Area Revolving Funds"

11 "Revolving Funds for Neighborhood Preservation, Lafayette Square, St. Louis"

25 "Establishing an Easement Program to Protect Historic, Scenic and Natural Resources"

38 "Routes of History"

42 "Introduction to Photographing Historic Properties"

48 "Basic Preservation Procedures"

50 "From Visitors to Volunteers: Organizing a Historic Homes Tour"

51 "Rescuing Historic Resources: How to Respond to a Preservation Emergency"

52 "Successful State Advocacy"

53 "The Economics of Rehabilitation"

55 "The Impact of the Americans with Disabilities Act on Historic Structures"

56 "Using the Community Reinvestment Act in Low-Income Historic Neighborhoods"

57 "Safety, Building Codes and Historic Preservation"

61 "Controlling Disaster: Earthquake-Hazard Reduction for Historic Buildings"

65 "Cultural and Ethnic Diversity in Historic Preservation"

67 "Organizing for Change"

68 "The Protection of America's Scenic Byways"

69 "Preservation and the Recent Past"

70 "Coping with Contamination: A Primer for Preservationists"

71 "In Search of Collaboration: Historic Preservation and the Environmental Movement"

73 "Heritage Education: A Community-School Partnership"

74 "Buyer's Guide to Older and Historic Houses"

76 "Preservation of Historic Burial Grounds"

77 "Rural Conservation"

78 "Preservation Revolving Funds"

81 "1994 Directory of Private Nonprofit Statewide Preservation Organizations"

86 "Archeology and Historic Preservation"

87 "Appraising Historic Properties"

88 "Regional Heritage Areas: Approaches to Sustainable Development"

89 "A Guide to Tax-Advantaged Rehabilitation"

91 "1995 Directory of Staffed Local Preservation Organizations"

Preservation of Special Building Types

16 "Preservation of Concert Halls, Opera Houses and Movie Palaces"

17 "The Preservation of Churches, Synagogues and Other Religious Structures"

31 "Rehabilitating Residential Hotels"

32 "Surplus Schools"

Illustration Credits

Figure 7-1	Courtesy of Old Salem, Inc., photo by Simons
Figure 7-2	Colonial Williamsburg Foundation
Figure 7-3	Colonial Williamsburg Foundation
Figure 7-4	From the collections of Henry Ford Museum and Greenfield Village
Figure 7-5	Courtesy Old Sturbridge Village
Figure 7-6	Historic Deerfield, Inc., Deerfield, Mass., photo by Jennifer Mange
Figure 8-1	*Post-Courier*, Charleston, S.C., photo by Bill Jordan
Figure 8-2	Historic American Buildings Survey, photo by Jet Lowe
Figure 8-3	Walter Smalling, Jr., Washington
Figure 8-4	National Trust for Historic Preservation, photo by Sue Brink
Figure 8-5	National Trust for Historic Preservation and Historic Madison, Inc., photo by Tom Moriarity
Figure 8-6	U.S. Coast Guard photo
Figure 9-1	National Trust for Historic Preservation
Figure 9-2	National Trust for Historic Preservation, photo by Walter Smalling, Jr.
Figure 9-3	National Trust for Historic Preservation
Figure 9-4	National Trust for Historic Preservation, photo by Walter Smalling, Jr.
Figure 10-1	Robert Z. Melnick, Land and Community Associates, for The Hanalei Project
Figure 10-2	National Trust for Historic Preservation
Figure 10-3	National Trust for Historic Preservation, photo by Marler, 1963
Figure 10-4	National Trust for Historic Preservation, photo by Edmund Barrett
Figure 10-5	Courtesy Historic Annapolis Inc., M.E. Warren, Photography
Figure 10-6	Courtesy Historic Annapolis Inc., M.E. Warren, Photography
Figure 11-1	National Trust for Historic Preservation
Figure 11-2	Nebraska State Historical Society
Figure 11-3	National Trust for Historic Preservation and North Carolina State Department of Archives and History, photo by Tony Wrenn
Figure 11-4	Bureau of Reclamation, U.S. Department of the Interior
Figure 11-5	National Trust for Historic Preservation, photo by James L. Ballard
Figure 12-1	Colonial Williamsburg Foundation
Figure 12-2	National Park Service, Golden Gate National Recreation Area
Figure 12-3	National Park Service
Figure 12-4	Colonial Williamsburg Foundation
Figure 13-1	National Park Service photo, 1979.
Figure 13-2	Photo of Chief Son-I-Hat's Whale House and Totems Historic District, Prince of Wales-Outer K. Borough census Area, Alaska 02000627 courtesy of the National Register of Historic Places, taken by Louis A. Thompson.
Figure 13-3	The photo is from the National Register of Historic Places collection of Ani-akchak Bay Historic Landscape District #97000016, Chignik, Dillingham Census Area, Alaska, Keith Trexler, photographer.
Figure 13-4	The photo is from the National Historic Landmark Bear Butte, Meade County, South Dakota. Photographer unknown.
Figure 14-1	Copyright © Kathleen Cohen
Figure 14-2	Corbus Digital Stock
Figure 14-3	Photo by Lawrence Freedberg
Figure 15-1	Wayne Clark, Jefferson Patterson Park and Museum, St. Leonard, Maryland
Figure 15-2	The National Colonial Farm, photograph by Mastracco
Figure 15-3	National Trust for Historic Preservation
Figure 15-4	Historic American Buildings Survey, photo by Lawrence Bradley
Epilogue 1	Schuylkill River National Heritage, Staff Photo
Epilogue 2	Photo by Brenda Barrett
Epilogue 3	Photo by G. Leslie Sweetnam.

Index

Aall, Hans, 78
Aborigines, Australian, 144, 145
Above-ground archaeology, 133
Abraham Brown House (Watertown,
  Massachusetts), 66
Academic training programs, xix
Accokeek, Maryland, National Colonial Farm, 161
Adaptive use, 6, 9, 99–106
  course of action for, 103
  defined, 99
  historic character-defining features in, 103–104
  house museums as, 63, 99
  integrity in, 101–103
  and patina, 104
  repair and replacements in, 104–105
  standards/guidelines for, 105–106
Adirondack Forest Preserve (New York), 110
Adler and Sullivan, 68
Advisory Council on Historic Preservation, x, 32
  contact information for, 205
  function of, 58
  legislative establishment of, 53
  and Office of Archaeology and Historic
    Preservation, 54
  working relationships of, 127
Aga Khan Trust for Culture, 205
Agricultural economy, 121
Agricultural land, xviii, 111–113. *See also* Rural
  preservation
Ainslie, Michael L., 32, 33
Alaska:
  Aniakchak Bay, 143
  St. Michael's Cathedral, Sitka, 7
  Son-I-Hat's Whale House and Totems Historic
    District, 144
Albert Memorial (Hyde Park, London), 4
Albright, Horace M., 26, 40
Alexander, Edward P., 82, 83
Alexander Ramsay House (St. Paul, Minnesota), 65

Alexandria, Virginia, 90, 92
  archaeological program in, 135
  architectural style restrictions in, 88
  Gadsby's Tavern, 68
  torpedo factory, 106
Alterations (for adaptive use), 105
American Architect and Building News, 18
American Association for State and Local History,
  26, 205
American Association of Museums, 205
American Express, 153
American Graves Protection and Repatriation Act of
  1990, 143
American Indian Religious Freedom Act of 1978, 143
American Institute of Architects, 26, 28, 41
American Institute of Architects Historic Resources
  Committee, 205
American Scenic and Historic Preservation Society
  (New York), 26
American Society of Civil Engineers, 26
American Society of Interior Designers, 69
American Society of Landscape Architects, 107
Amerindian artifacts, 39
Aniakchak Bay, Alaska, 143
Ankor Wat (Cambodia), 148
Annapolis, Maryland:
  visual cohesiveness of, 94
  William Paca House and Gardens, 117
Anthropology, 132
Antiquities Act of 1906, xviii, 49, 171
Appleton, William Sumner, 17–20, 22, 37, 64–66, 78, 134
APT, *see* Association for Preservation Technology
Archaeological Resources Protection Act of 1979, 143
Archaeology, 131–137
  above-ground, 133
  commercial, 133, 134
  conservation, 133, 134
  definitions of, 131
  historic, 133